Compassionate School

This book is a vital resource for all educators who are dedicated to promoting student mental health and well-being. Built on a solid foundation of research and experience working with schools, Christine Mason and her colleagues offer readers key principles and actionable strategies, stories that illustrate and inspire, exercises to reflect upon and apply lessons to one's own school, and references to numerous additional online sources. The heart and soul of this book are clear and present on every page—the centrality of caring, compassion, and community to the ability of students to thrive in school. I would highly recommend this book in ordinary times. In this period of uncertainty, unrest, and distress, it is indispensable.

Mark A. Smylie, Professor Emeritus
College of Education, University of Illinois at Chicago
Visiting Professor, Peabody College, Vanderbilt University
Coauthor of *Caring School Leadership* (2020) and
Stories of Caring School Leadership (2021)

This outstanding contribution to the literature on our students' mental health and well-being provides an exemplary blend of cutting-edge research, step-by-step practical interventions, and a true humanistic vision for the future of our schools and society. Before COVID-19 this book would have been important; today it is indispensable. Wherever you are teaching or working in the education sector, Compassionate School Practices *is essential reading for all of us, both during the pandemic and in the years to come.*

Dennis Shirley, Duganne Faculty Fellow and Professor
Editor in Chief, *Journal of Educational Change*
Lynch School of Education and Human Development, Boston College
Chestnut Hill, MA

As schools begin to shift away from the industrial model of education, we see many implementing student-centered and inquiry-based practices that are designed to help students develop their curiosity and become more proficient thinkers and problem solvers. While these practices are laudable, the unaddressed mental health needs of many students will stand in the way of desired progress for all. Thankfully, Compassionate School Practices *offers an easy-to-follow four-phase model and a series of nine principles to help school personnel, parents, and psychologists better support students' social and emotional well-being. Simply put, the authors' approach puts much needed structure into what for many educators may otherwise be just a vague directive. This book's compassionate voice and sound tools unlock the promise that* **successful** *schools going forward will balance students' acquisition and the demonstration of knowledge with proper attention to their social and emotional needs.*

Jeff Ikler and Kirsten Richert, Authors
Shifting: How School Leaders Can Create a Culture of Change

I started my career as a teacher in the New York City neighborhood of Bedford-Stuyvesant where many students came to class hungry, sick, abused, homeless, or all of the above. It was then when I first realized the health and welfare of our students surpasses the importance of their academic achievement. That was 1968. Fast forward to today. Suicides rates are the highest they've ever been. Drug use is just as alarming, which raises the question, "What's more important, scores on a test or keeping kids alive?" Compassionate School Practices *unpacks a myriad of informative principles that can help school systems build a framework to enhance their social and emotional programs. The well-being of a child is of the utmost importance, especially during this public health crisis. The demand for quality SEL is at an all-time high. I applaud the authors for creating this resource.*

Daniel A. Domenech, Executive Director
AASA, The School Superintendents Association
Alexandria, VA

Quality education cannot exist in the absence of compassion. And even if it could, it would be difficult— if not impossible—for such "education" to be applied in a way that would move humanity forward. This book provides a comprehensive and evidence-based blueprint for how to create a heart centered and compassionate school environment that allows all children— especially our most vulnerable—to heal, learn, and thrive.

Steve Gross, Chief Playmaker
The Life is Good Playmakers
Boston, MA

When it comes to children's mental health, school is among the biggest stressors that kids have to deal with. Compassionate School Practices *is the bridge that we need to redesign the school system in a way to meet the needs of youth. If we are able to implement at least some of the recommendations, all of us stand to substantially benefit!*

Akeem N. Marsh, Psychiatrist
Bellevue Hospital Center
Assistant Professor of Child and Adolescent Psychiatry
New York University School of Medicine
New York, NY

Compassionate School Practices *captures our imagination, with principles and action steps to strengthen student mental health and well-being. The authors offer a practical approach that goes beyond screening and identification as it promotes collective kindness and caring. Their blueprint for schools shows how to embed compassion into everyday interactions between teachers and students to bolster student self-esteem, while strengthening self-care practices. They show us how to uplift our neighbors and our communities so that schools first and foremost address what is most important—the lives, the hearts, the souls of students, families, and ourselves. An inspirational work that is so needed today!*

Paul Liabenow, Executive Director
Michigan Elementary and Middle School Principals Association (MEMSPA)
Holt, MI

An important new look at how we can foster mental health in schools. Educators have the capacity to buffer against adversities their students face, and schools can lessen the impact of trauma and toxic stress. At the same time, teachers themselves face unique stressors. Mason, Asby, Wenzel, Volk, and Staeheli present numerous practical suggestions for promoting mental health and well-being among students and teachers alike.

Kimberly Noble, Professor of Neuroscience and Education
Teachers College, Columbia University
New York, NY

In the midst of this horrific pandemic, there's more than learning on the minds of educators. Many youth depend on teachers and their schools to connect with peers and caring adults. Mason and her coauthors provide valuable insights as they tell the story of the New England Childhood-Trauma Learning Collaborative—stories from principals, social workers, teachers and school psychologists, about how they are building student self-esteem and resiliency, and how they are teaching while addressing the critical needs of students who are most at-risk. Whether learning is virtual, hybrid, or in-person, caring leaders will be inspired by the network of practices, guidelines, and resources that Compassionate School Practices *provides. An ideal book for book studies, an ideal blueprint for a brighter future, an ideal resource for transforming education and transforming lives!*

Mark Terry, Deputy Executive Director
Texas Elementary Principals and Supervisors Association (TEPSA)
Austin, TX

The social and emotional health of students is interdependent with that of teachers and school leaders. But one-size-fits-all or piecemeal programs won't improve true resilience. Compassionate School Practices *provides the tools you need to be intentional about identifying your learning community's current needs and your capacity to influence, no matter your position. And you'll discover research-based strategies for self-care, for assessing student needs, for increasing needed staff knowledge— and more—to create the safe and supportive environments that lead to serving and educating the whole child.*

Jane Kise, Principal
Differentiated Coaching Associates
Minneapolis, MN

This publication is a timely contribution to promote children and youth's social emotional development. It provides a useful ecological framework and specific practices that educators and specialists may incorporate into their daily work.

Songtian (Tim) Zeng, Assistant Professor
College of Education and Human Development
Research Director, Institute for Early Education Leadership and Innovation
University of Massachusetts
Boston, MA

Compassionate School Practices *exemplifies Mason's expertise in the field of mindful education and creates real-world learning for "whole educators" who truly wish to address social emotional issues with their students. Mindfulness, restorative justice, equity, trauma-informed care—it's all wrapped into a single cohesive message here with practical applications for the modern teacher. This is a book every educator must own.*

Jeffrey Donald, **Mindfulness Coordinator**
Montgomery County Public Schools
Rockville, MD

Teaching the facts of mental health challenges in schools is comparable to teaching students rote math facts without understanding the systems that numbers function in and how this is applied to solve problems. Having basic knowledge of a subject does not lend itself to deeper thinking to promote both individual and systemic growth. Without analyzing our data, identifying areas of need, and altering how we navigate mental health challenges, we will inevitably continue to repeat the same pattern of misunderstanding and inadequate treatment. Compassionate School Practices *provides thoughtful exercises to guide your district in identifying specific areas of need, integrating these into your district vision, and developing comprehensive professional development. This is not an expensive initiative that is implemented and forgotten, but rather a process to shift the collective understanding and treatment of mental health challenges. Building protective measures of resilience and compassion helps to vaccinate your students and staff against complacency and despair that affects generations.*

Rachel Santa, **Director of Special Services**
Fellow, Childhood-Trauma Learning Collaborative
Board Certified Special Educator, Cumberland School Department
Cumberland, RI

Our schools, our children, our society face a profound moment of reckoning with the global pandemic, climate crisis, political polarization, systemic and structural racial and social injustice, and more. These times call for a mindshift of being, thinking, and acting, and that begins with centering compassion, mindfulness, empathy, and kindness within our schools. This book is rich in solid research and practices that support teaching and learning through mindfulness, trust building, cultivating belonging and awareness, and more. It is a must-read for educators seeking to meet the challenges of our time with evidence-based, equity-centered practices that support growth and learning to heal our school communities and our world.

Valerie Brown, **Leadership Coach**
Coauthor, *The Mindful School Leader:*
Practices to Transform Your Leadership and School
New Hope, PA

The authors conceive of a heart centered, compassionate learning community bound together by trusting, safe, authentic relationships that include the child, family, educators, and the broader community. Central to their vision is a single caring adult who supports each student, and is embedded in both the school and surrounding community. This approach builds a trauma-informed school culture that enhances children's health and well-being. Their strategy is supported by tools and tips that makes the implementation of this creative vision possible. This visionary book would be transformative and is a must-read for everyone involved in helping children grow and thrive.

Ellen L. Bassuk, Founder
C4 Innovations
Needham, MA

Who better to guide our children's mental health than our educators? Compassionate School Practices gives a comprehensive blueprint to managing our mental health inadequacies in the 2020 pandemic/ post-pandemic world. Beyond medical diagnosis and pharmaceutical treatment, the book focuses on our most at-risk and underserved children. I have firsthand experience with a child who has thrived through services provided at school. As a physician who has worked with diverse communities, I recognize how compassionate public schools can be a healing force for vulnerable children.

Alex Thacker, Physician
Family Practice
Intercoastal Medical Group
Bradenton, FL

Finally! As crisis after crisis threatens the future of our children, we have a book that outlines specific and deeply researched ways to approach children's mental health and well-being from a truly holistic, heart centered, community-based perspective. Never has the need for inspiration and resources to change the future of education been greater than now.

Adam Grove, Physician
Head to Toe Holistic Healthcare
Anchorage, AK

Compassionate School Practices *provides useful tools for confronting the complex nexus of mental health, education, and trauma. Importantly, the authors realize that educators cannot pour from an empty glass and must maintain their own well-being in order to effectively support their students in the long term. Mason and her colleagues reassures her audience that while there are aspects of our reality that may be out of reach for improvement (teacher budgets, state curriculum policies, etc.), there are specific practices and strategies we can implement both on an individual and community level to combat teacher stress and burn out. The suggested resources and insights are invaluable, particularly in this era of wide-spread social instability.*

Norrell Edwards, Assistant Director
Prisons and Justice Initiative
Georgetown University
Washington, DC

Compassionate School Practices

Compassionate School Practices

Fostering Children's Mental Health and Well-Being

Christine Mason

Dana Asby

Meghan Wenzel

Katherine Volk

Martha Staeheli

CORWIN

FOR INFORMATION:

Corwin

A SAGE Company

2455 Teller Road

Thousand Oaks, California 91320

(800) 233-9936

www.corwin.com

SAGE Publications Ltd.

1 Oliver's Yard

55 City Road

London EC1Y 1SP

United Kingdom

SAGE Publications India Pvt. Ltd.

B 1/I 1 Mohan Cooperative Industrial Area

Mathura Road, New Delhi 110 044

India

SAGE Publications Asia-Pacific Pte. Ltd.

18 Cross Street #10-10/11/12

China Square Central

Singapore 048423

Acquisitions Editor: Ariel Curry

Associate Content Development Editor: Jessica Vidal

Editorial Assistant: Caroline Timmings

Production Editor: Gagan Mahindra

Copy Editor: Lynne Curry

Typesetter: C&M Digitals (P) Ltd

Proofreader: Rae-Ann Goodwin

Indexer: Integra

Cover Designer: Lysa Becker

Graphic Designer: Lysa Becker

Marketing Manager: Sharon Pendergast

Printed in the United States of America

ISBN: 9781071820490

This book is printed on acid-free paper.

21 22 23 24 25 10 9 8 7 6 5 4 3 2 1

Contents

List of Online Resources

To access online resources, visit the companion website at resources.corwin.com/compassionateschoolpractices.

INTRODUCTION

CHAPTER 1

CHAPTER 2

Foreword

When we first established the Program for Recovery and Community Health (PRCH) twenty years ago within the Yale School of Medicine Department of Psychiatry, our main goal was to transform the field of psychiatry to promote the recovery and community inclusion of persons with lived experiences of serious mental illness. Since that time, PRCH has become an internationally recognized center for research, evaluation, education, policy development, and consultation and technical assistance aimed at transforming mental health systems to provide strength-based, culturally responsive, and person and family-centered care to people living with psychiatric disability, their loved ones, and their communities. To carry out this work, PRCH has received funding from state agencies, most prominently from the Connecticut Department of Mental Health and Addiction Services, and from federal research institutions such as the National Institute of Mental Health, the Patient-Centered Outcomes Research Institute, the U.S. Substance Abuse and Mental Health Services Administration, and the National Institute on Drug Abuse. In addition, PRCH contracts with public and nonprofit organizations seeking evaluation and programmatic consultation in the areas of recovery, person-centered care, health disparities, and community inclusion.

At the center of our work remains a passionate commitment to aiding individuals in their own recovery process, and in promoting their pursuit of their own aspirations and interests, beyond the illness- and deficit-based paradigm from which the mental health system has historically operated.

Early in PRCH's history, Dr. Martha Staeheli and I became focused on middle and high schools as places where we might be able to combat the shame and stigma that clings to a diagnosis of mental illness. Together, we developed a curricular program to educate students and their teachers about the facts of mental illness and the reality, and experiences, of people in recovery. At that time, it was difficult to gain school-based support for such a curriculum, and we were consistently met with skepticism about whether children suffered from such conditions, or had much awareness of members of their families who might, and the ever-present concern that talking about mental illness might precipitate symptoms in teenagers and risk of suicide.

As a result of our work, we have come to understand that a curriculum about mental illness is not adequate, and that school communities cannot combat the stigma around these issues by simply teaching "facts" about mental illness and raising awareness; it requires a transformation in their perspectives toward, and attitudes about, mental illness as a whole, and the development and enactment of compassion toward students considered to be at risk.

In the time since PRCH was established, the field of psychiatry has begun to evolve to include the voices of those with lived experience of mental illness and to make room for the diverse ways that people with a diagnosis of serious mental illness express and create their own recoveries. Although we, within the field, are often at odds in how to create systems that help people with lived experience, we are heartened by the expansion of perspectives to include the voices of the people at the center of this work. Heartening, too, is the movement in school systems toward taking on a broader, and much richer, role in promoting the mental health of students.

While the incidence of student mental health concerns continues to grow, so, too, does the awareness by educators, parents, and policy makers that we must work together to identify the needs of those children who have experienced trauma, who struggle with challenges at home, or who may have emotional or developmental challenges. We now understand that many students with diverse emotional and educational needs rely on schools and educators to provide multiple pathways to learning, gaining access to mental health and behavioral assistance, and to a support system of nurturing adults.

Through the New England Mental Health Technology Transfer Center (MHTTC)'s School-Based Mental Health Initiative, PRCH recently established the Childhood-Trauma Learning Collaborative (C-TLC) in partnership with the Center for Educational Improvement. Through the C-TLC, and under the direction of Dr. Staeheli and CEI's Dr. Mason, PRCH has been able to come full circle back to our roots in advocating for child-centered, trauma-informed, and culturally responsive school-based mental health, this time with a broad base of national and local help through the MHTTC network to address the mental health needs within school communities. This book reflects the ideals that underpin all of the work we do within and beyond PRCH; children, educators, families, and communities are best served when we address the emotional needs of students with compassion and respect, finding joy and connection in their perspectives and experiences.

As in the larger mental health system, schools, too, can be caught between the competing needs and demands of educators, politics, families, mental health providers, and children, which serves to create layers of complexity and bureaucracy that can become barriers to establishing efficient and effective services for students. ***Compassionate School Practices: Fostering Children's Mental Health and Well-Being*** provides the foundation for an antidote to this complexity, through practical and well-researched advice to inform schools and mental health support systems. Through the perspectives of a deep evidence base, members of our C-TLC, and the voices of school leaders, families, and students themselves, this book challenges traditional practices and our own worldviews, to reorient schools toward courage and compassion. The need for transformation in our schools has never been greater than in the present moment; we hope that readers find this book useful in their efforts to bring about such changes in their own communities.

Larry Davidson, PhD

Professor of Psychiatry; Senior Policy Advisor,
Department of Mental Health and Addiction Services
Yale Program for Recovery and Community Health, Yale School of Medicine

Preface

We know that educators, even as they are overworked, provide a haven of safety and security for children who leave the school building to return to home environments complicated by poverty, racism, abuse, neglect, substance misuse, and mental illness. And while these caring adults can make all the difference in a single child's life, a few educators cannot move mountains that must shift to establish a safer, more equitable and just future.

We wrote this book for educators whose hearts were weary long before the COVID-19 pandemic and widespread police brutality against Black Americans revealed systemic inequities causing pervasive disease that can no longer be ignored. We wrote this book for the many children who have experienced extensive trauma and need more immediately available assistance. We wrote this book knowing that we are all a step away from unspeakable trauma, and we (educators, children, and families) all benefit from the model we are using in New England schools, a Compassionate School Mental Health Model. This model shows school leaders and educators how to leverage the abundance of resources that already exist in their schools, communities, and most importantly, themselves.

The process of transforming your school into a compassionate community where everyone in the building is thriving, growing, and making a difference in their neighborhood and beyond can easily become overwhelming if you're the only one steering the effort. (Ch. 9, "Time for Reflection Allows for Visioning")

In *Compassionate School Practices: Fostering Children's Mental Health and Well-Being,* we will show you how to use Heart Centered Learning®, an approach to leadership and social emotional learning that relies on mindfulness as a foundation for transformational change and cultivating compassionate school communities. You will learn about a collaborative visioning process that provides a frame for elevating compassion through dialogue, policies, and protocol to address the needs of *all* of your school community members.

This book tells the story of the needs and successes of the collaboration between the Program for Recovery and Community Health (PRCH) at Yale University, the Center for Educational Improvement, and the Childhood-Trauma Learning Collaborative (C-TLC), a network of twenty-four Fellows (school administrators, social workers, counselors, and psychologists). [See Chapter 5, "The Substance Abuse and Mental Health Services Administration: National Leaders in Mental Health Support"]

Why Is This Book Important Now?

Before COVID-19 and racial injustice unleashed (or revealed) a public mental health crisis, youth mental health and well-being were already on a sharp decline. Youth suicide, now the second leading cause of death for individuals ages ten to twenty-four, has spiked in the past decade, with a 56 percent increase in teen suicides between 2005 and 2017 (Abbott, 2019). Although one in five children has a diagnosable mental, emotional, or behavioral disorder, only 20 percent get a diagnosis or receive care, let alone quality, evidence-based, and person-centered care focused on resilience and recovery (NAMI, 2020b; Kessler & Bromet, 2013). The increase in students of color with mental health crises requiring emergency care has outpaced the rise for white students (Abrams et al., 2019). According to Children's National Medical Center researcher and pediatrician Anna Abrams, "It's really disheartening. Community resources for mental health, especially for youth, are incredibly scarce" (Fox, 2018).

We know that despite funding and staffing cuts, schools are increasingly becoming the *only* point of care for youth mental health in many areas, especially rural communities. We know that teachers and administrators are facing unbearable levels of stress exacerbated by the complexities of distance learning during a global pandemic and widespread racial discrimination and violence. Increasing compassion and emotional and mental well-being is an equity issue. Systemic trauma exists within the school building and it disproportionately affects students of color and continues to impact their lives into adulthood. Schools can be a powerful force in dismantling that systemic injustice.

Who Should Read This Book?

This book offers any adult working with youth a framework for not only self-care, but community care in the context of youth mental health. It is not just for the school psychologist or classroom teacher who spends time with a child with a diagnosed mental illness or emotional disorder; it is for any adult who works with or lives with youth. Rather than providing another program, curriculum, or prescription that may or may not work for your unique community, we offer a mindshift that will help your school or district rethink how they use their available resources to transform into a caring, compassionate community that promotes well-being and justice for all students, by strengthening relationships and building the holistic skills students and teachers need to cope with the burdens of stress. We know that students cannot learn until they feel safe and loved. This book provides a path toward this well-being, for youth and the adults who work with them.

What Will I Be Able To Do Once I Finish This Book?

If you're a decision maker in your school or district, this book will provide you with examples, strategies, resources, and reflection exercises that will help you take the steps to reenvision your team as a trauma-skilled, compassionate school community that creates joy and possibility for every member. If you are an educator or mental health service provider on the ground with students, you will have new tools and knowledge that can help you change the hearts and minds of your colleagues and the students you work with to step onto this transformational path.

To do that, we've structured this book in a way that provides you with a variety of tools, resources, and strategies. You can read this book from cover to cover, or you can skip ahead to the chapter that addresses your school or district's most dire needs now. As you read, look out for these features and benefits:

- *Key Principles* orient the reader to the main takeaway for each chapter.

- *Strategy Boxes* explain evidence-based tools for you to take into the classroom immediately.

- *Story Boxes* provide a lens into classrooms, schools, and programs that have found success using aspects of our model with students in their community. Readers can use these exemplars as inspiration for their own transformational journeys.

- *Info Boxes* give the reader additional information to understand the complexities of mental health through research, statistics, and deeper explanations.

- *Online Resources* will be indicated throughout the book at the end of each chapter. Visit this book's companion website for printables, evidence-based resources, and even more strategies and tips to benefit youth mental health. The companion website can be found at resources.corwin.com/compassionateschoolpractices.

- *My School Exercises* provide the reader with an opportunity to reflect on their school's journey to becoming a trauma-skilled, compassionate school community.

Acronym Guide

Our work is informed by the collaborators we've been working with, both new and old. We know that remembering these organizations' names and acronyms can become confusing, especially with all of the acronyms used for the various frameworks and models we will share. Please consult this acronym guide as needed:

Behavior Intervention Monitoring Assessment System 2 (BIMAS-2)

Bridging Resilient Youth in Transition (BRYT) model

Centers for Disease Control and Prevention (CDC)

Childhood Trauma Learning Collaborative (C-TLC)

Compassionate School Mental Health Model (CSMHM)

The Collaborative for Social and Emotional Learning (CASEL)

The Comprehensive Behavioral Health Model (CBHM)

Heart Centered Learning (HCL)

Massachusetts School Mental Health Consortium (MASMHC)

Mental Health Technology Transfer Center Network (MHTTC Network)

Multi-Tiered Systems of Support (MTSS)

National Alliance on Mental Illness (NAMI)

National Institute of Mental Health (NIMH)

New England Mental Health Technology Transfer Center
(New England MHTTC)

Positive Behavior Intervention Supports (PBIS)

Program for Recovery and Community Health (PRCH)

School-Compassionate Culture Analytical Tool for Educators (S-CCATE)

School Health Assessment and Performance Evaluation (SHAPE) System

Substance Abuse and Mental Health Services Administration (SAMHSA)

Suicide Prevention Resource Center (SPRC)

Why Is This Book Important Outside of New England and the United States?

While our recent work, which informed this book, with the Childhood-Trauma Learning Collaborative (C-TLC; see Chapter 1, Partnerships for Building Student Mental Health and Well-Being) has taken place in New England, we also work with educators and mental health service providers across the country and globe. Many of the concepts and suggestions we provide have been used by diverse voices serving populations in various domestic and international settings. We have also looked to other U.S. regions and countries, like Ireland, to find exemplars for youth mental health services.

In 2015, the National Educational Psychological Services, a service provided by the Department of Education and Skills of the Irish government, issued a statement of guidelines for mental health, which suggested the following:

Mental health should permeate all aspects of school life and learning. Effective schools should therefore put systems in place to promote mental health and well-being and thus build resilience in both staff and students to help prepare them to cope with a range of life events. (p. 8)

Like the Irish, and in our work with the Yale Program for Recovery and Community Health (PRCH), we see well-being experienced at the personal level and extended to, and influenced by, the world beyond. From our analysis of the international response to youth mental health concerns, these factors seem particularly important to us:

- Acknowledging that mental health permeates all aspects of school life and learning

- Building resiliency in staff and students

- Promoting dynamic, optimal development and flourishing for everyone in the school community

- Conceptualizing well-being as an experience at the personal level that is connected to risk and protective factors at the individual, relational, community, cultural, and societal levels (see Figure 0.1)

A Framework for Cultivating Well-Being in Schools

FIGURE 0.1   Compassionate School Mental Health Model

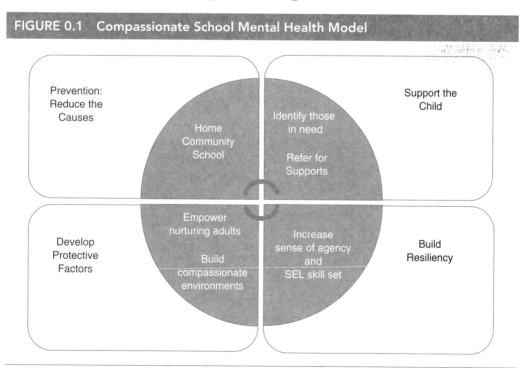

From Mason, C., Wenzel, M., Asby, D., & Staeheli, M. (2020). *A compassionate school response to children's mental illness: A Childhood-Trauma Learning Collaborative resource guide.* New England Mental Health Technology Transfer Center. Used with permission from the New England MHTTC.

Our Compassionate School Mental Health Model provides a framework for educators interested in reaching the hearts and minds of children and youth who are most vulnerable and in helping others expand their vision for listening more carefully and responding more fully, while continuing to engage students in powerful academic lessons. Rather than focusing primarily on the diagnosis and treatment of mental illness, as the traditional medical model for mental health treatment has in the past, the Compassionate School Mental Health Model asks the school community to work with students, families, and other stakeholders to holistically address mental health at every stage through:

- *Prevention: Reducing the Causes.* When schools work to address the social determinants of health, systemic injustices, trauma, and other causes of mental illness that exist in society and within their own walls, they provide a caring environment that lessens the impact of trauma and toxic stress. Working with families to replicate these strategies breaks the cycle of intergenerational trauma that is the root of many mental illnesses.

- *Supporting the Child.* We know that some children will experience levels of trauma, toxic stress, or mental illness that require extra care and attention. We give trauma-informed recommendations for screening, assistance, and treatment options that reduce the stigma associated with the labeling of mental illnesses.

- *Building Resiliency.* All humans will experience stress and challenges at some point in life, so every student will benefit from direct instruction of social emotional and stress-coping skills at the schoolwide level. We also know that students who have experienced trauma will need opportunities to regain a sense of self-esteem and agency, but they must feel a sense of belonging in their school to develop these traits.

- *Developing Protective Factors.* The strongest buffering factor for a child who has experienced trauma is the presence of a single caring adult. We explain how to cultivate a compassionate school environment filled with heart centered educators who care for their students.

Reducing Stigma. Our model seeks to drastically reduce the stigma of mental illness and its symptoms by enhancing compassion. Speaking out about mental illness can be intimidating and risky. However, there are youth and adults who realize the importance of sharing their experiences. We have been inspired by the brave individuals who use their lived experiences of recovery from mental illness in their work with the Program for Recovery and Community Health (PRCH) in the Department of Psychiatry at Yale University to reduce mental health stigma, which believes that personal accounts, like the one shared below, can be a powerful force in reducing stigma.

Being Judged for My Mental Illness Was So Damaging.

> I was diagnosed with depression and anxiety when I was sixteen years old and started counseling sessions. I was so ashamed of it that I would lie about where I was going. I didn't want people to know I was having counseling in case they labeled me "crazy" or "insane" (Time to Change, 2017).

To understand more about how the voices of individuals most at risk have informed our approach, we urge you to take a few moments, as we did, to reflect on your own life and your experiences with stress and/or mental health challenges. Although not all of us have experienced a mental health crisis, been hospitalized, diagnosed, or labeled, many, if not most of us, have had extremely stressful, sad, or panic-inducing acute experiences—especially in this new world impacted at the same moment by a global pandemic and racial violence. When we focus on these experiences, we realize that there was something more that others could have, should have, or might have done if they had realized our need. Sometimes we can recall the person or persons who helped us through our time of distress, those who truly made a positive difference in our lives. Sometimes we also recall our own inner resilience, the compassion we felt for ourselves, and the positive steps we took on our own behalf.

During COVID-19. During the COVID-19 pandemic, many children and youth experienced an extreme sense of loss as they missed their friends and let go of plans for proms, athletic milestones, or even high school graduation. However, without minimizing the burden that we all experienced, the impact of COVID-19 was certainly more traumatizing for some children and families than others. Some experienced greater risks, greater anxieties, and greater loss. Families with functional coping skills flourished while those with dysfunctional patterns of adult interaction may have led to feelings of fear and insecurity for children. One Massachusetts principal said of his most vulnerable students, "We come into these homes and tell them to stay inside to keep them safe, but we look around and wonder how safe those homes really are" (PCTV, 2020).

With the pandemic came a greater need to help children and adults with their own self-care and a greater need to help build resiliency and protective factors into our lives. Educators who had previously focused largely on academics realized that their roles as protective factors—the adults who can be counted on to show up virtually, to establish some sense of a new normalcy and a new connectedness—have expanded in critical ways for so many children and families.

The Trauma That COVID-19 Brought to Our Community

- Consider your local community, families, and students. What are some of the most serious consequences? _____

  _____

- Consider educators at your school and in your community. What are some of the most serious consequences? _____

  _____

- What are some of the most critical needs for your community, families, and schools? _____

  _____

- Have you gained any new realizations regarding trauma, its impact, and what educators can do to help alleviate stress?

  _____

How can schools improve children's well-being not only with COVID-19 and racial inequity and violence but also for the future? How does mindful leadership help schools vision collaboratively for their collective destiny? We invite you to enter our world, listen to the community we are building and helping, and consider how you can become another essential thread in the cloth we are weaving to create more justice throughout our country and the world. The cloth we are weaving ensures that we are supporting the hearts of those students and families who we fight for every day, as together we reduce stigma, deepen resolve, and further compassion and community care.

Key Principles

This book addresses nine key principles, one for each chapter:

1. Schools have an opportunity and an obligation to help strengthen student mental health and well-being using evidenced-based practices to alleviate trauma and build teacher and student self-care, resiliency, and coping.

2. Student mental health and well-being is interrelated with staff well-being and school climate and culture. By addressing self-care, increasing mental health literacy, developing a collective vision, and furthering a sense of belonging and community,

complete with mental health supports, schools can take critical steps to alleviate stress and trauma and develop resiliency in children and youth.

3. Student mental health and well-being is best aided when solutions are implemented thoughtfully and flexibly; accommodating the individuality of students; seeing them as people first and responding to them in the context of their individual needs and strengths, school climate, families and culture, and communities.

4. Teacher and staff mental health and well-being is best facilitated when schools provide time and resources for teacher and staff self-care and options for modifying working conditions.

5. School leaders have an obligation to increase their knowledge and insights into people and develop their compassion and communication skills.

6. Caring, competent leaders who are most attuned to the needs of vulnerable students are also attuned to the strengths of these students. They lead with a mindset of inclusion, inspiring others, and are always aware of self-care and the wisdom of establishing a sense of trust and elevating compassion, courage, and confidence in their school communities.

7. School leaders are uniquely positioned to set the tone for a culture of compassionate community in their schools and work collaboratively with community organizations and agencies to meet the holistic needs of students and staff.

8. Families and educators need to work as a team to convey consistent and responsive efforts to strengthen the mental health and well-being of students.

9. With a positive mindset, self-care, thinking big, and caring, we can shape our destiny, even in the midst of strife.

Acknowledgments

Our heartfelt thanks to Dr. Larry Davidson, director of the Yale Program for Recovery and Community Health (PRCH) and principal investigator of the New England Mental Health Technology Transfer Center (MHTTC) and Maria Restrepo-Toro, the project manager of the New England MHTTC. Thanks especially to the other faculty, staff, and people with lived experience at PRCH, to their years of dedication and research to advance the recovery of persons living with mental illness, and to the team at the Center for Educational Improvement implementing Heart Centered Learning® and the New England MHTTC. Through a related affiliation with Dr. Hilary Hodgdon at the Trauma Center at the Justice Research Institute, we have also had firsthand guidance regarding trauma, neuroscience, and neuroplasticity.

Our work is also grounded in research in education, psychology, and mental health. We established a way to tie positive outcomes in schools to a childhood trauma learning collaborative and we developed an instrument to encourage educators to measure progress and help schools celebrate success. We are mindful of the passionate, dedicated efforts of the twenty-four Fellows in the New England MHTTC's Childhood-Trauma Learning Collaborative (C-TLC). We are also grateful to the staff at TeachLink who designed and manage the technology platform that powers our tool to measure compassion in schools—the "School-Compassionate Analytic Tool for Educators" (S-CCATE, Mason et al., 2018). We also want to thank a host of researchers who have conducted similar investigations into the power of mindfulness and compassion, including Dr. James Doty and the team at Stanford University for the insights obtained through the Center for Compassion and Altruism Research and Education, Mark Greenberg and researchers at the Pennsylvania State University, and Vicki Zakrzewski at the Greater Good Science Center. Related research on mindset (Yeager & Dweck, 2012), systems change (Senge, 2006), and the knowledge of the power and value of yoga and yogic movements, as well as meditation (Davidson, 2003; Frank, et al., 2014; Seppala, 2009) and executive functioning (Zelazo & Lyons, 2012) have given us confidence in the recommendations we make to schools and educators.

Teams of researchers, focusing on person-centered planning and self-determination have also shaped our views and our beliefs in the power of listening to individuals and taking a strengths-based approach. These include Drs. Maria O'Connell, Janis Tondora, Michael Wehmeyer, Carolyn Hughes, Bonnie Jones, and David West.

The Center for Educational Improvement's expanded network of believers who helped us shape our vision also helped us gear up for our work in New England schools through the initial design, conceptualization, and pilots to reach our goals. This includes Paul Liabenow, the president of CEI; Shlomo Sawilowsky, the statistician at Wayne State University who guided the S-CCATE valida-tion research; and fellow authors, educators, and researchers: Dr. Michele Rivers Murphy, Suzan Mullane, Matt Bergey, Jill Flanders, Kate Retzel, and Dr. Kathleen Sciarappa. The Center's board of directors—and particularly Dr. Nancy Phenis-Bourke, Dr. Melissa Patschke, and Mary Woods—helped us conduct pilot studies using S-CCATE.

Our work has also been informed by three recent books, two coauthored with Drs. Michele Rivers Murphy and Yvette Jackson (*Mindfulness Practices: Cultivating Heart Centered Communities Where Students Focus and Flourish*, 2018 and *Mindful School Communities: The Five Cs of Nurturing Heart Centered Learning,* 2020), and one with Paul Liabenow and Dr. Melissa Patschke (*Visioning Onward: A Guide for ALL Schools,* 2020).

Over the past seven years, a group of virtual interns at the Center for Educational Improvement aided us by conducting background research and developing blog posts and e-newsletter articles that focused on compassion, mindfulness, trauma, and mental health concerns. Special appreciation goes to Kaela Farrise Effie Cummings, Vien Nyugen, Deidre Dunin, Lauren Keisel, Kelsey Remeis, Joanna Marzano, Dalveer Faur, Sofia Duenas, and Aisha Powell, and to others who have assisted with editing, revisions, communications, and providing the glue that holds our work together—particularly Ingrid Padgett.

Our thanks as well to Ariel Curry, Lynne Curry, Gagan Mahindra, Jessica Vidal Desiree Bartlett, Caroline Timmings, and others from Corwin Press for under-standing our passion and commitment and for their loving care, guidance, and expertise in the editing and production of *Compassionate School Practices*.

Our deepest love and thanks to our families and communities. As we wrote this book during a time of global crisis, we relied on loved ones in our homes and far away to provide the assistance necessary to devote our time to this topic while also living through the pandemic ourselves. A special note of appreciation to Chris's siblings for their compassion and kindness, her dad who died at the very young age of forty-seven, and particularly to her mom who left this planet under hospice care as we were finalizing our edits. It has taken many, many years to fully understand the intergenerational impact of early childhood trauma and how our brains and actions are influenced by significant trauma—including how we may not really understand ourselves and our actions during or even after traumatic experiences. Martha expresses a similar tribute, to her dearest friend, Christopher Barker, who was the father of her goddaughter and recently died after a long battle with leukemia. Martha says, "He was the very best teacher I know, encouraged me to become a teacher, and talked through every aspect of our initiative and C-TLC when it was being developed, including the grant application. He met every student with love and compassion, accepting them for who they were and believing they could be even better."

We thank each and every person for their kind words, ready ears, and open hearts. And finally, a heartfelt thank you to the wonderful group of educators who were the inaugural class of C-TLC Fellows. Without your passion, drive, and vulnerability to let us into your schools, share your needs, and allow us to guide you in helping to meet them, this book and this work would not be possible. We are grateful for the work you do for your school communities, and we are honored that you let us share your story with the world.

About the Authors

Christine Mason, PhD, is an educational psychologist and founder and executive director of the Center for Educational Improvement. She is also director of Childhood-Trauma Learning Collaborative at the New England Mental Health Technology Transfer Center, a researcher, a yoga instructor, and lead author of three recent books: *Visioning Onward: A Guide for ALL Schools (2020), Mindfulness Practices: Cultivating Heart Centered Communities (2019), and Mindful School Communities: The Five Cs of Heart Centered Learning* (2020). Chris has served as a researcher, professor, senior scientist in disability education, university professor, evaluator, consultant, and entrepreneur. She has also served as an interim principal at the Miri Piri Academy in Amritsar, India; director of professional development for the Student Support Center in Washington, DC; a senior research scientist with CESSI in McLean, Virginia; and the senior director for research and development with the Council for Exceptional Children in Arlington, Virginia. She has received awards for her research in early childhood education, disabilities education, and most recently an award from the Ashoka Foundation for her pioneering work in Heart Centered Learning.

Dana Asby, MA, MEd, is the director of innovation and research support for the Center for Educational Improvement where she conducts research and writing, oversees management of the School Culture Analytical Tool for Educators (S-CCATE) assessment, and is the copy editor of the *Compassion Action* newsletter. She is also education coordinator at the New England Mental Health Technology Transfer Center where she helps manage several projects including the Childhood-Trauma Learning Collaborative. She is cofounder of Parent in the Moment, where she teaches families how to use mindfulness to reduce stress and increase the bond of love. She studied child development and neuroscience under Dr. Kimberly Noble in the Neurocognition, Early Experience, and Development lab, as well as early childhood and family policy under Drs. Jeanne Brooks-Gunn and Lynn Kagan at Teachers College, Columbia University and educational psychology and creativity under Dr. Bonnie Cramond at the University of Georgia. She was a preschool, early elementary, and junior high school classroom teacher in Missouri, Georgia, New York, and Japan. She is also a trauma-informed yoga teacher, trained at Shaktibarre and Exhale to Inhale.

Meghan Wenzel, MA, is a researcher and writer with the Center for Educational Improvement. With a background in developmental cognitive neuroscience and education, Meghan is interested in early brain development and its implications for learning. She studied cognitive neuroscience at Brown University, as well as neuroscience and education during her masters at Teachers College, where she worked in Professor Kimberly Noble's lab on neurocognition, early experience, and development investigating how socioeconomic inequality impacts brain development. Meghan has worked in a policy and advocacy nonprofit focused on improving the health, safety, education, and economic well-being of Rhode Island's children and in an edtech company building an adaptive learning platform to provide more personalized learning experiences. Currently, she infuses positive psychology into performance management software in order to unlock the potential of every member of the global workforce.

Katherine Volk, MA, is a child development specialist with a particular focus on early childhood and families living in poverty. She has worked with hundreds of community organizations to provide training and technical assistance in the United States and Australia, specifically focused on implementing trauma-informed practices. Katie understands the multidimensional needs of vulnerable children and families, the needs of the paraprofessionals who serve them, and the systems and contexts in which they live and work. Katie is currently a site director with C4 Innovations at the New England Mental Health Technology Transfer Center.

Martha Staeheli, PhD, is a faculty member at the Program for Recovery and Community Health in the Yale School of Medicine Department of Psychiatry and the director of the School Mental Health Initiative for the New England Mental Health Technology Transfer Center. Trained as a secondary English teacher, and with a PhD in public health, she has extensive experience in population health and epidemiology; qualitative and mixed methods research design, analysis, and evaluation; and community and clinical intervention implementation. Her research interests are focused on recovery within substance use and mental health disorders, issues of health disparity and equity, and the health and wellness of under-resourced community, clinical, and educational environments.

Needs and Approaches

The Why?
What? and How?

1

This chapter includes three sections: (I) Why – background on the needs and suggestions for what we should and could be doing, (II) What – solutions we propose, and (III) How – an introduction to successful methods.

I. WHY *Is a Focus on Children's Mental Health and Well-Being So Critical Right Now?*

Natural disasters, war, health concerns, and the current political climate have many people on edge. With the COVID-19 virus causing great uncertainty and anxiety in 2020, people around the globe are adjusting to physical distancing, isolation, and long-term disruptions to the status quo. Adults and children alike were thrust into situations requiring large-scale compliance to new mandates and protocols. Everyone is getting used to a world that requires increased vigilance and cleanliness inside and out of the home, exacerbating anxiety for many. These are just the most recent significant stressors.

In recent years, immigrants, families escaping violence or war-torn nations, and families fearing deportation faced increased levels of stress and anxiety, were more likely to live in poverty, and were more vulnerable to mental health disorders (SAMHSA, 2018a; Hameed, et al., 2018; Zayas & Heffron, 2016). In addition, more children and youth from a variety of racial, ethnic, and socio-economic backgrounds have been directly impacted by school shootings and schools' responses to these shootings. Responses such as lockdown drills can be traumatizing in their own right (NASP, 2019). Children in these situations

FIGURE 1.1   Impact of Childhood Trauma on Emotions and Learning

Childhood exposure to Trauma

Heightened fear, anxiety, and depression

Difficulty regulating emotions and behavior, learning, and interpersonal relationships

are particularly vulnerable. As Bill Adair (2019) points out in *Emotionally Connected Classrooms,* "Young children are particularly vulnerable to anxious emotions others consciously or unconsciously share" (p.47) (see Figure 1.1).

The National Association of Elementary School Principals (2018) reported that the top-ranked concern of principals was addressing the increase of students with emotional problems. Principals were also concerned with related issues including the management of student behavior, student mental health issues, absenteeism, lack of effective adult supervision at home, and student poverty. Interestingly, none of these issues were identified as major concerns just ten years earlier in 2008 (see Figure 1.2).

Trauma and Stress

Trauma and stress for children and youth are manifested in many ways; we are seeing a substantial increase in children dying by suicide and those suffering from self-injuries, particularly among teens. Half of U.S. states reported a 30 percent increase in suicide fatalities between 1999 and 2016 (CDC, 2018). Although the rate of suicide remains highest for teenage boys, there is an alarming increase in the number of girls attempting suicides as well. Additionally, the rate for LGBTQ youth is estimated to be two to seven times higher than for their heterosexual peers (Haas et al., 2011).

FIGURE 1.2   Comparison of Elementary School Principal Concerns 2008–2018

	2008	2018
Percentage of principals with extreme or high concern with the increase in the numbers of students with emotional problems	63.1%	73.7%

Level of principal concern with the increase in the numbers of students with emotional problems

	MAJOR	MINOR	LITTLE TO NO
2008	63.1%	26.9%	10.0%
2018	73.67%	18.8%	7.6%

Source: Adapted from the National Association of Elementary School Principals reports (2018).

Educators as Protective Factors

Educators play a crucial role in promoting well-being and identifying and responding to mental illness in children as soon as possible. We can help children develop a positive, growth mindset; we can provide nurturing environments and assist in developing a sense of resiliency. Each of these protective factors can reduce the impact of traumatic events.

A Social Worker Helps Alleviate Stress Using the Compassionate School Mental Health Model

Cumberland High School in Rhode Island was not a trauma-informed school. The district had begun encouraging the schools to implement mindfulness practices, but the high school had not yet begun. I saw students increasingly reaching out to me for service for panic attacks and generalized anxiety, so much so that I had started a "Relaxation Strategies Group" during 2018–2019 to try to reach more students. After becoming a Fellow with the C-TLC (the Childhood-Trauma Learning Collaborative), it became clear to me that if I could reach our teachers, then they might be able to cultivate a more

(Continued)

(Continued)

compassionate culture in the school that could then result in improved mental health for all.

The faculty participated in the School Compassionate Culture Analytical Tool for Educators (S-CCATE; see Partnerships for Building Student Mental Health and Well-Being later in this chapter] in June 2019, and I shared the results with them when we returned to school for the 2019-2020 school year. This guided the professional development I presented to them monthly on topics such as the effects of trauma on the brain as well as mindfulness experiences and resources. I encouraged them to explore practices that were positive for them. My hope was that when they became comfortable with mindfulness practices on their own, they would be ready to bring them to the classroom. They then participated in the S-CCATE again in June 2020 and showed improvements in all areas.

Although teachers were not required to use mindfulness strategies in their classrooms, administrators observed mindfulness activities being offered by many teachers. Mrs. M, a special education resource teacher who uses Heart Centered Learning, reported that her students were more focused and settled (had better inhibition). She often uses a quick guided meditation from the Internet when students arrive to her class. She says that more students are completing assignments and are less likely to avoid their work with trips to the bathroom, nurse, or water fountain.

I met "Sarah" at the end of her junior year when her sister was getting ready to graduate and go to college. Sarah was a high-achieving student athlete who was experiencing panic attacks for the first time. She was dropping in or requesting support multiple times per week. Every time, we started with breathing and mindful relaxation. She was given a referral for therapy to help her with continued support over the summer. When Sarah returned to school in September 2019, she was a different girl. She was no longer in therapy and was watching her sleep hygiene carefully. She had a daily practice of meditation and yoga, which she knew to employ at any time outside of her regular schedule. More importantly, she now saw her fears as something she could handle with these new tools. She even became a school "reporter," participating in a monthly video news production.

Lisa Parker, LICSW

School Social Worker

Fellow Advisor for the Yale Childhood-Trauma Learning Collaborative (L. Parker, personal communication, July 2020)

Educators can also promote equity and empower youth as schools become more trauma-skilled. We can start by providing more culturally responsive outreach, education, and services. Hiring a diverse workforce allows students to develop strong relationships with people with more shared experiences and culture. Because youth mental health treatment relies on a positive relationship between the young person and the service provider, respect, shared trust, and open communication are paramount. When more counselors, therapists, and other mental health service providers look like the students struggling with their mental health, the more likely they are to seek out and continue treatment (McGuire & Miranda, 2008). Additionally, nurturing students' strengths, instead of focusing on weaknesses, will inspire learning and higher intellectual performance (Jackson, 2015). Replacing punitive consequences with restorative justice can facilitate building healthy relationships, repair harm, empower youth, and promote justice and equity. Schools that remove zero-tolerance policies can improve equity, retention, and academic performance (Gregory & Evans, 2020). What else is needed? Consider the following:

- Empowering teachers by providing cultural responsiveness training around youth mental health topics

- Becoming more trauma-skilled as a school community

- Identifying and nurturing students' strengths and interests

- Examining school policies like tracking and labeling

- Teaching all students the highest quality curricula that accelerates creative and critical thinking

- Teaching students about how the brain works and cultivating a growth mindset

During and after a mental health crisis, educators, including teachers, administrators, psychologists, and social workers, have a vital role to play. During a crisis, schools can respond compassionately and respectfully, identify immediate needs and concerns, gather information, suggest coping and stabilization mechanisms, and connect students with personal assistance and relevant mental health professionals (MHTTC, 2019). After a crisis, schools can aid staff and students as they make sense of what happened. Teachers can create open, welcoming, and compassionate environments, model positive coping mechanisms, and invite students to talk with them or other trusted adults as needed.

However, currently, many educators feel unsupported and ill-prepared to recognize and address mental health concerns. We need to better assist teachers—often our first-line responders—and provide them with the necessary resources and training to aid students in dealing with mental health issues. As a first step, the Mental Health Technology Transfer Center Network (MHTTC Network) compiled existing resources to help educate, train, and guide educators in promoting mental health (MHTTC Network, 2020). One of its resources, *After a School Tragedy,* was "designed to help schools better support students and families in the aftermath of violence and trauma." It provides strategies to assist schools and communities with readiness, response, and recovery to support resilience in the face of a tragedy (MHTTC Network, 2019).

Currently, many educators feel unsupported and ill-prepared to recognize and address mental health concerns.

Why Are Teachers and Schools Not Better Prepared?

A large percentage of educators report a high level of concern for student mental health needs (93 percent) and the need for further training in mental health (85 percent) (Moon et al., 2017).

Below are some trends from the past two to three decades that have helped shape where we are today, with teachers, administrators, and schools underprepared to deliver effective services to at-risk youth.

- Our focus has been elsewhere: consider *No Child Left Behind,* high academic standards, STEM/STEAM, and competition with others around the world (Mason, Liabenow, & Patschke, 2020; Ravitch, 2016).

- Schools have historically shied away from going too deeply into the realm of social emotional learning and character development (Tate, 2019).

- We have used a system of "referral" to others, leaving a lot of the hard work to therapists and families. There aren't enough psychiatrists and counselors to meet growing demand for these services, and often people are asked to wait months before they're able to get an appointment (Johnson, 2016).

- We are caught in a cycle of trauma and stress, and frankly we have been taken by surprise—the severity of the concerns has gradually emerged over the past two decades—and we just have not been alert to the needs (APA, 2011).

- Schools and educators have missed the moral imperative to address foundational needs of youth and societies (Shirley, 2009).

- At the pre-service level, change is sometimes difficult and assisting universities in coming up with strategies to stay abreast of the most recent developments is time consuming and not always productive (Adams, 2013).

- Educators for the most part have not kept up with the arena of neuroscience and knowledge about executive functioning and how children learn (Mason, Rivers Murphy, & Jackson, 2019).

- Many of the strategies and approaches that have been recommended are complex and take considerable bandwidth to implement. There are issues around funding, personnel, infrastructure, and decision making (Walker, 2018).

My Biggest Mental Health Concerns

Look at your school and community and think about your own "whys." What are your biggest mental health concerns? Take a minute to record your thoughts for each of the four environments below.

	Biggest Mental Health Concern(s)	How much do you know about how adults are responding to youth mental health challenges?	What else would you like to know about how to respond with compassion?
My classroom			
My school			
My state			
Our nation			

Risk Factors Influencing the Increase in Behavioral and Emotional Challenges

In 2019, EAB (formerly known as the Education Advisory Board) conducted a survey of over 1,900 educators and found that 34 percent of the respondents reported an increase in students with behavioral and emotional challenges. Of that 34 percent, 29 percent represent those respondents who reported a significant increase in students with those same challenges. When asked to explain these sizable increases in disruptive behavior, educators ranked potential causes:

1. History of trauma in the family

2. Untreated mental health conditions

3. Modern-day changes in parenting

4. Overexposure to electronic devices

5. Inadequate amount of daytime recreation

6. Increased academic pressure

The survey also found that districts and schools lack clear and consistent guidelines to aid teachers in managing student behavior, and teachers feel ill-prepared to address and manage behavioral disruptions (EAB, 2019).

Other risk factors for behavioral and emotional challenges include drug use, the recent opioid epidemic, poverty, economic hardships, family conflict, community violence, and abuse and neglect (Takeuchi et al., 1991; Welsh et al., 2018). In households with parents experiencing increased stress, drug use, poverty, and uncertainty, families are likely to also experience conflict, fatigue, caregiver depression, maladaptive parenting, and lower levels of family communication, emotional support, or dependability (Sheidow et al., 2014). These factors are associated with both externalizing (disruptive, aggressive) behaviors and also the more difficult to identify internalizing (withdrawal, depressive) behaviors.

In a recent report, the Centers for Disease Control and Prevention (CDC) declared childhood trauma a preventable public health crisis (Chatterjee, 2019). While it is preventable, it will take considerable, concerted effort on many levels, from many sectors.

The large percentage of the population that is impacted by trauma suggests that trauma is not something that simply impacts individuals; it is a societal concern that calls for collective efforts. At a societal level, reducing episodes of violence, increasing a feeling of community

ACES: The Numbers

The CDC found that about 60 percent of Americans have experienced at least one adverse childhood experience (ACE) and 15.6 percent have experienced four or more distinct types (Chatterjee, 2019). These experiences range from the death of a loved one or the loss of a pet to bullying or illness. However, not everyone reacts to a situation in the same way—what may be traumatic for one person may not be considered traumatic by another.

safety, and fostering the development of parental skills, for example, may pay off many times over.

Trauma and stress touch all of us. For some, trauma is particularly adverse due to the absence of caregiver support, reassurance, or emotional attachment. However, none of us is immune to trauma or its aftermath. A stress overload can result in elevated cortisol and adrenaline levels, signaling for the brain to focus on anxiety and perceived threats rather than a sense of well-being and learning (NIH, 2002). When cortisol levels are chronically elevated, hyperarousal, hypervigilance, and an overly sensitive threat-detection system may take over, often resulting in insomnia, anxiety, fear, and reactive anger (Greenberg, 2018).

> Trauma is not something that simply impacts individuals; it is a societal concern that calls for collective efforts.

The Developmental Consequences of Prolonged Exposure to Trauma

Although other factors, such as genetic predisposition, are associated with mental illness, trauma is often a precursor (Fryers & Brugha, 2013; Breslau et al., 2014). Children exposed to trauma may experience significant barriers to learning, sometimes with lifelong repercussions. For children and adolescents, trauma affects cognitive, academic, and socio-emotional-behavioral functioning (Perfect et al., 2016). For individuals with trauma, academic difficulties may present as learning or hyperactive ADHD disorders.

Prolonged exposure to trauma and adversity undermines normal development of brain circuits, installing significant barriers that impede the ability to cope with stress, establish healthy relationships, and regulate attention, emotions, and behavior (Perry, 2009). Executive functioning, which regulates attention, memory, and decision making, is often impaired by chronic stress and trauma (Hair et al., 2015). In extreme instances, disassociation, hallucinations, and psychosis may occur, as they may provide a self-protective escape valve for an individual who has suffered severe psychological distress (Rosen et al., 2017).

The Influence of Trauma on Mental Health

Some of the common signs of an increased risk of mental illness include drastic changes in behavior, sleep patterns, or personality; increased agitation; lack of interest in everyday activities; difficulties thinking clearly; and intense worries or fears that interfere with normal activities. Children and youth may also experience sudden overwhelming fear, severe mood swings, or severe out of control risk-taking that may cause harm to themselves or others (NAMI,

2020b). There are multiple ways that prolonged and relentless stress influences the behavior and actions of individuals—common reactions to trauma are to "flee, fight, or freeze" (Seltzer, 2015).

Children who are in the midst of considerable stress and anxiety may be inattentive, fearful, or hypervigilant, putting them on constant alert, ever waiting for the next storm of thunder and lightning. In some cases, it may be difficult to ascertain whether trauma or a neurological dysfunction is the underlying condition. In *Finding Audrey*, a novel for teens that gently explores mental illness, Sophie Kinsella writes, "Our house is like a weather system. It ebbs and flows, flares up and subsides. It has the time of radiant blue bliss, days of gray dismalness and thunderstorms that flare up out of nowhere. Right now, the thunderstorm is coming my way, thunder-lightning, thunder-lightning . . . " (2014, p. 20). Imagine waiting as thunder and lightning draw ever closer each moment and trying to focus on reading or math.

Equity Issues in Access to Mental Health Support and Advocacy

Not everyone experiences trauma, mental health symptoms, or mental health treatment to the same degree and with equitable access to quality supports and treatment options. These disparities exist because of differences in access to health insurance or financial means, systemic (and often historic) prejudices of the healthcare system, rural or urban health care deserts, and cultural or educational differences in how we understand and trust mental health providers. Within educational settings, these disparities are often clearly evident and are sometimes magnified, but schools can also provide opportunities to work with the goal of equity through ready access to aid for children and families, a reduction in the stigma surrounding mental health disorders, and opportunities for advocacy for families and communities.

Inequities, Prejudice, and the Need to Reframe Our Perspectives

 Dr. Orinthia Harris, the Early Childhood STEAM instructor for the Center for Educational Improvement, elaborated on equity issues she discussed during a webinar on equity, justice, and children's well-being:

Since inception, America has legally and socially sanctioned privileges and rights to one group of people . . . while at the same time denying these rights to others . . . often to the point of death in the form of genocide, slavery, interment, lynching, immigration, and naturalization laws. Our education system has not escaped these inequities, and students who do not fall on the right side of privilege continue to face the negative impacts of an unjust system daily. I've seen these systemic inequities as a board member in Washington DC, and as a teacher in Howard County, Maryland.

Many of the inequities my students faced in the district were due to flawed governance, mismanagement of funding, and lack of quality programming. As a teacher in Howard County, I noticed many students of color being misidentified as special needs or learning disabled, as well as being denied access to quality programming.

In one specific case, I had two students score one point shy of passing the Gifted and Talented entrance exam for the following year. As a teacher, we could recommend students for the program who were within one to two points of the cut-off. I recommended both students, one a White male and one an African American female. They admitted my White student with no questions. They denied my African American student. When I questioned their decision, I discovered it was based on their perception of her not being capable enough to handle the rigor. As their teacher for the full academic year, I assured them that they were both up for the challenge. The next reason they gave was that she may not have the support at home, at which point I bluntly stated that this was a race issue and that either they both needed to be admitted or denied. Thankfully, they admitted both students, but only because I spoke up.

Advocacy is key if we want to make sustainable changes within our education system. As the world of education begins a massive paradigm shift due to the COVID-19 pandemic, we have an opportunity to change the systemic injustice that has sought to tear down communities of color. We cannot allow COVID-19 to further exacerbate the many systemic inequities that have persisted throughout our education system. Instead, we must use this time to thoughtfully create a plan that gives all students equal access to a high-quality education, both in the classroom and virtually. This cannot be done by simply giving all students a device without considering if they have Internet, electricity, or may be facing homelessness. The barriers and challenges many students of color face in both rural and urban schools is very real. These issues must be addressed from the lens of a broken system rather than a broken child. We must recognize the racial prejudices that exist in our own lens and be willing to question and reframe our perspective of students when necessary. Adversity does not predestine children to poor outcomes. (O. Harris, personal communication, May 2020)

Barriers to Service Delivery in Rural Areas

Rural areas also face unique mental health challenges, including a shortage of qualified service providers, lack of school investment, lack of coordinated systems of care, provider discrimination, and underlying assumptions that leave clinicians less able to accurately read the severity of symptoms among students of color. In rural areas, the suicide rate for youth is twice that for urban or suburban areas and only 33 percent of emergency rooms report having policies for responding to children's mental health crises (Remick et al., 2018). Dennis Mohatt, Vice President for Behavioral Health at the Western Interstate Commission Mental Health Program, provided "the hard facts" (2018):

> More than 60 percent of rural Americans live in mental health professional shortage areas, that more than 90 percent of all psychologists and psychiatrists and 80 percent of [professionals with a] Masters of Social Work, work exclusively in metropolitan areas. More than 65 percent of rural Americans get their mental health care from a primary healthcare provider, and the mental health crisis responder for most rural Americans is a law enforcement officer.

Being a Part of a Marginalized Community

Being part of a marginalized community takes its toll in many ways. Zaretta Hammond (2014) describes how this contributes to needing to be on constant alert: "When we look at the stress some students experience in the classroom because they belong to marginalized communities because of race, class, language, or gender, we have to understand their safety-threat detection system is already cued to be on the alert for social and psychological threats based on past experience" (p. 45).

Gayle Macklem in *Preventative Mental Health at School: Evidence-Based Services for Students* (2014) writes of the barriers these students encounter to receiving services:

> Disparities in mental health care have been well documented. Sixteen- and 17-year-old boys are the least likely of all school-aged students to be given help for mental health problems. Lesbian, gay, bisexual, or transgender adolescents; homeless teens; incarcerated teens; children under the child welfare umbrella; uninsured adolescents; and adolescents in rural areas have particular difficulty accessing treatment. Publicly funded insurance is available to some students, but even in this case, many states have limits on those services. (p. 2)

When a Crisis Strikes

Educators are interested in not only providing preventative and general support services for youth facing emotional challenges; they also want to know what to do if a mental health crisis arises. According to the National Alliance on Mental Illness (NAMI), effective response systems for handling mental health crises include 24-hour crisis lines, walk-in clinics, psychiatric urgent care centers, and mobile crisis centers (2020a). Individuals and families receive pre-assessment screening, counseling, triage, information, and referrals, and hospitals have guidelines and policies to provide for the immediate safety of youth in crisis. If resources permit, it is useful to designate a specific room in the school building as a calm space for these youth (Feuer et al., 2018).

> The National Suicide Prevention Lifeline (1-800-273-TALK) provides free and confidential guidance twenty-four hours a day, seven days a week. Over 150 local crisis centers participate in the Substance Abuse Mental Health Services Administration (SAMHSA)-funded Lifeline, which also has web-support for families and individuals in crisis.

For youth who have experienced a mental health crisis, trauma does not end when they enter a treatment program. In treatment, they encounter risks of dislocation from normal life, family, friends, and normal psychological and social development as well as risks of learning unhelpful behaviors and forming unhealthy relationships (Edwards et al., 2015).

Youth may have trouble during the transition "back to normal" since they were suddenly disconnected from their community during the treatment process, often in another town or remote location unable to speak with friends and family. *The more often treatment can be provided in the least restrictive environment possible—one that is more reflective of day-to-day life—the easier it will be for a young person experiencing a mental health crisis to return to their regular life.*

The Bridge Program: A Mental Health Transition Program at Methuen High School in Massachusetts

The Bridge Program at Methuen High School in Methuen, Massachusetts is a short-term (six to eight week), intensive general education program that aims to serve some of the highest need students as they navigate returning to "normal" after an extended absence or hospitalization due to a serious medical or mental health challenge. It is modeled after the Bridging Resilient Youth in Transition (BRYT) model created by the Brookline Center for Community Mental Health in Brookline, MA. The BRYT model has now been adapted and implemented in 137 schools across Massachusetts and

(Continued)

(Continued)

beyond, collectively enrolling 140,000 students (The Brookline Center for Community Mental Health, 2020).

Alison Sumski, a Bridge Program Support Specialist (and also a C-TLC Fellow), works with the student's parent(s) and his or her school counselor to organize a reentry meeting for students returning to school after a hospitalization. They develop a scaffolded plan for the student's reintegration. This might include modifying the school day, meeting the student at a separate entrance in the morning to limit peer interaction, walking them to and from classes, and more. Students typically spend their first few days back in school in the Bridge room, which is a dedicated therapeutic space exclusively used for the program.

Below is a case study of a student, Jim* (*name has been changed to protect confidentiality), who successfully graduated from the Bridge program in the 2018-2019 school year with tremendous gains academically, socially, and emotionally. Jim is one of twenty-eight students who have benefited from this Tier-III intensive mental health program over the course of two school years at Methuen High School.

In September 2018, Jim, a sophomore, seemed depressed following a recent break-up, declining grades, self-image issues, and an overall feeling of lack of purpose and direction. Previously a high-achieving student, Jim has had difficulty focusing in class, socializing with peers, or even getting out of bed in the morning, eventually leading to an alarming increase in suicidal ideation. His self-esteem was quite low, largely due to his insecurities over chronic cystic acne. Jim reported spending upward of forty-five minutes in the bathroom each morning just looking in the mirror and feeling horrible about himself, which fed into his negative thought spirals, introversion, and unwillingness to be seen in public, including at school.

In the Bridge intake process, Alison worked with Jim to set up therapeutic goals around setting routines, addressing self-esteem issues head-on, and breaking down cognitive distortions regarding his self-worth and place in the world.

One particularly useful strategy was behavioral activation scheduling, a cognitive behavioral therapy technique designed to intentionally plan activities into each day, hour-by-hour, to help break up the vicious cycle of depression. For Jim, this meant breaking down his daily routine, limiting time allowed looking in the mirror, making time to eat nutritious meals, and incorporating some kind of physical activity into each day. Alison would also check in with Jim daily, facilitate communication and makeup work with his teachers, and have a standing forty-minute counseling session with him each week. As tracked through a psychosocial progress monitoring, Jim "graduated" from Bridge in nineteen weeks with a 100 percent decrease in depressive symptom presentation (Moderate to None/Minimal on the Patient Health Questionnaire-9), an 11.1 percent increase in self-esteem (Normal on the Rosenberg Self-Esteem Scale), a 146.6 percent increase in behavioral activation (Low-Average to High on the Behavioral Activation for Depression Scale-Long Form), and a 90 percent increase in school and class attendance (beginning with attending 0 classes in December 2018 and ending with attending 90 percent of classes in May 2019). These tremendous gains reflect Jim's resilience in a dark period of his life and speak volumes to the necessity of quality mental health services in schools to prevent students from what can oftentimes be dire alternatives.

Whatever approach your school uses to handle mental health crises, *it is essential that explicit protocols are in place to assist students as they return to school.* Children and adolescents are extremely impressionable and need access to caring, compassionate adults to grow—especially when they have experienced something as traumatic as a mental health crisis.

Where Does Your School Stand on Mental Health Crises?

☐ We have a protocol for assisting youth during and after a mental health crisis.

☐ We have implemented this protocol effectively.

☐ We need to improve our plan.

II. WHAT Do We Need?

Children and youth need guidance from trusted adults and peers, as well as structure and participation in activities that will build resiliency and coping strategies (Milaniak & Widom, 2015). Both schools and parents can provide valued assistance by openly discussing mental health and creating a safe space for youth to feel comfortable disclosing sensitive information. Teachers can also help alleviate student stress through mindfulness interventions, which will also assist in strengthening cognitive performance, student achievement, executive functioning, prosocial behavior, and socioemotional competence (Bakosh et al., 2016; Flook et al., 2010; Mason, Rivers Murphy, & Jackson, 2019, 2020; Schonert-Reichl & Lawlor, 2010). Scientific evidence is showing mindfulness-based therapies are effective in alleviating many symptoms of mental illness. The Center for Mindfulness Studies (2015) suggests the following:

> Mindfulness practice increases compassion over time. It does this by developing the capacity to be kind to ourselves, accepting ourselves for who we are and not what we imagine we "should" be; therefore, allowing us to accept others as they are, and not as we imagine they "should" be. In this practice, we begin to understand the necessity of community and inclusivity (for more information see Chapter 7).

National organizations such as SAMHSA, NAMI, and the Suicide Prevention Resource Center (SPRC) have valuable resources to help schools build a caring, responsive community that are available at no cost online. *What a Difference a Friend Makes* is just one of many SAMHSA initiatives designed to promote peer supports to aid the recovery of youth. This initiative explains how friends can offer reassurance, companionship, and emotional strength through expressing interest and concern. NAMI has a related campaign, *Say It Out Loud,* which provides adults with a toolkit to use to talk with youth about mental health. The toolkit includes a short film, a discussion guide, and fact sheets. Additionally, SPRC has a guide, *Preventing Suicide: The Role of High School Teachers,* that provides training around how to identify and respond to students at risk as well as a list of relevant resources and materials (SPRC, 2019).

III. HOW Can We Approach Mental Health in Schools?

Various efforts in the past two decades have addressed mental health concerns—many of which we describe in Chapter 3. However, we choose to begin here with a framework and approach that we consider most critical and viable to scaling up a proactive response that addresses a multitude of stressors and concerns, the Compassionate School Mental Health Model (see preface, Figure 0.1.). Our intention is to aid schools in guiding individual children as educators cultivate a sustainable community that is structured to foster trust and build resilience.

To address the needs of students facing the most serious behavioral and emotional challenges, schools have an array of options that fall into the following areas (see preface, Figure 0.1):

- Prevention: Reduce the Causes

- Support the Child

Children and youth need guidance from trusted adults and peers, as well as structure and participation in activities that will build resiliency and coping strategies (Milaniak & Widom, 2015).

- Develop Protective Factors

- Build Resiliency

Although traditionally a mental health approach has followed a medical model and focused on prevention and treatment of the individual child, research on evidence-based practices confirms the importance of systems that address environmental changes. This research supports the wisdom of strengthening the environment and encouraging children and youth to build positive interpersonal relationships (Harvard Center on the Developing Child, 2017). Such an approach helps to develop inner capacity and sense of self, while restructuring interpersonal dynamics away from threats, bullying, and hardships.

Each of the factors in the Compassionate School Mental Health Model plays an important role in assisting children and youth cope with stress and providing relief from exacerbated mental and emotional challenges. However, costs and benefits are associated with each. Consider the following:

Prevention: Reduce the Causes

Teachers can aid prevention through classroom rules, procedures, discipline strategies, and activities that enhance student self-esteem and encourage children to feel good about themselves. When teachers and others know the signs and warning signals of deteriorating mental health, they can aid students in getting needed assistance sooner, often bolstering the child's inner resiliency and interrupting a chain that could result in more serious mental health concerns.

Support the Child

Cognitive behavioral therapy, and for younger students, play therapy, can help children and youth understand their emotions and cope with daily concerns. Art, music, and dance therapies can be effective tools to help students in expressing and processing difficult emotions. Therapists can also provide youth with strategies to handle their mood swings, anxieties, or depression more effectively.

Schools have the potential to better connect students with the services they need. "Treating children in schools can powerfully overcome issues of cost, transportation, and stigma that typically restrict children from receiving mental health services" (Castro, 2018). Mental health services blended into routine academic instruction in the classroom are particularly effective, compared to pull-out services or implementation of a separate mental health curriculum altogether. Moreover, treatments that are implemented multiple times per week are more than twice as effective as treatments that are only implemented on a weekly (or less) basis (Castro, 2018). However, funding, the availability of staff, the stigma attached to therapy, and the child's reluctance to reveal his or her vulnerabilities to the therapist all present substantial barriers that may limit the effectiveness of this treatment. Therapy, although important, is best provided in a compassionate setting that is simultaneously developing peer supports, resiliency, and protective factors.

Build Resiliency

Resiliency, or the ability to bounce back or recover quickly from challenges and setbacks, can be nurtured in classrooms and community settings. Resiliency is strengthened by a sense of optimism, effective problem solving, flexibility, and perseverance. Teachers can assist students in preparing for adversities they may face in the future through providing constructive feedback and scaffolding success as they present challenges to students.

Resiliency During the COVID-19 Pandemic

Paul Liabenow, the president of the Center for Educational Improvement and the executive director of the Michigan Elementary and Middle School Principals Association, spoke with us about his view concerning resiliency:

> COVID-19 has taxed school principals across the country with challenges never before experienced. Their courageous and innovative leadership has helped to reduce public anxiety and led to wide scale daily feeding programs supporting millions of needy students. Our use of distance learning platforms built and loaded with quality learning resources replete with motivating videos to encourage student engagement is unprecedented.

> As devastating as COVID-19 has been, it has exposed massive gaps in education equity and quality. It has led to school, district, and state level planning for closing equity and resource gaps like never before. Key leaders in state legislatures and departments of education are recognizing the need to build social emotional skills; this is leading to policy changes and additional funding for resources.

Post COVID-19, K-12 education will make mindfulness, resilience, and all of social emotional learning a top priority. Increased student engagement and achievement, as well as a general improvement of quality of life, will be the result.

A Sense of Purpose Creates Resiliency

 Research has shown that having a sense of purpose can aid people in increasing their resiliency to stress and mental health challenges. Journalist Emily Esfahani Smith (2020) interviewed philosophers, religious leaders, psychology researchers, and "other luminaries" about what makes their lives meaningful and she identified some commonalities, which she names the four pillars of meaning:

1. Belonging

2. Purpose

3. Storytelling

4. Transcendence

When we are able to connect to others and share our stories with them, we are better able to find a sense of purpose, of what we are meant to be doing, and why we are meant to be here. Understanding and expressing one's life as a narrative can be a powerfully healing process. Schools can cultivate moments of transcendence by allowing for time in the day to slow down and reflect, perhaps using mindfulness (Esfahani Smith, 2020):

> Transcendent experiences are those moments when we're lifted above the hustle and bustle of daily life and come into contact with something bigger. They are experiences of beauty and awe that take us outside our own head, make us feel smaller, and at the same time more connected to the world and people around us. There are lots of ways to experience transcendence, like in nature, through religious or spiritual practices like meditation, music, dancing, and so on. These experiences bring us into the present moment.

Coping is directly tied to resiliency. When researchers and psychologists examined who copes well in a crisis, it turns out that people who have adopted a spirit of "tragic optimism," meaning they are able to find hope and meaning in life, are the most resilient. One study tracked a group of young adults after the September 11 terrorist attacks and found that those who were able to find some good in what was happening around them were less likely to develop symptoms of depression (Esfahani Smith, 2020). Providing the space and time for students to find their purpose can be powerful for the prevention and treatment of mental health challenges.

Develop Protective Factors

Nurturing adults can help rebuild neuropathways for children with attachment disorders who may have failed to form normal attachments with a primary caregiver during the first few years of life. *Nurturing involves listening to students, honoring their choices, guiding them through difficulties that emerge, and helping them develop healthy relationships with others.* One nurturing adult, who could be a teacher, can aid in developing a child's sense of safety and security (Harvard Center on the Developing Child, 2017). Additionally, consistency in rules and routines can foster a feeling of safety and trust for children who may have experienced chaotic parenting.

 Suzan Mullane, a former high school counselor and teacher in Anchorage, Alaska:

During summer school, I noticed a student angrily scratching his arms during a credit recovery assignment on *Romeo and Juliet*. I had observed this behavior before, but not in this student. Privately, I invited this student, who I'll call Sam, to talk to me after class. We had established a positive working relationship so I was hopeful he'd disclose his obvious angst. I felt Sam's trauma was fresh, painful, and urgent. The night before, Sam disclosed to his parents he was gay and it was then they told him to pack his bag, because he was going to hell. Sam's sense of shame, fear, and betrayal were very real and interfering with his credit recovery, which he needed in order to graduate. I knew if Sam had dropped out, that would increase his sense of shame and possibly delay employment. Assuring me he was safe and staying with a neighborhood family, I invited Sam to come up with a plan to complete a paper—one that would help him focus and process his grief and anger. Sam chose to write about his family rejection; he wrote sixty-two pages! He compared his family pressure to Romeo's quest for love, freedom, and acceptance. In the end, Sam quit scratching, completed the paper, and processed his grief through writing. He ultimately graduated.

Establishing a warm, trusting classroom gives students a sense of safety. Rather than making a referral for mental health testing, it is less restrictive and less stigmatizing if accommodations can be made in the classroom— accommodations that offer choice that gives students a sense of purpose, joy, or comfort. When students have an opportunity to talk in a safe environment, where trust is established, they can often discover solutions to their own personal dilemmas—the art of self-determination. Weaving STEAM and music into the curriculum can also give students a sense of purposeful joy. Joy and purpose promote emotional regulation, which is the foundation for all learning. (S. Mullane, personal communication, May 2020)

How We Support Student Mental Health at My School

☐ We have implemented prevention strategies.

☐ We have systems in place to help treat individual children and youth who most need assistance.

☐ We are strengthening protective factors.

☐ We are building resiliency.

Partnerships for Building Student Mental Health and Well-Being

In 2018, the Program for Recovery and Community Health (PRCH) at Yale University was awarded SAMHSA funds to establish one of ten regional Mental Health Technology Transfer Centers (MHTTC) around the country, focusing on New England states (Connecticut, Maine, Massachusetts, New Hampshire, Rhode Island, and Vermont). One of the aims of the New England MHTTC School Mental Health Initiative is "to enhance school culture and prepare school personnel to improve the mental health of school-aged children in the New England region" (MHTTC, 2020). There are three goals:

Goal 1	Foster alliances to address the needs of children and youth who have experienced or are at risk of experiencing significant trauma.
Goal 2	Provide publicly available, free training and technical assistance to early childhood, elementary, and secondary teachers, principals, school psychologists, and other school staff.
Goal 3	Accelerate adoption and implementation of evidenced-based mental health practices through the C-TLC for New England.

PRCH is completing its work through a contract with the Center for Educational Improvement, a small nonprofit organization whose signature program is Heart Centered Learning®, a theoretical framework for social emotional learning and community building.

With a strengths-based approach, recovery for persons with mental illness involves identifying and building on personal and family strengths and aligning plans for recovery with the person's own values, preferences, and goals. Larry Davidson and colleagues (Davidson et al., 2009) describe this process as a way to give people tools to rebuild their lives: "The definition of recovery that we have used in our own system transformation efforts, for example, describes recovery as 'a process of restoring a meaningful sense of belonging to one's community and positive sense of identity apart from one's condition while rebuilding a life despite or within the limitations imposed by that condition'" (p. 29).

In step with PRCH's belief in the power of healing environments, the Center for Educational Improvement's foundational approach (shown in Figure 1.3), Heart Centered Learning®, is designed to strengthen children's healing and resiliency through boosting five key evidenced-based elements: consciousness (mindful awareness), compassion, confidence, courage, and community (Mason, Rivers Murphy, & Jackson, 2019, 2020) (see Figure 1.3).

FIGURE 1.3   The Five Cs of Heart Centered Learning (Mason, Rivers Murphy, & Jackson, 2020)

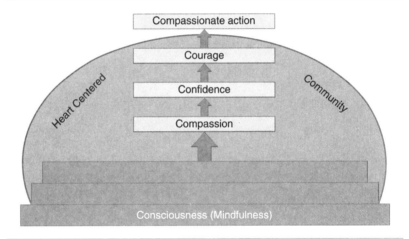

Source: Used with permission. From *Mindful School Communities: The Five Cs of Nurturing Heart Centered Learning* by Christine Mason, Michele M. Rivers Murphy, and Yvette Jackson. Copyright 2020 by Solution Tree Press, 555 North Morton Street, Bloomington, IN 47404, 800.733.6786, SolutionTree.com. All rights reserved.

Where Should Schools Begin?

 Developing a plan for enhancing the mental health of children in schools begins with a self-assessment and a visioning process. Some schools, like those who needed to quickly pivot to distance learning during the COVID-19 pandemic, might have to embark on this journey in the middle of a crisis. In early 2019 when they joined the C-TLC, many of the Fellows described an unaddressed crisis of trauma and mental health challenges in their schools, disrupting the lives of those experiencing them, their teachers, and their classmates. They overwhelmingly agreed that when their schools were thrown into collective trauma a year later, the need for this visioning work—starting with some kind of needs assessment—was even more pressing.

To assess their school climate, the C-TLC used the School Compassionate Culture Analytical Tool for Educators (S-CCATE). Validated on a national sample of over 800 educators, S-CCATE provides a step-by-step online process for synthesizing data on individual perceptions of proficiency (Mason, et al., 2018). S-CCATE is also aligned with Heart Centered Learning and our recommendations for school leadership. Using a four-point Likert scale, with S-CCATE, respondents answer forty questions, rating implementation from "Needs Improvement" to "Exemplary."

S-CCATE is based on current research regarding the factors that improve well-being, executive functioning, and neuroplasticity among children and youth—all of which help students gain resiliency, alleviate trauma, and overcome barriers to learning and decision making. S-CCATE results provide users with feedback on the assessment of students' sense of safety, leadership skill development, development of student confidence, and compassionate school policies and protocols. S-CCATE results include ratings, means, and percentages based on a national norm group, with a comparison to local school or district results.

When schools complete S-CCATE or similar school climate assessments, they gain information that can help shape a vision for their school. School leaders can use these data to consider how to implement components of heart centered practices. Schools may want to consider the eight-step iterative visioning process we describe in *Visioning Onward* (Mason, Liabenow, & Patschke, 2020).

Other school climate assessments may also be useful, although few of them have the direct reference to childhood trauma, neurobiology, and mindfulness that can be found with S-CCATE. Most of the other available instruments have not undergone a validation study and/or may measure only some of the components that are included in S-CCATE. These other instruments include the *Comprehensive School Climate Inventory* developed by the National School Climate Center (Guo et al., 2011) and school climate surveys that have been developed for various states, such as Delaware, Maryland, and California (Bear et al., 2011; Bradshaw et al., 2014; Hanson & Voight, 2014; Kohl et al., 2013). See also research by Wang and Degol (2016) and social emotional learning assessment reviews by the Collaborative for Academic and Social Emotional Learning (CASEL, n.d.).

School leaders can also consider their school community and how they use heart centered practices to strengthen their school climate (see Figure 1.4 below).

FIGURE 1.4   Heart Centered Practices

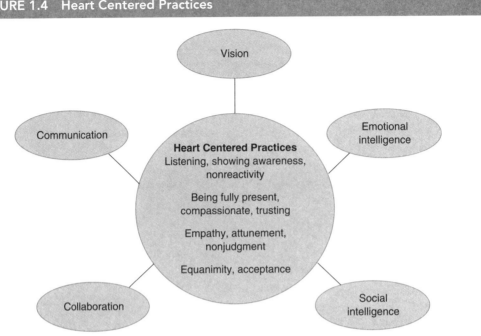

Source: Mason, Rivers Murphy & Jackson (2020) p. 157, as adapted from Goleman & Boyatzis, 2008; Goleman, et al., 2002; Wells, 2015.

As Daniel Goleman and Peter Senge (2014) have written, "As more parents, educators, and students bring social and emotional learning and systems thinking into schools, we will see happier, calmer, and more personally mature students succeeding in their lives and contributing to vital societal changes" (p. 8).

To review, we recommend beginning by assessing needs, developing a vision, and then ensuring that staff have adequate professional development so that they have sufficient knowledge and skills to infuse compassionate, Heart Centered Learning® practices into their instruction throughout the academic school day (see also Chapter 2).

How My School Is Implementing Compassionate Practices

☐ We have conducted a needs assessment.

☐ We have developed a vision for service delivery.

☐ We have ensured that staff have adequate professional development.

☐ We have a plan for infusing relevant instruction to enhance youth understanding of emotions, compassion, and related skills throughout the academic school day.

Implementation of Heart Centered Learning (HCL) in New England

The C-TLC is implementing HCL in New England. In 2019, Fellows reported the following:

- Their knowledge increased regarding trauma and brain development; implementing yoga, meditation, and mindfulness (95 percent reported an increase); early intervention (89 percent reported an increase); and student self-regulation; needs and concerns of families; mental health concerns; and compassionate discipline (84 percent reported an increase).

- They are actively involved in implementing innovative programs (95 percent reporting some to considerable involvement; 63 percent reporting considerable involvement).

There is great value in both aggregating quantitative data and using individual narratives to understand the complete story of how trauma-informed a school's climate is and on which areas to focus for growth. In our face-to-face meetings, C-TLC staff and Fellows have had opportunities to do informal, qualitative needs assessments. A common thread throughout the most successful methods of providing mental health service was a community-based approach that brought together stakeholders at every level.

The Power of Community-Based Approaches

One of the guiding principles of the New England Mental Health Technology Transfer Center is that "resiliency and recovery are holistic," that there is a need for team-based care that can address prevention, crisis intervention, self-care, family needs, and a coordinated array of natural supports and alternative services. Another of the principles is that "resiliency and recovery are community-based and promoted through collaboration." This includes shared responsibilities for "developing, implementing, monitoring, and evaluating each individual care plan in partnership with child/youth and family or adult" (New England Mental Health Technology Transfer Center, 2019). The power of this approach is reflected in the other guiding principles, including the value of mutual support and peer groups, advocacy, and networking. This approach provides options and opportunities for building on strengths, navigating through crises, making informed decisions, involving youth in their own recovery, fostering alliances, and providing for continuity of care.

Comprehensive Behavioral Health Model (CBHM) in Boston Public Schools

The Comprehensive Behavioral Health Model (CBHM) provides a holistic approach to meeting students' mental health needs in Boston Public Schools (BPS). It is one of the best examples of a comprehensive, compassionate school district response to student mental health we have seen in our years of working with schools around the country to benefit youth well-being. Furthermore, it has shown enormous promise for prolonged benefits for students with positive improvements in attendance, academics, and emotional health for students enrolled in the program.

BPS currently serves over fifty thousand students from diverse backgrounds in 125 schools; around 70 percent identify as Latinx/Hispanic or African American/Black, two-thirds qualify for free lunch, one-third are English Language Learners, and families come from 139 countries and speak more than seventy-five languages. In 2010, the school psychologists and pupil adjustment counselors in BPS created CBHM to organize a system-wide approach to promote positive behavioral health and reduce barriers to learning for all students. Partnering with community agencies, BPS has built an infrastructure for the district as it strives to meet the social, emotional, and behavioral needs of students (Pearrow et al., 2016).

Andria Amador, senior director of behavioral health services in Boston Public Schools, notes, "We strongly believe we need to teach social and emotional skills as intensively and purposefully as we teach reading and math. These skills also teach perseverance, which helps keep kids in school and enables them to push through the tough times all adults experience" (Amador, 2020).

Following Brofenbrenner's (1977) theory, BPS's approach began with a review of contextual variables at the macro-level, including a review of cultural context, social values, and cultural values. Next, leaders examined the exosystem, reviewing settings or events such as caregivers' employment, media, or politics that are not directly connected to the child. Then, leaders considered the meso- and microsystems, examining variables that had a direct influence on the child and the relationship among those entities—health services, family, peers, and teachers.

Ten schools participated in the 2012—2013 launch year with another ten schools joining each subsequent year. In 2020, sixty-nine schools, serving more than 34,000 students, participated in CBHM.

Early on, the CBHM emphasized the recommended staffing ratios from the National Association of School Psychologists (NASP, 2010), increasing both the number of school psychologists and also their responsibilities. Over time, the role of the school psychologist in BPS has expanded to include the provision of services in ten domains of practice as recommended by NASP (2010). After receiving training in evidence-based practices to reach all students through prevention services and supports, school psychologists also became more knowledgeable about Positive Behavior Intervention Supports (PBIS), functional behavioral assessments, crisis intervention, leadership, and implementation strategies.

The following curricula have been instrumental in the implementation of its CBMH in Boston:

- For PreK-8th grade, the *Second Step* social-emotional learning curricula are used (Second Step, 2020).

- For high school, topical curricula are used, along with *DBT Skills in Schools* (Mazza et al., 2016), *Break Free from Depression* (BCHNP, 2017), and *Signs of Suicide* (MindWise, 2020) (see Figure 1.5).

FIGURE 1.5   Theory of Change BPS Comprehensive Behavioral Health Model

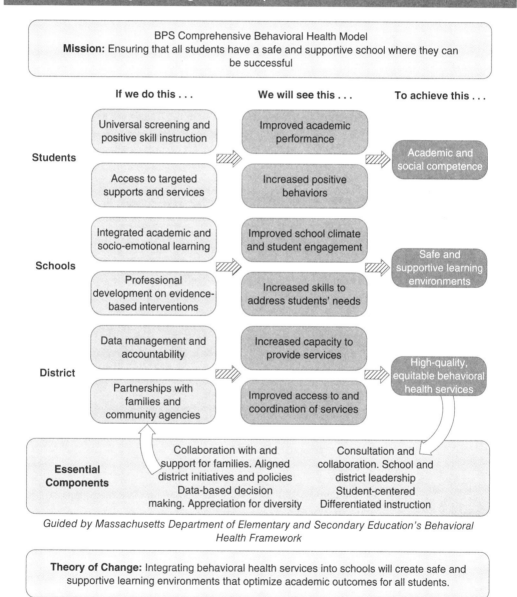

Guided by Massachusetts Department of Elementary and Secondary Education's Behavioral Health Framework

Theory of Change: Integrating behavioral health services into schools will create safe and supportive learning environments that optimize academic outcomes for all students.

Source: Boston Public Schools Behavioral Health Services (2013). *Comprehensive Behavioral Health Logic Model.* https://cbhmboston.com/wp-content/uploads/2013/03/Logic-Model.pdf

DBT Skills in Schools includes thirty lesson plans with explicit instructions for teaching mindfulness, distress tolerance, emotional regulation, and interpersonal effectiveness (Mazza et al., 2016).

In BPS, a Multi-Tiered System of Support (MTSS) is used, with Schoolwide Positive Behavior Intervention Supports (SWPBIS) used universally (Tier I). The *Behavior Intervention Monitoring Assessment System 2* (BIMAS-2) is used for screening to identify students with increased risk for developing behavioral issues and to match students to appropriate targeted/Tier II evidence-based interventions. Intensive supports (Tier III) are provided for students who exhibit serious needs or are not responding to Tier II interventions with referrals to partnering behavioral health community services as needed (see Chapter 3).

Note: The *Behavior Intervention Monitoring Assessment System 2* (BIMAS-2; McDougal et al., 2011), includes two adaptive scales (social functioning and academic functioning) and three behavioral concern scales (conduct, negative affect, and cognitive attention).

With CBHM, BIMAS-2 is administered twice yearly. Results over the course of implementation (eight years) show significant changes in all five areas of the BIMAS for students found with risk. For example, effect sizes for Conduct and Academic Functioning are +1.0 and +0.9 accordingly (see Figure 1.6).

CBHM has had a significant, positive impact on students and schools in the program, including the following:

- Scores on the Massachusetts Comprehensive Assessment System (MCAS) for participating schools are higher than scores for other Boston schools.

- Attendance rates and social skills of CBHM students have improved.

- Disciplinary referrals have decreased.

- A majority of students demonstrated "low risk" on the BIMAS-2 concerns scales.

- Students with the highest level of risks demonstrated the greatest gains.

The school mental health support staff who saw the need and created the collaborations to make the CBHM a reality had the courage to take compassionate action to address youth mental health in BPS. We'll discuss more about the importance of their collective efforts to bring wraparound services to schools in Boston in Chapter 7. We'll begin the discussion of how to cultivate a school culture that leads to compassionate action in Chapter 2.

Source: Boston Public Schools. Used with permission.

FIGURE 1.6 Examples of Effect Sizes for BIMAS-2

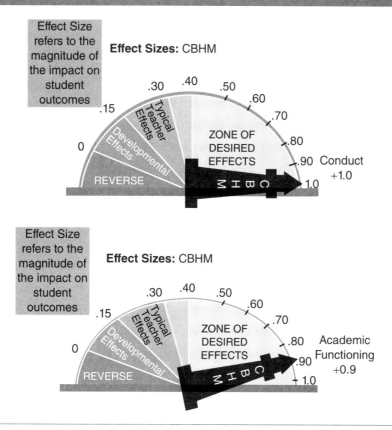

Source: Amador, A., (2019, November). Comprehensive Behavioral Health Model in the Boston Public Schools. Community partnerships to support school based behavioral health. https://cbhmboston.com/wp-content/uploads/2015/04/CBHM-annual-report.pdf

Reflections on Mental Health and Well-Being

Student mental health and well-being need to take priority in our decisions about curriculum and instruction. Trauma and violence are so pervasive that it will take considerable effort over many years to turn the tide. We are encouraged by the many efforts underway right now to assist schools in becoming trauma skilled (see Chapter 2). Some practices, such as turning first to reprimands and negative consequences for misbehavior, need to end. However, they have been implemented in schools over such a long period of time that we might not even be aware of how they contribute to the problem and not the solution.

We now have a clearer understanding of why children's mental health is a top concern of educators around the country and what we can do to begin addressing it. Stress, anxiety, and trauma can compound and lead to behavioral and emotional challenges, mental illness, and even suicide if left unchecked. We need to be aware of inequities in health and access to treatment and meet students where they are. We need to help students develop resilience and protective factors, so they can live long, healthy, and productive lives. Having open dialogues with students, forging healthy and caring relationships, and teaching positive coping strategies are a few of the many ways teachers can help students. We also need to provide teachers and administrators with adequate training so they can better support students experiencing mental health challenges—teaching them to identify the signs and symptoms of mental illness as early as possible and connecting students with the relevant resources and services.

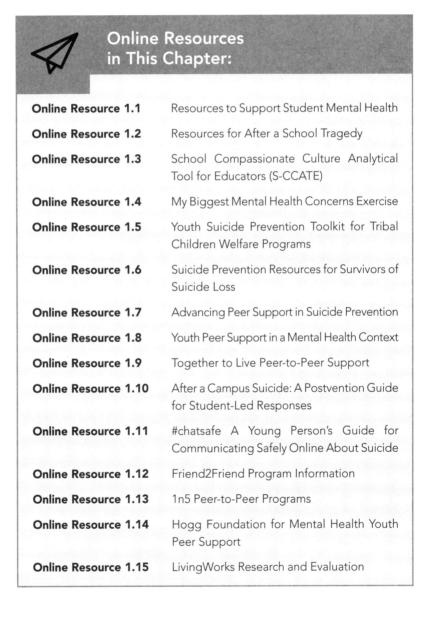

Online Resources in This Chapter:

Online Resource 1.1	Resources to Support Student Mental Health
Online Resource 1.2	Resources for After a School Tragedy
Online Resource 1.3	School Compassionate Culture Analytical Tool for Educators (S-CCATE)
Online Resource 1.4	My Biggest Mental Health Concerns Exercise
Online Resource 1.5	Youth Suicide Prevention Toolkit for Tribal Children Welfare Programs
Online Resource 1.6	Suicide Prevention Resources for Survivors of Suicide Loss
Online Resource 1.7	Advancing Peer Support in Suicide Prevention
Online Resource 1.8	Youth Peer Support in a Mental Health Context
Online Resource 1.9	Together to Live Peer-to-Peer Support
Online Resource 1.10	After a Campus Suicide: A Postvention Guide for Student-Led Responses
Online Resource 1.11	#chatsafe A Young Person's Guide for Communicating Safely Online About Suicide
Online Resource 1.12	Friend2Friend Program Information
Online Resource 1.13	1n5 Peer-to-Peer Programs
Online Resource 1.14	Hogg Foundation for Mental Health Youth Peer Support
Online Resource 1.15	LivingWorks Research and Evaluation

Best Practices for a Healthy School Climate and School Culture

2

Key Principle #2

Student mental health and well-being is interrelated with staff well-being and school climate and culture. By addressing self-care, increasing mental health literacy, developing a collective vision, and furthering a sense of belonging and community, complete with mental health supports, schools can take critical steps to alleviate stress and trauma and develop resiliency in children and youth.

How Can Schools Improve Children's Well-Being?

School leaders are beginning to recognize that a sustainable and effective approach to positive school culture and climate—two interrelated, but distinct aspects of schools—requires a collaborative approach to foster holistic well-being. Students, families, staff, school and district leaders, and community stakeholders work in tandem toward this shared goal. Well-meaning schools wishing to transform their culture and climate to become more trauma skilled often experience frustration that a single training or a single trial implementation of a social emotional learning program isn't the silver bullet to solving the academic and mental health effects of trauma.

In this chapter, we provide evidence-based strategies for the whole school as well as a community-based framework to building or redesigning your school's mental health support system, known as the Compassionate School Mental Health Model. By engaging with students, staff, and community members at the beginning of this transformational journey, schools will be able to build the culture that they and those they serve have been dreaming of, a culture that encourages connection and joyful learning for *all* members of the community.

Compassionate school communities are born out of school climates that provide the safe space and time for honest and empathetic feedback, so that all members of the school community feel that their voices are not only heard, but also respected. School climates are dependent on the culture that district and school leaders perpetuate. The culture is a product of the underlying beliefs and values of a school; the climate is how those beliefs are translated into action. In addition to reflecting on the policies that affect well-being, we urge leaders to also consider the environment in which these policies are enacted.

A Model for School Cultures That Foster Mental Health

To address trauma and children's health and well-being, we designed the Compassionate School Mental Health Model, which we presented in the preface. We based our model on research and practical considerations for eight features that we believe are essential to providing the most needed services for children and youth whose emotional well-being is most at-risk. These include the following:

1. *NO STIGMA*: The desirability of a school culture that reduces stigmatization, including a reduced need to identify, label, and provide select services to a group of students who may represent up to 20 percent of our student population (Holm-Hadulla & Koutsoukou-Argyraki, 2015).

2. *INCLUSIVE*: An approach that is applicable across an array of conditions: ages and grade levels; varying ability levels; gender; cultural, ethnic, racial, and socioeconomic groups; family constellations; geographic conditions; and rural, urban, and suburban areas.

3. *COST-EFFECTIVE*: The quest for a process that is easy to implement in schools without extensive additional resources, training, or funding.

4. *SUSTAINABLE*: Evidence that the approach can be implemented schoolwide and is scalable and sustainable.

5. *MEETS THE NEEDS OF ALL COMMUNITY MEMBERS*: An understanding that teachers' morale is low, and their own stress, trauma, and attrition is significant—hence the need for ways to decrease teachers' stress.

6. *RESEARCH-BASED*: Research documenting the relationship between stress, ACEs, and student mental illness.

7. *EFFECTIVE*: Research substantiating the approach—its impact on neuroplasticity, reduction of trauma, and an individual's well-being, all reducing the likelihood that a serious mental health challenge will emerge and increasing the likelihood that students will be happier, better able to focus and learn, and more resilient.

8. *RESPECTED*: Anticipation that the approach will be highly regarded by students, family, and schools.

> Compassionate school communities are born out of school climates that provide the safe space and time for honest and empathetic feedback.

We searched for an approach that will empower teachers and students to make decisions about implementation, while also furthering joy, happiness, equity, cultural understanding, and a sense of belonging. We also looked for a way to measure growth or progress to aid in guiding decision making, implementation of interventions, and report our successes for such purposes as school improvement planning (SIPs) or documenting progress for ESSA and state assessments.

Throughout this chapter, we will share how schools around New England are using our suggested process to reduce office referrals and suspensions, retain teachers, and get more students the services they need. We will also share stories of schools and districts looking beyond their walls to bring comprehensive services to staff and students. In doing so, schools not only create a stronger sense of belonging, but foster deep relationships that benefit both students and staff, as well as their families, local businesses, and many more members of the community.

As portrayed in Figure 2.1, *schools can prepare to address the well-being and mental health needs of students not only through the four quadrants*

FIGURE 2.1   Ring of Supports to Address Mental Health Options in Schools

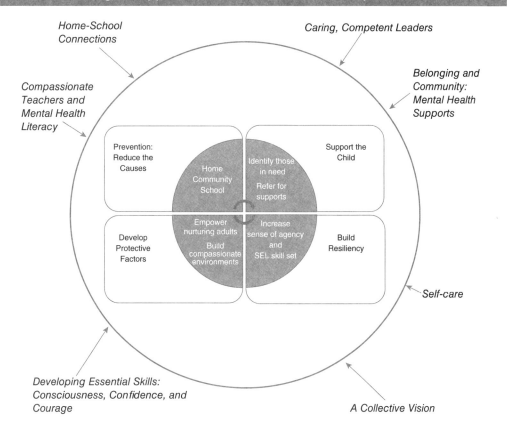

of our wheel of services, but also through a "ring of supports" that relies on caring, competent leadership, compassionate school culture, and other elements that each contribute to the health of the school and the well-being of students and staff. Each of these elements is described more fully in Chapters 3—8 of this book.

With the recent COVID-19 pandemic, and the turn to virtual schooling, our model stands out as an effective way to use limited resources to help get an array of needed supports to students and staff without undue burdens of high costs or large amounts of time. Our model only asks that schools use their resources differently. When you collaborate, you actually save time, money, and energy that can go toward realizing your school's vision rather than constantly putting out fires that only reignite.

Implementing Mental Health Supports at My School

As you read through the following, consider what you are doing at your school and which areas could use further development to improve implementation and results.

- **Prevention: Reduce the Causes.** Prevention begins with an understanding of the developmental needs of students and the early warning signs of distress. School leaders use an iterative community visioning process to reexamine policies, procedures, and discipline strategies through the lens of compassion. Staff and students are taught social emotional and self-regulation skills, which alleviate the emotional distress that can lead to mental health challenges. Restorative justice is used more frequently than punitive measures like suspensions and expulsions.

Ways our school practices prevention:

_____

_____

_____

_____

Practices we need to develop further:

_____

_____

_____

_____

- **Support the Child.** Educators view children with emotional and behavioral difficulties through a more holistic lens as they design and implement treatment options that are more child- and family-centered. Families feel empowered as their preferences are heard and integrated into treatment plans. Mindfulness (Chapter 4, Practical Solutions to Improve Educator Mental Health and Well-Being; Chapter 6, Self-Care Exercises) is used alongside therapeutic interventions to encourage emotional regulation skill development.

Ways our school supports the child:

_____

_____

_____

_____

Practices we need to develop further:

_____

_____

_____

_____

(Continued)

(Continued)

- **Build Resiliency.** Schools help all children, but especially those who have experienced trauma, find confidence in themselves and their team to make lasting change in their community and beyond. Schools create structures, systems, and supports to guide students to the tools and resources they need to be happy, fulfilled, and connected to others.

Ways our school builds resiliency:

_____

_____

_____

_____

Practices we need to develop further:

_____

_____

_____

_____

- **Develop Protective Factors.** Educators promote a sense of belonging that allows all students to develop a secure connection with a caring adult through establishing routines, traditions, and norms.

Ways our school develops protective factors:

_____

_____

_____

_____

Practices we need to develop further:

_____

_____

_____

Providing Structure and Rituals

Poliner and Benson (2017) describe the value of structure and rituals in building resiliency.

Provide structures and rituals that help students in processing their inevitable disappointments on the road to academic success.

Start a class conversation by asking, "What helps when you don't do as well as you wish you did?" The question lets students know that it is inevitable to have difficult times. Many teachers, anticipating that their students will have rough days, set up a space for reflection, post the steps to get help, and make available books that encourage reflection and balance, such as *Chicken Soup for the Teenage Soul*. Deciding together to build that support space in class brings teenagers into the conversation as central players (p. 173).

The Five Cs of Heart Centered Learning: Strategies to Take a Schoolwide Approach to Assisting Staff and Student Well-Being

The Compassionate School Mental Health Model we first introduced in the preface is coherent with the guidelines and principles of Heart Centered Learning (HCL). We have seen schools beset with trauma work seeming miracles with "problem" students who become engaged, whose attitudes shifted, and who suddenly showed a deepened interest in learning. We have seen resistant staff who, after learning about the neuroscience behind trauma and acting out behaviors, came to understand students in a new light. These staff, by reaching out and reaching in, facilitated a connection with themselves and others. With our model, we have seen a sense of belonging emerge that has formed a protective buffer, contributed to a sense of resiliency, and led to compassionate and courageous actions.

FIGURE 2.2   Compassionate School Mental Health Model Implementation With Heart Centered Learning

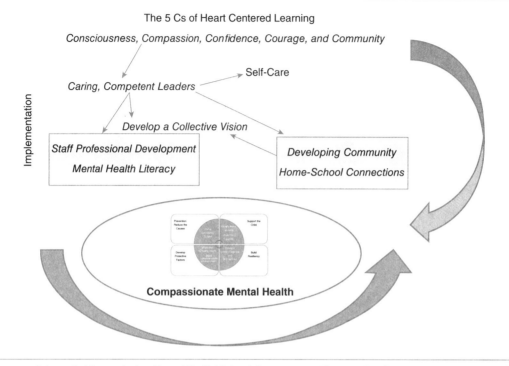

The 5 Cs of Heart Centered Learning

Consciousness, Compassion, Confidence, Courage, and Community

Self-Care

Caring, Competent Leaders

Develop a Collective Vision

Staff Professional Development
Mental Health Literacy

Developing Community
Home-School Connections

Compassionate Mental Health

Implementation

Source: Adapted with permission. From *Mindful School Communities: The Five Cs of Nurturing Heart Centered Learning* by Christine Mason, Michele M. Rivers Murphy, and Yvette Jackson. Copyright 2020 by Solution Tree Press, 555 North Morton Street, Bloomington, IN 47404, 800.733.6786, SolutionTree.com. All rights reserved.

Improving Belonging, Improving Mental Health

When schools purposely choose to build respectful relationships and meaningful connections with students, staff, and families, a sense of safety, belonging, and trust takes hold. When students feel valued, connected, and supported by their school community members, mental health and well-being are just two of many improvements (Mason, Rivers Murphy, & Jackson, 2020).

When students, staff, and families feel like they belong to a school community that cares about them, they have the confidence to take the courageous action necessary to address the injustices they see. They are able to have courageous conversations about mental health, bullying, and injustice that can lead to solving a problem before it changes the trajectory of a youth's development, academic career, and life. As we become more aware of what needs to change in order to serve all students well, we begin to understand the value of connection and the importance of relationship building (see Figure 2.2).

Heart Centered Learning (HCL), the research-based framework for infusing mindfulness and social-emotional skills into a school community to support holistic well-being, is an easy-to-implement process of teaching both staff and students practical strategies to promote positive mental health and cope with mental health challenges. In our Compassionate School Mental Health Model, HCL helps schools apply more compassionate practices at every level.

We know that issues of toxic stress, violence, and trauma affected large numbers of youth before COVID-19, but this global pandemic significantly increases these instances during the duration of the stay-at-home orders and we will see ramifications in the form of PTSD and other mental health challenges for years to come. We, as a society, cannot ignore the obvious warning signs of a looming global mental health crisis.

Implementation takes time and requires caring, competent leaders. To bring the Five Cs to your school community most effectively, we recommend introducing them slowly, perhaps focusing on one C for one to two months at a time before moving on to the next one. Staff are more likely to buy into the practices for themselves and begin teaching them to their students if they see them being modeled effectively by school leaders. For this reason, we encourage school leaders to spend time trying out each recommendation for themselves before presenting them to staff, students, or families.

The Five Cs

Consciousness

Before educators can teach children how to regulate their emotions, we must first teach them how to be aware of them. Far too many adults don't understand their own emotions, much less how to tell others about them. In some families, the typical response to hardship was to "suck it up," and any expression of disappointment, sadness, or hopelessness was dismissed as whining. When we ignore our feelings and stuff them deep down inside, they don't go away. Instead, they become larger and burst out of us when we least expect it. We can all bring to mind an angry boss who exploded over a misplaced stapler or a child who flipped over a plate of peas seemingly out of nowhere. It's highly unlikely that the stapler or the peas were the root of the problem, but when constant stress or trauma raise our blood pressure and heart rate and pump us full of cortisol, our nervous systems and brains have a lower capacity to handle that one additional stressor. Chances are that if your boss had had a chance to express his disappointment over his performance in a big meeting or your child had been able to release the tears she's been holding back at school all day after her friend wouldn't play with her at recess, the explosion could have been avoided.

> **The 5Cs**
> Consciousness
> Compassion
> Confidence
> Courage
> Community

Schools can help young children better understand their emotions by teaching them to name their feelings when they arise and by naming the emotions of characters in books. For older children, bringing emotions into the conversation during history lessons can bring a new layer to the conversation, which might even help them better relate to the people who have shaped societies. Before staff and students can start to recognize the signs and symptoms of mental illness and risk of suicide—important knowledge that can save lives—they have to have the basic language to talk about their own feelings.

Emotion Coaching

 One way teachers can guide young children as they process emotions and reflect on unhealthy ways of expressing emotions is to use emotion coaching (Asby, 2020):

1. Get down on the youth's level and make eye contact. Parents or teachers can also put a hand on a child's shoulder or give a hug when appropriate, avoiding any restraining actions.

2. Validate their emotions; for example, "I understand why that made you so angry."

3. Help them reflect on their actions; for example, "Was it safe to throw that chair?"

4. Brainstorm solutions; for example, "What can we do next time instead? Could we tell an adult we need help?"

Give gentle reminders the next time a similar situation occurs; for example, "Remember when this happened yesterday? You had some really good ideas for how to solve this problem safely."

Mental Health Literacy: Youth Mental Health First Aid

 When staff and students understand the risk factors, warning signs, and symptoms of various mental illnesses and suicide, youth are able to get the assistance they need much earlier. This can prevent lifelong difficulties or fatalities that result from untreated mental illness. *Youth Mental Health First Aid* is a training program that teaches school communities, both youth and adults, what mental health problems look like in adolescents, why early intervention is so important, and how to intervene or who to get help from in a crisis.

Through role-play and simulation, students and staff learn how to assess a mental health crisis, choose appropriate interventions, and help youth in making connections with professionals, peers, and the wider community. The eight-hour training also promotes awareness of emotional and mental states that require extra care and the understanding that regularly taking care of oneself will help prevent those mental health challenges in the first place.

Regulating Emotions – Important for Prevention and Resiliency

Once students have the words to use to express how they feel, it's important to directly teach them strategies to regulate those emotions, so those unprocessed big emotions don't later lead to a clinical mental illness. Schools can help prevent youth mental health challenges by directly teaching staff and students about the neuroscience of trauma and how toxic stress can affect their prefrontal cortex's ability to make wise decisions and plan effectively, can reduce the hippocampus's effectiveness at memory storage, and can overstimulate the amygdala so that the flight or fight response is overly sensitive—all of which make learning new information and thinking and acting rationally more difficult (Shonkoff et al., 2011).

Schools and districts can bring in local and national experts to do professional development sessions on the neurobiology of trauma, growth mindset, and neuroplasticity to educate staff about these important concepts and teach them how to respond with compassion rather than react with punishment when issues arise in the classroom.

Consciousness Exercise: Affirmations

 To build a sense of positive self-regard, teachers work with students on identifying between one and three affirmations they can repeat daily.

1. Ask students to write between one and three things about themselves that they may want to improve. These should be written as a positive statement, such as *I want to get better grades,* or *I want to be kinder to my friends.*

2. Guide students in transforming sentences to positive, present-tense affirmations, such as *I am getting good grades,* or *I am kind.*

3. Give students three minutes each day to write down the positive affirmation they wrote in step two.

Students write the affirmation as many times as possible during the three minutes. Or, instead of writing the affirmation for three minutes, students could say their affirmation aloud for two minutes. Whatever format it takes, students can practice this affirmation at various times during the day over several weeks.

Anxiety Is a Time Traveler

As Bill Adair (2019) says in his book *The Emotionally Connected Classroom*:

Anxiety is a time traveler: It can tell any painful story it wants in the past or future. Arm students with mindfulness strategies that aid them in staying grounded in present moment safety. Monitor emotions and thought patterns during lessons to "check in" to the truth of the present moment. (p. 180)

Affirmations are just one of many mindful strategies to foster a deeper mind-body-emotion connection that can empower members of your school community to learn how to regulate their emotions through mindfulness practices. Visualizations, meditation, breath work, yoga, and other mindfulness activities help staff and students better understand and regulate their emotions. Most C-TLC Fellows began their transformational journeys to becoming trauma-skilled schools with consciousness, because their staff and students' biggest need was stress reduction and emotional regulation skills.

Conscious Awareness of Emotions and Stress was the lowest scoring S-CCATE factor for both our pilot study of 814 participants (Mason et al., 2018) and during the spring 2019 administration to 430 additional participants in New England (New England MHTTC, 2020). In the years of work we have done assisting schools create compassionate school communities, we have seen that teachers and administrators, as well as students, need help understanding how to soothe extreme emotions. Unregulated educators will find it nearly impossible to teach self-regulation skills to students until they themselves have acquired them.

Compassion

A regular mindfulness practice allows a person to stay in the present longer and begin to forgive those involved in their trauma, primarily oneself. Many people who experience trauma blame themselves for the abuse. Their narrative of trauma likely includes a false explanation that their abuser may have fed them, perhaps suggesting that the individual is complicit in their own pain. Or the person may have constructed a false narrative to help make sense of a senseless act. Low self-esteem and the resultant risky behaviors meant to soothe pain—such as unsafe alcohol and drug use, unprotected sexual acts, and in the most unfortunate cases, suicide completion—can be the result of a lifetime of blaming oneself for the abuse endured.

Traditional reactions to "bad" behaviors—that is, non-suicidal self-injury, substance use, and so forth—can actually drive young people deeper into these methods of escape from stress and trauma. These coping mechanisms, although unhealthy, provide very real and necessary comfort to those who engage in them. Many adults in recovery from mental illness and/or substance misuse become avid advocates of recovery-oriented practices that focus on understanding, acceptance, and healthy coping skills because they wish someone in their communities had assisted them in gaining these valuable tools when they were adolescents.

Instead of shaming youth for the choices they make to attempt to deal with their mental health challenges on their own, adults can respond with compassion by practicing a form of emotion coaching.

Strategies for Emotion Coaching in Response to Risky Teen Behaviors

- *Acknowledge that there was a legitimate reason for their use of an unhealthy coping mechanism*; for example, "I understand that you feel upset about your parents' divorce. That's a really difficult situation to be in. It makes sense that you would turn to alcohol to feel good when everyday activities no longer make you feel as good as you did before the divorce."

- *Explain the long-term consequences of continuing with the unhealthy coping mechanism* and its inability to solve their problem; namely, "I know it may seem like the alcohol is what is making you feel better, but really, it is just numbing your pain. If you continue to drink, your brain chemicals will change to the point where you'll grow more and more dependent on alcohol to make you feel ok, much less good."

- *Ask them what they think might be a better way* to get their needs met; for example, "Before your parents' divorce, what kinds of things used to make you feel good? How can we help you get more of those things back in your life?"

- *Provide them with* strategies to get those needs met depending on their ideas; that is, "While you won't be able to rejoin the basketball team this season after your drunk driving incident, there are other opportunities for you to play sports in the community. What about mentoring a younger student or starting a neighborhood game? Let me connect you with someone at the YMCA looking for volunteer coaches for the youth league."

- *Provide them with opportunities to build healthy coping skills* using mindfulness and process their stress or trauma in a safe space; for example, "Let's also get you a time with our counselor. She's going to teach you some great tools to help you feel better without alcohol."

- *Check-in with them regularly to provide encouragement and find new solutions*, if needed; that is, "How is the youth basketball coaching going? Is it helping you pump that dopamine up? Well, maybe we could see if you can keep score at tomorrow's home basketball team so you can be near your teammates."

When educators remove their judgment and look beyond a behavior to see its genesis, they begin to better understand their students' struggles and are more able to respond compassionately rather than reacting reflexively.

Teaching youth how to use simple mindfulness techniques; for example, repeating a grounding phrase such as "Everything is ok right now," when they feel out of control can aid them in beginning to show themselves more compassion when they experience mental health challenges. Research has shown that people who meditate regularly have higher rates of compassion and self-compassion (Mahon et al., 2017). Although we recommend caution if you bring someone who has recently experienced a trauma to meditation, since they may be still processing this experience, mindfulness techniques can be great for increasing self-esteem, an essential part of the healing process.

After developing self-compassion, it becomes easier to show compassion for others. In families, communities, and cultures where it is common for intergenerational traumas to lead to a climate of protection rather than vulnerability, stigma around seeking mental health treatment can be especially high. Instead of viewing therapy, medication, or other traditional mental health treatments as tools to help recovery from an illness, whether it is temporary or chronic, some people see them as pointless, something only weak or "crazy" people need, or something potentially dangerous. When discussing mental health with students or families who you know to carry stigma against mental health, approach the topic with compassion by putting yourself in their shoes and remembering your own first experience with mental health and how scary or overwhelming that might have been.

Restorative Practices. One of the most powerful and compassionate policy changes a school leader can make is to shift away from punishment-based consequences and toward restorative justice.

Restorative justice is a formalized discipline response that focuses on respect, dignity, accountability, and mutual concern in order to build healthy relationships, repair harm, empower youth, and promote justice and equity (Gregory & Evans, 2020). Research has found that using restorative justice can result in fewer suspensions (Augustine et al., 2018), and reduce disparities in suspensions (Hashim et al., 2018) and discipline referrals (Gregory & Clawson, 2016); while improving relationships, interpersonal skills, graduation rates, school climate, and teachers' relationships with students (Jain et al. 2014; Ortega et al., 2016; Youth Restoration Project, 2016). Restorative justice aids both perpetrator and victim of a conflict so that they can better understand why an incident occurred, provides a forum of expression for the victim's preferred resolution, and holds a space that allows for an opportunity to repair the pain for both parties. For example, instead of automatically suspending a student who started a fight, restorative justice would bring both the victim and offender together into a circle of communication with others who may have been affected by this fight. All stakeholders are allowed to share their stories and, together, find an appropriate consequence to bring about healing.

In addition to reducing distractions, conflicts, and harmful behaviors, restorative practices give teachers more time for instruction and allow students to learn more effectively. They encourage students to explore the reasons and effects of their offenses, enabling real change and transformation:

> "When you get these kids talking, you learn about the traumas they have faced. Maybe their brother was killed, or their father was sent to prison. If you can get to the root of the cause of the offense, you're truly stopping the cycle" (WeAreTeachers Staff, 2019).

Restorative justice can be incorporated at any school level. One preschool teacher describes how she incorporates restorative justice practices in her own classroom: "I simply have the offender ask the victim, 'Can I help you feel better?' The offender offers solutions like hugs, high fives, funny faces, or volunteers to fix something broken. The victim accepts the solution or offers another idea until they mutually agree. Oh, how I love the way this has improved my classroom culture!" (Ledbetter, 2018).

Creating a Compassionate School Culture

 When a school has a compassionate school culture, it's obvious the moment you walk through the door. Youth feel loved and want to be at the school. This is accomplished through many ways:

- Model kindness and compassion with each other, families, guests, and students.

- Teach students about compassion using fiction and non-fiction.

- Create and teach norms around classroom behavior that encourage compassion (i.e., during classroom discussions students share opposing opinions respectfully with sentence starters like, "I understand X's opinion, but I disagree because . . . " and use supporting evidence.)

- Avoid yelling, sarcasm, and other practices that erode self-esteem.

To achieve a compassionate school culture, transformational leaders will need to vision with the entire community to understand what staff and students need to thrive, not just survive (Mason, Liabenow, & Patschke, 2020). But to do that, they must have confidence.

Confidence

To truly foster change, to transform a school from one where everyone feels as if they are barely getting by, putting in their all and feeling as if there's nothing to show, into one that thrives and overflows with joy and love, school leaders must have confidence in their vision and they must cultivate confident leaders in their staff and students.

Like compassion and emotional regulation, confidence is a skill that should be, but often is not, directly instructed. However, let's remember that children come into the world confident and ready to take appropriate risks. Babies are actually quite good at knowing their limits and only testing them when the time is right. But when they see their caregiver look worried about their prospects of completing a risky behavior, they are more hesitant and less likely to take the risk (Waters et al., 2014). Fear can be socialized. Anxiously attached caregivers— helicopter parents who hover around their children picking them up after every fall and padding the sidewalks so they don't fall again or bulldozer parents who go in front of their children to remove all obstacles to success so they aren't burdened by any small inconvenience—can actually contribute to low self-esteem.

All students, regardless of whether or not they've experienced trauma, need to build resiliency. Every human experiences stress, setbacks, the death of a loved one, and other events that put our minds, bodies, and emotions under immense pressure. It's easy to fall into anxiety and depression if you haven't built the confidence that you can get through any situation. Teachers and counselors can promote resiliency by teaching resiliency skills, such as cognitive reframing (i.e., a student experiencing seasonal affective disorder could turn their frustration about a cold, snowy day into an opportunity for gratitude by saying, "I'm so glad I get to throw snowballs and make a snowman with my friends today.").

The Most Compelling Factor

The most compelling factor to buffer against the ill effects of trauma is the presence of a single caring adult in a child's life (Murphy et al., 2013). Those caring adults exude compassion every day, but they can only reach out and help directly when students develop the confidence that gives them the courage to speak out about the injustices they themselves have experienced and/or the injustices they see their family, friends, and neighborhood experiencing.

Once students become confident, they begin to develop the twin skill of vulnerability. The truly confident feel brave enough to ask for help. This can be very difficult for students who have experienced trauma, especially if their home environment requires them to be a de facto parent to younger siblings. They may be distrustful of adults because asking for assistance or advice led to an inappropriate exchange. To be a deeply compassionate community, schools must enable students to feel safe—safe enough that they are confident to tell their stories, whether that is through journaling, to a counselor in one-on-one sessions, or to a peer.

Courage

Transformational leaders have the courage to stand up for the needs of their communities. Once conscious awareness has opened the community's eyes to the need for increased compassion toward those who are suffering from trauma or mental illness and members of the school community feel confident enough to tell their stories, school leaders can have challenging conversations about equity, perhaps using the Courageous Conversations framework we describe below. Good leaders don't blindly decide a school's goals; instead they consult various stakeholders in the school community—teachers, bus drivers, social workers, families, the students themselves—to help guide conversations about what their school deserves. Having these conversations gives voice to many who are rarely invited to the table. Including their perspective may also strengthen equity and belonging in your school and help ensure that no one is getting left behind.

Banding Together

When educators share stories of youth who have the courage to stand up to those in power to get more equitable treatment, students make connections with their own lives and start to gain the confidence needed to take the next step of action in their own community. For example, some of the students who survived the horrific Parkville shooting banded together to form the gun safety nonprofit organization Every Town for Gun Safety to educate people on gun safety and fight for more protective gun laws (Every Town for Gun Safety, n.d.). Sometimes, the best motivation to do something about your problems is hearing stories about other people who solved their problems by speaking out and making sure people listened.

When students hear the stories of other young people—especially those that look like them—standing up to injustice, they are inspired to think about the injustices in their own lives and speak out. Many young people around the country spoke out against racial injustice by bringing their voices to the streets to demand changes in police training and funding. Those youth were ready for these conversations because adults in their lives gave them the confidence that their voice mattered and could make a difference.

For example, the powerful testimony quoted below came from one of the high school students presenting the case for allowing students to take mental health days when necessary as Oregon state legislators debated House Bill 2191, which was passed into law and amended the state's school attendance laws to allow for excused absences related to mental health. The students' voices, like senior Derek Evans, were important in convincing lawmakers of this important accommodation that individual schools and districts may have the ability to make for their students:

> There's a bigger problem at hand than students missing school, which is students taking their own lives into their hands with risk of suicide and stuff like that. So, although absenteeism might go up, it might save lives and, in my opinion, that's well worth it. (Fox 12 Staff, 2019)

Facilitating Courageous Conversations in Your School

 Courageous Conversations™ is an "award-winning protocol for effectively engaging, sustaining and deepening interracial dialogue" developed by researcher and educational consultant Glenn Singleton (Courageous Conversation, n.d.). Some schools and organizations have expanded these conversations to include other equity issues—many of which are interrelated to race—that are stigmatized in their communities (i.e., poverty, incarceration, substance misuse). Singleton and his colleague, school improvement researcher and author Curtis Linton (2006), share three key elements of a Courageous Conversation:

1. Engages those who won't talk

2. Sustains the conversation when it gets uncomfortable

3. Deepens the conversation to a point where a meaningful action occurs

Often, when we engage in dialogue with another person, we have difficulty practicing active or reflective listening. Instead of using eye contact, refraining from judgment or interpretation, and confirming that we've understood our conversation partner, our instincts often have us formulating our response before we've even given the other person a chance to finish their thought. In some cases, we interrupt them to share what *we* think rather than truly listening to what *they* think. If we aren't actively listening to each other, we are rarely having the same conversation.

That is why Singleton and Linton (2006) developed four agreements that those entering into a Courageous Conversation must commit to before the dialogue can begin:

1. Stay engaged.

2. Speak your truth.

3. Experience discomfort.

4. Expect and accept nondisclosure.

These four conditions are what allows everyone involved to feel like there is a safe space to express what's on their hearts and minds without fear of judgment or aggressive confrontation. When everyone in the room is using the same norms for conversation, there is more room for growth and less room for contention.

It takes enormous courage for students to stand up for their rights regarding mental health and racial equity, but supportive school environments and compassionate communities create the safe environment that allows students to find that courage.

A Heart Centered Community

To come together as a team, working toward a common goal that truly meets the needs of all stakeholders, the groundwork of conscious awareness through mindfulness leads to compassion for self and others that allows confidence to blossom so that everyone has the courage to work side-by-side toward greatness as a community.

To reach every student, a heart centered community cultivates a culture of joy and respect. Students feel like there is at least one adult in the building they can turn to in times of need. Youth Mental Health First Aid training helps staff respond to student's mental health crises with compassion (see Mental Health Literacy: Youth Mental Health First Aid, this chapter).

Red Blanket Project

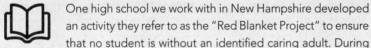

One high school we work with in New Hampshire developed an activity they refer to as the "Red Blanket Project" to ensure that no student is without an identified caring adult. During a professional development day, each student's name in the school was written on an index card and placed around the room by grade level. Each staff member circulated around the room and wrote their name on the back of cards of each student they felt they had a personal connection with. During an advisory period, a few days later, each student was given an index card and was asked to write the names of each adult in the building they had a connection with and would go to in a crisis situation.

"The Red Blanket activity was an amazing exercise for our school community to identify where we needed to improve our efforts around building relationships with our students. We believe, as a school community, that building and maintaining positive relationships is the single most significant factor in student academic success and emotional well-being," said principal Jim O'Rourke.

If staff members don't feel like a team, creating comradery in the larger school community will be difficult, too. Gossip and competition can be devastating to a sense of belonging and building effective professional learning teams. Engage in team building exercises to foster a sense of community in your staff. Next, move to the classroom level. Help teachers understand how to encourage community in homerooms or grade team levels. Celebrating teamwork and kindness will lead to a compassionate school community.

Connection to Community: It's All About Relationships

 Parent advocate Jenna White (2020) tried everything to assist her second-grade son who had struggled to "fit in" and learn successfully with his peers. Her son's Fairfax County, Virginia, elementary school worked with her to assess him for mental illness and provide the appropriate accommodations and supports, which included building emotional regulation skills and one-on-one counseling. He jumped from one type of unsuccessful therapy and behavior plan to another. Then, Ms. White went to a presentation about trauma and where she gained new information that led to a new understanding.

There wasn't something wrong with her child. There was something wrong with his situation. She had been so caught up in her own stressors that she didn't realize how her son's home life was affecting his emotional well-being.

Ms. White began reading articles and books about how trauma impacted children's mental health and behavior. She realized that her son hadn't found a sense of safety in any of his school's staff members. Because of his frequent behavior problems, he had difficulty making friends with children and adults.

Strengthening Protective Factors. Ms. White worked with her son's second grade teacher to make a plan to form a bond. Playing basketball was one of the rare moments he could focus and feel a sense of accomplishment as the ball swished through the hoop. His teacher decided to spend just fifteen minutes each Wednesday morning in the gym, cheering him on, making jokes, building a relationship, and eventually teaching some emotional regulation skills. This caring and consistency enabled Ms. White's son to form a secure attachment that provided him with a safe space in his school.

Many of his behavioral challenges disappeared; he was able to get along better with peers and complete his work. Ms. White's son went on to love school and find academic and social success throughout the rest of elementary school, all because one teacher took the time to foster a positive relationship with a young boy deeply in need of a connection.

> To sustain a heart centered community, schools vision with their stakeholders regularly.

To sustain a heart centered community, schools vision with their stakeholders regularly. They further *home-school connections* and monitor their progress regularly by measuring essential 21st-century skills not traditionally captured by standardized tests, such as social emotional learning, school climate and culture, and leadership ability.

**Implementing Heart Centered Learning
With a Strategic Visioning Approach**

Implementation of Heart Centered Learning (HCL) can be enhanced by the use of "Core Learning Teams"—which might be professional learning communities, grade level, or cross-grade level teams, a practice from MIT's brilliant strategist and systems thinker, Peter Senge. Senge has authored several books guiding practitioners through team approaches to aid "learning organizations" that are able to adapt quickly to new circumstances (Senge, 2006; Senge et al., 2012). He stresses the importance of three core components or principles—what he refers to as the three legs of a three-legged stool: *fostering aspiration, developing reflective conversation, and understanding complexity.*

When Core Learning Teams meet, they review data about program effectiveness; reflect on their needs and progress; and decide on directions, goals and strategies. As they continue to implement HCL, educators discuss their own efforts, problem solve together, and consider ways to enhance the overall implementation, which programs to pilot and/or expand, and how to monitor progress. The S-CCATE can be useful throughout this process.

The School Compassionate Culture Analytical Tool for Educators: A Trauma-Informed Progress Monitoring Tool

 The following is excerpted from the Center for Educational Improvement's website.

S-CCATE (School Compassionate Culture Analytical Tool for Educators) is a cutting edge, 21st-century social emotional learning tool that helps educators vision, plan, and monitor progress toward the implementation of compassionate, trauma-informed practices in classrooms. The tool, a brief, validated assessment to be completed by teachers and other school personnel, is uniquely designed to guide teams of educators and whole school communities through the process of transformational change.

The approach, developed by the Center for Educational Improvement over a six-year period with school leaders, is an outgrowth of its signature approach to social emotional learning and mindfulness, Heart Centered Learning®. Data from S-CCATE can be used to show progress in becoming a trauma-skilled school and in making improvements in school culture and social emotional learning.

(Continued)

(Continued)

S-CCATE also:

- Aids in interpreting results of social emotional learning, identifying strengths and needs, and planing professional development and interventions.

- Reports progress on "non-academic" factors aligned with ESSA (Every Student Succeeds Act).

- Fosters alignment to address the needs of children and youth who have experienced or are at risk of experiencing significant trauma.

- Accelerates adoption and implementation of mental health evidence-based practices.

- Provides publicly available, free training and technical assistance to elementary and secondary teachers, principals, school psychologists, other school staff, and the wider school community.

Using Heart Centered Learning to Build Compassionate School Communities in New England Through Visioning

In New England, through the Childhood-Trauma Learning Collaborative (C-TLC), we have been building transformational leadership capacity in twenty-four school leaders who have engaged in an iterative visioning process with us that they took back into their own communities. We used the S-CCATE assessment to understand the needs of New England schools, designed professional development opportunities to respond to those needs, introduced the HCL framework, and used the collaborative as a Core Learning Team to facilitate exchanges that helped everyone learn from each other.

Impact of Heart Centered Learning on C-TLC Fellows, Staff, and Students

 Lisa Parker, a C-TLC Fellow and school psychologist at a Rhode Island high school, described the first year of implementation of HCL at her school:

This is the first year that our high school teachers have had any exposure to HCL. I am offering them experiences, resources, and encouragement to explore practices that are positive for them.

> My hope is that when they become comfortable with mindfulness practices on their own, they will be ready to bring it to the classroom. Some have already begun!

During Year 2 of implementation, Lisa provided this update regarding the benefits observed with students:

> Teachers reported anecdotally that students were more focused and settled (better inhibition). Some of my students in these classes also reported decreased anxiety when doing their assignments as well as improved memory of the concepts they had studied the night before.
>
> (L. Parker, personal communication, April 2020. Used with permission)

Mental Health Literacy and Professional Development. Introducing HCL and the Five Cs will be most effective if staff receive intentional professional development sessions on topics like the neurobiology of trauma, restorative practices, mindfulness, and other heart centered interventions discussed below. Free trainings and technical assistance are available online, which can introduce staff to these concepts (visit the Mental Health Technology Transfer Center's website for free access to hundreds of trainings).

Visioning for a Comprehensive Behavioral Health Model in Boston Public Schools

In 2010, Boston Public Schools' (BPS) Comprehensive Behavioral Health Model (CBHM) was launched in a handful of schools. Knowing that their task was far too great for their current mental health support staff to meet alone, they brainstormed solutions that would meet the needs of the most students without putting further burden on social workers and counselors. The CBHM team capitalized on the great work other institutions in their city—like Boston Children's Hospital and University of Massachusetts-Boston's school psychology program—were doing with children's mental health. Both stakeholders became partners who provide essential services the schools couldn't.

(Continued)

(Continued)

This intentional process of assessing the district's needs, looking out into the community for partners already doing effective work, and merging strengths has resulted in a resilient and adaptable system. When COVID-19 forced behavioral health services to switch from in-person to telehealth delivery systems on a moment's notice, the CBHM team was able to get their program running online in record time. Andria Amador, Senior Director of Behavioral Health Services at Boston Public Schools, says, "The reason we were able to pivot is that we already have structures for how people work and also robust partnerships."

(Boston Public Schools, personal communication, April 2020)

Developing Community and Belonging Through Partnerships. Taking the time to form relationships with behavioral health agencies, universities, hospitals, community programs, juvenile justice programs, foster care, and other stakeholders doing excellent work in youth mental health can relieve an enormous amount of burden from school leaders who may feel underqualified and overwhelmed in this realm. Together, communities can build a mental health support system that acknowledges the importance of mental health screening, diagnosis, and treatment, but prioritizes the connection and community that *prevents* mental illness.

 Becoming a Therapeutic Setting.

Stacy Bachelder-Giles describes how she worked with her school to address mental health concerns:

To overcome challenges that teachers face, we worked with one another to collaborate and share strategies to create a therapeutic setting. What we had been doing wasn't working. We needed to approach the challenges as an entire school community instead of triaging and being reactive. We took a Tier I approach to reach every staff member and every student. We provided professional development to assist teachers with knowledge and strategies for working with the most challenging students. The missing piece was trauma-informed teacher training.

The S-CCATE was a valuable tool to use as a leader and change agent. The results and recommendations showed staff a purpose and need for change. Over the past year as a C-TLC Fellow, I have been able to provide training and information to staff about the effects of trauma on the brain and strategies to cultivate a more compassionate environment. Staff willingly participated in a C-TLC book study on *Mindfulness Practices* (Mason et al., 2019) and implemented techniques from the book in their classrooms.

Our school redesigned recess, partnered with a local university to improve SEL, piloted SEL curricula such as *Choose Love*, and held additional book studies to connect with the most challenging students. Teachers and students were calmer, more connected, and more compassionate. I am confident that the leaders who emerged from this process, will continue this work. (S. Bachelder-Giles, personal communication, April 2020)

The Five Cs of Heart Centered Learning can provide a powerful approach to increasing well-being. Both the research base supporting the inclusion of the specific elements and our results of pilot studies and work in New England substantiate the impact of each of these Five Cs (see Figure 2.3).

FIGURE 2.3 Results of Heart Centered Learning Interventions		
	INCREASES	**DECREASES**
Mindfulness (Consciousness)	Sense of well-being, calmness, readiness to learn; better understanding of self/one's emotions and others; student metacognition; self-care, insights into the present moment; ability to provide the most needed assistance	Anxiety; disruptive behaviors; office referrals; suspensions/ expulsions
Compassionate Exercises	Empathy, support for peers, positive mindset, kindness, understanding of justice, self-compassion	Reactivity to others, discrimination, racism; harassment; bullying
Confidence	Enhanced self-esteem, sense of self-efficacy, growth mindset, academic success, leadership, understanding and acknowledging one's own vulnerability	Sense of failure, reluctance to approach new or difficult tasks
Courage	Resiliency, ability to withstand hardships	Bullying, fear
Community	Sense of belonging, equity, family involvement with school	Sense of isolation, alienation
Overall	*Improved memory, decision making, attention, academic skills*	*Impulsivity*

The Five Cs at My School

Consider the Five Cs: Consciousness, Compassion, Courage, Confidence, and Community.

- What is your overall sense of how well your school is doing?

- What are your strengths?

- Elaborate on two or three of those strengths. What evidence can you point to that demonstrate those strengths?

- What Cs would you like to work on and improve?

- How might you start working on that goal?

Connecting With Other School Communities

When your school is implementing an approach that is similar to others in your district, state, or region, it is easier to gain assistance and advice by asking questions of others as you share your progress. By connecting with national leaders, and looking abroad to other countries, we are better positioned to gain insights that strengthen both our resolve and the impact of our actions. With our Compassionate School Mental Health Model (see preface), we urge you to build new and existing networks so that your leaders, staff, and students can leverage resources and broaden your arena of impact, as well as your causes for celebration.

The most effective schools and districts will take the time to involve a variety of stakeholders—most importantly students struggling with trauma and mental illness and their families—into the visioning process to become a trauma-skilled school that responds to the challenges presented by mental illness. Schools can respond with compassion and community to heal, aid, and encourage all students to embody their full potential.

Reflections on Strengthening Student Mental Health and Well-Being

As individuals who are living with mental illness tell us, the stigma associated with mental illness is huge. Schools can play an important role in reducing that stigma through normalizing discussions about health and well-being and intentionally setting out to build resiliency. During times of national and international stress and trauma, helping individuals understand their emotions is critical, and schools provide an infrastructure to have a reach that is far and wide. Being a nurturing, compassionate presence is a role that educators can take on, whether we are meeting in person or virtually with students. Our calm, reassuring, and accepting presence matters.

**Online Resources
for This Chapter:**

Online Resource 2.1	C-TLC's Archived Webinars
Online Resource 2.2	*Youth Mental Health First Aid*
Online Resource 2.3	S-CCATE: Online Technology Designed to Enhance Social Emotional Learning

Tiered Systems and Mental Health Screening

3

In the last two chapters, we discussed some of the mental health issues that our students are facing and the growing movement for educators to employ trauma-responsive school practices. We also presented what we consider to be some of the most effective evidenced-based practices, providing examples of usage in schools and districts. In this chapter, we provide a brief summary of where the United States is at this moment, so that we have a common understanding and can think critically to adapt these strategies to meet the challenges we are facing and the needs of *all* students and educators. We will then present mindful strategies for implementation and our recommendations for executing best practices.

With the COVID-19 pandemic, and its profound effect on all of us, our approach to addressing children's trauma and stress (see Chapter 2) is becoming more and more relevant and necessary now and will continue to be in the coming months and years as we recover from loss, uncertainty, isolation, and closures of our institutions and structures. As we have stated before, there is a continuum of stress that begins with unpleasant garden variety stress and ends up with disassociation, hallucinations, paranoia, and severe anxiety and depression. With the COVID-19 pandemic in mind, it is critical to consider systems to address stress and mental health and well-being. In a way, the bar for accepting a solution is higher, the stakes are greater, and the potential impact is even more as we realize that how we choose to address stress and trauma can impact an increasingly larger percentage of our school population.

Learning From History

Before turning attention to tiered systems of treatment—the primary topic of this chapter—let's pause for a moment and recall the history of treatment of people with mental illness, including youth in the United States. The mental health hygiene movement in the early 1900s was a first step in a series of slow but evolving practices to get better and more appropriate assistance to adults and youth with mental illness. Since the early 1900s, we have seen residential service delivery, family therapy, crisis hotlines, shock therapy, and in-patient treatment. There have been summer camps, out-patient mental health clinics, crisis treatment, pharmacological interventions, behavioral and cognitive treatments, prevention programs, institutionalization and de-institutionalization, circles of support, and an array of school-based programs for youth with emotional and behavioral problems (Weisz et al., 2005). At times, society has been worried that persons with mental illness were "dangerous"; at other times, we have seen significant evolution in views of mental illness that focus on the importance of understanding lived experience or that might include mental illness in disability rights or chronic illness models. While some services and systems have operated in ways that perpetuate stigma and inadequate or harmful treatment, there has also been progress in the development of interventions and systems that respect the rights of individuals, and the dignity and recovery of people within, despite, and because of their symptoms or illness. Today's mental health system, including the diagnosis and support of people with mental health disorders, has evolved from what we have practiced and learned over the decades of services that preceded, and there has been enormous progress in mental health conventions, stigma, and treatments. There is still much progress to be made, and our work supports the continued evolution of these practices and ideas; we hope they will center, more and more, on the rights, dignity, lived experience, and recovery of people with psychiatric illness, symptoms, or disability, while promoting culturally and contextually responsive practices and supports.

When it comes to youth mental health, strategies and practices remain varied. We have seen programs that deal with mental health related issues such as juvenile delinquency and substance abuse; there have been programs established for youth needing guidance with depression, suicide, anger management, and trauma. There are many evidenced-based practices that are effective in providing an array of supports delivered by therapists, social workers, psychologists, psychiatrists, and teachers. And elements of many traditional approaches have been helpful for many youth.

As with much of the work we discuss in this book, we approach the tiered framework and universal screening with a lens of curiosity and critical thinking, one way of thinking about school mental health practices. Our approaches are not prescriptive; there are many educational approaches that are concerned with fidelity to models, often to very powerful effect. Our approach, though, is one of reflection and compassion, and ultimately, developing tools to thoughtfully and flexibly consider what we are doing and why, especially as we enter a new era in education where we have an opportunity to take some time and space to think about what's best for our schools. This will require an honest assessment of where we are now and how we got here, as discussed in the preface and in Chapter 1.

One Educator's Experience With Youth Mental Health Across Time and Space

Rita Benecke had an aching feeling in her heart to help others that led her to the idea that "I just needed to be a teacher." Her long career began in the 1980s in rural Missouri at the Boys Town, which serves youth—boys and girls—by providing "compassionate treatment for the behavioral, emotional and physical problems of children" in communal living settings (Boys Town, n.d.).

At Boys Town, Rita found the stories of the girls who had been sexually abused most devastating, because while others wanted to pathologize and diagnose their emotional and behavioral problems, she was able to see how much they needed a venue for telling their stories. There wasn't a clearly structured curriculum, so Rita incorporated art, dance, storytelling, and writing into her work with the students. When it was hard for unregulated students to learn a dance, she found rhythmic music students could connect with and create their own expressive dances to process their grief. She constantly adapted her teaching to meet the unique needs of her students.

After becoming frustrated at the administration's strict adherence to the medical model, prescribing medications more often than therapeutic opportunities to build self-regulation skills and process traumas, Rita sought out an opportunity to learn from a more progressive youth in-patient facility in Colorado. There, she was able to use the creative therapies she saw help young people in crisis in a more holistic educational environment. The youth she worked with there were given a chance to rehabilitate in nature with a community rather than going to juvenile detention for crimes with roots in trauma. She saw violent, angry young men find a sense of calm and peace, Many of them were able to leave the facility once they turned eighteen—a second chance in life that many other youth serving sentences in juvenile detention centers don't get. Unfortunately, some students, even those who were making enormous strides, could not overcome their past traumas in every

(Continued)

(Continued)

moment. She had to witness more than one student being escorted out of the classroom in shackles after a moment of dysregulation resulted in throwing a chair or attacking another student or staff member. Reflecting on this experience, Rita shared, "You know, I never stopped to think about how hard all of this was on me. I just had to watch this stuff happen, but you know . . . what am I supposed to do? Here I am the teacher, but I'm crying while they tell me their stories. You can't work there too long; it just tires you out."

Rita came back to teaching after taking some time off to raise a family of five children. When she reentered the field as a substitute teacher, back in rural Missouri, an 8th grade girl approached her and shared, "They tell me I'm bipolar," with a stricken look on her face. Rita remembers her reaction: "She suddenly had this label. I knew she was going to have trouble getting through that, let alone her issues."

Now, Rita is a special education teacher on the small, rural island of Lanai in Hawaii. She loves working at a school that lets her use the best tool she knows helps kids struggling to learn in classrooms: compassion. When she speaks about how she works with students, you can see why Rita's method for responding to students' emotional and behavioral challenges has been working for her for decades: "These are just kids with emotional needs that require adjustments from schools. These kids are great, because if you work with them one-on-one, you unlock their magic. You just have to figure them out. There are no bad kids. Give them confidence and away they go!" As a teacher, Rita has always followed her heart and listened to what her students tell her they need, because they usually know and the answer is often a compassionate ear and the tools to tell their story.

ACES and Social Emotional Learning: More Background and Context

In the twenty years since Felitti et al.'s (1998) seminal work in the Adverse Childhood Experiences (ACEs) study documented the long-term effects of trauma on children, we have begun to understand both how common these traumatic events (and many others) are and how that trauma manifests in myriad, complex ways throughout the lifespan. The ACEs study established both a new area of academic investigation into the effects of childhood trauma and served as the foundation for changes in public policy, health and educational programming, legislation, and funding (Brown et al., 2009; Felitti, 2019; Hartas, 2019).

As we have become more aware of the experiences of trauma in children and the sources of what we used to consider "problem behaviors," we have also become more aware of the experiences of people with disabilities, and have expanded our ideas about what mental illness *is* (and is not). As a result, schools have developed strategies to incorporate this evolving awareness and the value of lived experiences into their structures and curricula to address the behavioral and emotional needs of students. Although some approaches may be informal, many schools are implementing and investigating a variety of programs to teach social emotional skills, mental health literacy, bullying prevention, and other so-called "non-academic indicators" as measured in the Every Student Succeeds Act (ESSA). Further, many schools and principals are interested in implementing these programs and looking for resources to provide the needed teacher professional development (DePaoli et al., 2017). Most schools are now aware that students cannot learn until their basic needs of sustenance, safety, and belonging are met (DePaoli et al., 2017; Grant et al., 2017; Plumb et al. 2016).

The Multi-Tiered Systems of Supports

The secret in education lies in respecting the student.

–Ralph Waldo Emerson (2020)

To help address the social emotional needs of individual students, an approach that is widely used in the United States is the Multi-Tiered Systems of Support (MTSS). With the updated Individuals with Disabilities Education Act (IDEA) of 2004, the Response to Intervention Model sought to make more intensive supports available to students who needed them, primarily through special education (Individuals with Disabilities Education Act, 2004). From this model, the MTSS framework grew to address the behavioral and emotional needs of all students in a *proactive* approach rather than waiting until needs were urgent and students had "failed" in some way.

MTSS is a framework that promotes research-based strategies and the recognition that student academic success and behavior are interrelated—brain and behavior are crucially linked—by contextualizing them within the larger school environment, systems, and community. Within the MTSS model, a multilevel, tiered approach efficiently organizes resources via team-based leadership, a selection of evidence-based interventions and instruction, comprehensive screening and assessments, and data-driven decision making and evaluation. This structure organizes resources and implementation along a tiered continuum, from Tier I, the whole school population, to Tier II, smaller group interventions, to Tier III, intensive and individualized assistance, and is often portrayed in a pyramid figure (Figure 3.1). Although not a specific training package or curriculum, MTSS is a school behavioral health framework of school-based supports that can include social emotional learning (SEL), positive behavior guidance, universal screening programs, and the older Response to Intervention (RTI) models, among many others.

FIGURE 3.1   Multi-Tiered Systems of Supports

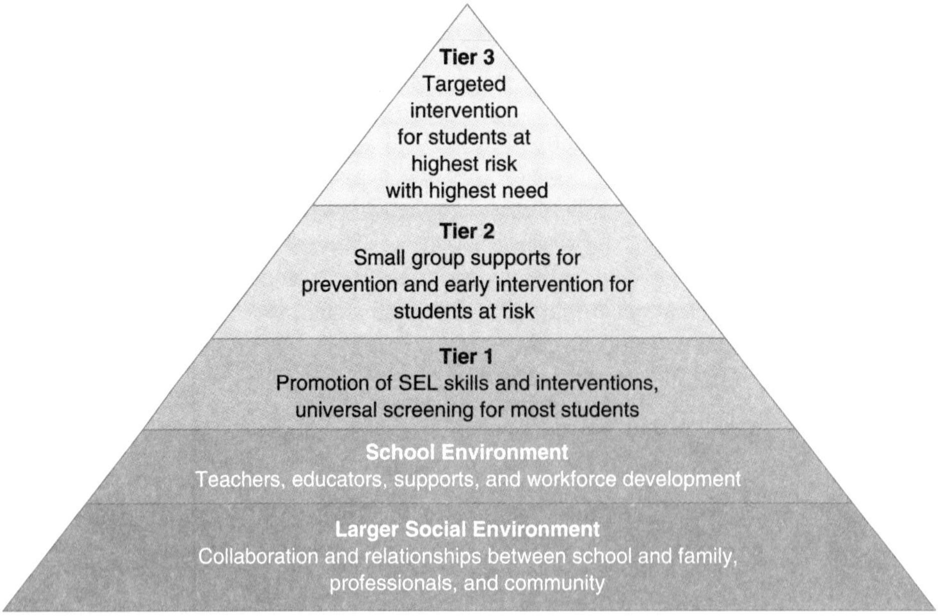

Tier 3
Targeted intervention for students at highest risk with highest need

Tier 2
Small group supports for prevention and early intervention for students at risk

Tier 1
Promotion of SEL skills and interventions, universal screening for most students

School Environment
Teachers, educators, supports, and workforce development

Larger Social Environment
Collaboration and relationships between school and family, professionals, and community

Examining MTSS With a Higher Bar

MTSS is a powerful and compelling model for American schools to address the needs of children equitably and thoughtfully and has represented a profound advancement in the ways schools approach assisting students with varied emotional and behavioral needs, including children who have experienced trauma. MTSS and other tiered models have increased teacher effectiveness and collaboration and improved student achievement. Its success and widespread adoption lead to its inclusion in the Every Student Succeeds Act (ESSA), resulting in funding for professional development for this model (Grant et al., 2017). MTSS allows for the flexibility for students to move between the Tiers at different points in their development or according to their needs, benefiting from the more generalized Tiers before they need individualized assistance. Those students who are struggling the most and require targeted intervention will still receive the more universal Tier I intervention.

Many thoughtful researchers and educators have written extensively about the history and implementation of MTSS models and many progressive schools, districts, and states have adopted MTSS to further the causes of equity in education, student achievement, health promotion, and improvements in school culture. To inform your own use of the model, you can review some of the innovative models and methods many educators are employing in an MTSS model to great success.

MTSS: Let's consider them in light of a higher bar—will MTSS help us meet the needs of what could potentially be a larger number of students with a need for healing, connection, and support? Further, how will MTSS operate when many children may be served virtually, some children may be difficult to locate or serve, and many more children and families may be stressed due to ongoing anxiety, fears, and precautions?

Let us look back at Figure 3.1 at the MTSS model in the context of our discussions on our heart centered approach and our model of creating compassionate schools. Using that lens, you might notice that there is no space or mention of the actual *child* in the MTSS model. Although the foundation of the MTSS pyramid is the larger social environment that includes family, school, and community relationships, this intended focus on the relationships that children form with the caring adults in their schools and the overall school climate, which we know are profoundly important factors in student well-being and achievement (Brody et al., 2002; Liu et al., 2020; Short & Nemeroff, 2014), is often minimal or missing altogether. In the discussions on Tiers and achievement and behavior and evidence, we are concerned that the actual needs, experiences, ambitions, traumas, and joys of children (and educators) have become lost, or, at least, obscured by a framework that is driving much of our educational models.

Often obscured, too, are the cultural, linguistic, and familial contexts from which children come, where they return at the end of the day, and which play such a central role in how we understand, identify, and address the complex behavioral and emotional needs of the children in our classrooms. This is not to imply that there are not *many* examples of MTSS frameworks and MTSS-informed approaches that center on the experiences and contexts of children, or that are not profoundly concerned about issues of culture and equity. This definitely exists; some of them are included in our examples on the previous pages and in the resource list. We know, too, that MTSS largely makes good on its promises to promote research- and data-informed strategies for addressing the needs of students.

However, it is worth returning our focus and our work toward the needs of the people most central to models such as these: the children that schools are serving. How are diverse needs and strengths being addressed, how are contexts and community considered, and with what sorts of input from the children and families themselves? Secondarily, it is worth thinking very carefully about the needs and experiences of the other people in these models and the relationships being formed between and within these groups, as well as how all of these factors affect and contribute to the overall school culture. How are the needs of teachers, administrators, and other school staff being addressed in terms of time, energy, and collegiality?

Will MTSS help us meet the needs of what could potentially be a larger number of students with a need for healing, connection, and support?

My School and MTSS Exercise

Now, take a few moments to think beyond your school's mental health supports to your school, district, or state's systematic approach to serving students with diverse emotional and behavioral needs.

- Does your school or district currently use an MTSS framework? If not, how has your leadership articulated their approach to serving students with different behavioral and emotional needs?

- What model or structure does your school/district use in their MTSS framework?

- What are the strengths or benefits for students of these models? What *is* working well?

- What are the challenges or pitfalls in these models? What **is** *not* working?

- How are the students in your school included in the implementation of these activities?

Universal Screening in Schools

Children love and want to be loved and they very much prefer the joy of accomplishment to the triumph of hateful failure. Do not mistake a child for his symptom.

—Erik Erikson (2020)

A key component of evidence-based multi-tiered approaches to school behavioral health, and an essential component of MTSS is universal screening. Many of these screenings identify students who are at risk of suicide, have experienced ACEs and trauma, are anxious, exhibit symptoms of disordered eating, or are developing anxiety disorders or other mental health concerns.

Screening, Diagnosing, and Funding

Following an MTSS approach, students may be screened and then receive a diagnosis prior to receiving more intensive services or supports. Diagnoses made may fall under several categories according to the *Diagnostic and Statistical Manual* (DSM-5; American Psychiatric Association, 2013), including the following: Tourette's syndrome, autism spectrum, attention deficit/hyperactivity (ADHD), anxiety, post-traumatic stress (PTSD), disruptive mood dysregulation, specific learning, obsessive compulsive, oppositional defiant, or eating disorders. (See also Centers for Disease Control and

Prevention, n.d.; Substance Abuse and Mental Health Services Administration, 2016.) If a child receives educational services under an Individual Educational Plan, the eligibility determination and diagnoses may differ, with services provided to individuals who have been identified as having serious emotional impairments, autism, traumatic-brain injury, health impairments, or specific learning disabilities (IDEA Section 1401 [3]). Under current regulations, sometimes a diagnosis may be needed to receive funding or reimbursement for services, whether that funding comes from the state, district, or private insurance providers.

The usefulness, advisability, and disadvantages of a formal diagnosis have been debated by many; certainly, a diagnosis can be accompanied by a painful ordeal as individuals and families struggle to understand all the implications of the new identity that individuals then wear as an invisible or not-so-invisible cloak, or as a means to access services, assistance, or treatments. However, diagnoses are subject to cultural contexts and mores, historical timing or developmental stage, clinical variability or training, and (explicit or implicit) biases including racism, sexism, homophobia, or transphobia. Individuals are not their diagnoses and their diagnoses do not own them or describe them as *people*. Rather, diagnosis represents, at best, only one part of a person, along with all of the other traits, interests, experiences, gifts, joys, and concerns that anyone has. Given how complex and delicate diagnosis is for many, screening as the first step in diagnosis should be implemented within a full complement of school-based mental health and/or special education services and serve as the gateway and impetus for students to receive the help that they want and need (Weist et al., 2007).

Screening and diagnosis remain an important way for many children to receive aid within schools. Thus, universal screening is widely endorsed, and there is a significant evidence base for its effectiveness in identifying kids at risk, although screening on this scale currently only happens in 15 percent of schools in the United States. (Bruhn et al., 2014). Universal screening has been recommended by many, including the National Association of School Psychologists, the University of Maryland National Center for School Mental Health, the Institute of Medicine, the American Academy of Pediatrics, and a Framework for Safe and Successful Schools, among others.

Screening is also a useful tool for schools to assess how and why their interventions are working in order to do continuous quality improvement. A further advantage of universal screening is the reduction of stigma around mental health issues; if everyone is already being screened, those who are screening positive for an underlying issue might not feel singled out. Screening also helps raise awareness within school communities about issues of mental and behavioral health; screening provides an opportunity to begin a conversation with students and school staff about signs to look for and what to do if you're concerned about a student.

The SHAPE System: Evidence-Based Screening, Resources, and More

The effectiveness and impact of universal screening begins with the selection of the right screening tool. How do you find a screening tool to meet your needs? The University of Maryland's National Center for School-Based Mental Health has developed the School Health Assessment and Performance Evaluation (SHAPE) System, which is a publicly available, web-based platform for schools and districts to improve their school-based mental health quality and capacity. The SHAPE System (National Center for School Mental Health, 2020), at www.theshapesystem.com, can provide evidence-based resources developed over many years and with the input of countless experts and schools, on universal screening and more.

An Overview of SHAPE's Use in New England Schools

Excerpted from the Center for Educational Improvement's website:

initial access to the SHAPE program involves an investment of time in creating the baseline data forms that will then be entered into a national database. The initial forms include the reporter's assessment of Teaming, Needs Assessments and Screening, Mental Health Promotion Services, Early Intervention and Treatment, Funding and Sustainability, and Impact. Each of these six assessments are updated by the school point person over the course of a school year, and results and suggestions are shared confidentially.

When you begin to explore the SHAPE website and its varied offerings, the volume of valuable information can be overwhelming. However, when used strategically, the SHAPE support and resources can enhance what schools and districts are already doing to improve students' mental health outcomes.

Becoming a part of the SHAPE program gives the enrolled school or district access to the National School Mental Health Curriculum and the National School Mental Health Learning Collaborative (supported by MHTTC). Once enrollment is completed, teams will then be able to access assessments on school mental health resources, quality, sustainability, and trauma responsiveness, as well as other free school mental health tools.

Using SHAPE in Your School or District: Our Perspectives

Heather Pach, a C-TLC Fellow and school psychologist at Cheshire Public Schools, describes the benefits of SHAPE:

As a practicing school psychologist, I see the greatest benefit of SHAPE in its evaluation of the strengths and needs of your overall program. It allows your district or school to more fully engage in a data-driven Scientific Research Based Intervention (SRBI) selection process for mental health. This will be most helpful for districts that truly are committed to digging deep to create or revamp their SRBI process. Once a school/district initially registers, they receive a message from a partnered organization, for example, the Child Health and Development Institute in Connecticut. These non-profit organizations provide free technical assistance and support to schools or districts using SHAPE.

Jillayne Flanders, former elementary school principal and current social emotional education/early childhood advocate in Massachusetts, concurs:

As a former public elementary school principal, I can see the value of the SHAPE System and I wish this kind of resource had been available during my tenure. My school served the youngest children in our district: pre-school, kindergarten, and first grade. We had a marvelous student support team with a behavior therapist, a school psychologist, a special education team leader, a teacher, a paraprofessional, the school nurse, and myself. It would have been a tremendous support to have this team collaborate in submitting the SHAPE forms, establishing our baseline, and learning where we could and should improve our services. My one concern would be the amount of time needed to begin the process, but it would be time well spent. (H. Pach & J. Flanders, personal communication, May 2019)

How Are We Screening and Why?

Undoubtedly, there are kids with intellectual deficiencies or neurological problems. But a lot of kids shunted into special education classes are deficient only in a willingness to conform to the school pattern. They are just honest, brave kids who say, "I just won't take that, and I don't believe in what you're doing." If you give them an alternative to the usual classroom, they break free of a lot of inhibitions and bad associations, and they begin to learn.

–Seymour Papert (Evenson, 1997)

For what are we *actually* screening? It is an essential question, even if it seems like the answer is already obvious. We have presented a very brief overview on some aspects of screening and the tiered system, understanding that there is a wealth of research, implementation, and real-world information about how and why these are essential components of the modern school-based mental health system. That evidence base is important but may not truly get at the types of practices and models we are proposing. As mindful educators, intent on helping schools to be more trauma-skilled, culturally responsive, and compassionate, we must constantly raise, and answer, the questions of "why" and "how." That question is not offered as a challenge to screening practices but as an invitation for reflection.

So, take a moment to consider these questions, in the context of your own educational practice, and in your own schools: *Why are we screening?* For many educators, the answer is that we have been told to, or that is what is recommended, or because it is state/district/school policy, or because it is part of school-based mental health best practice. We want to acknowledge that these are all very important considerations that offer real-world challenges and demands that are often intractable. However, we think it is essential that we really deeply consider the question of universal screening and some of the common pitfalls, as well as some of the best practices for implementing universal screening in a thoughtful, meaningful, and equitable way.

Role of Prevention and Screening in School Mental Health

Alison Sumski, a C-TLC Fellow from Massachusetts, shares her thoughts on prevention and screening:

By implementing prevention methods such as universal mental health screening, social emotional learning strategies, and behavior curricula such as Positive Behavioral Intervention & Supports (PBIS), schools can position themselves to better safeguard against the potential development of serious mental health issues in their students (Center on Positive Behavioral Intervention & Supports, n.d.). When thinking in the context of Multi-Tiered Systems of Support (MTSS), prevention efforts fall under the Tier I umbrella.

Implementing Tier I prevention efforts such as social emotional learning can have profound impacts. Researchers from the Collaborative for Academic, Social, and Emotional Learning, have conducted two large meta-analyses (213 studies in 2011; 83 studies in 2017) to examine the impact of social emotional learning programs on student outcomes (Durlak et al., 2011; Taylor et al., 2017). They found a 24 percent increase in social behavior, a 24 percent decrease in self-reported emotional distress, and a 22 percent decrease in conduct problems (Durlak & Mahoney, 2019). (A. Sumski, personal communication, May 2020)

The Differences Between Screening, Assessment, and Diagnosis

We conduct screenings for groups of people or populations to detect or rule out the risk or presence of disease, most often with a "yes" the condition is probably present, or, "no," it is probably not. We can do this via:

- Biometric tests, such as height and weight for obesity, or high-blood pressure screenings.

- Signs of disease, or the physical manifestation of illness or disease that can be seen by someone else, such as a rash or a pattern of behaviors in autism spectrum disorder.

- Symptoms, or the experiences of an illness by the person who has it, such as pain in a broken arm or lack of interest in activities in depression.

- Assessing risk by detecting the earliest presence of an illness, as in an elevated blood glucose level for diabetes, or by evaluating risky behavior, such as having multiple sex partners without using condoms.

Screening helps professionals determine whether a person needs an *assessment* in which more detailed and specific information is gathered in order to determine the nature of the problem—which might involve a *diagnosis* of a specific condition or illness. Understanding the nature of the problem, and sometimes a diagnosis, helps professionals create an individualized plan for treatment or intervention.

Potential Issues in Screening

Many common screenings have dramatically improved our health—for high blood pressure, colorectal cancer, substance use disorders, and many other health conditions or risk behaviors—throughout the history of public health.

With the COVID-19 pandemic and its profound effect on all of us, our approach, which does not necessitate formal screening, diagnosis, or even necessarily using the MTSS model, is becoming more and more relevant and necessary now as trauma and stress are growing concerns and will continue to be in the coming months and years. While the Compassionate School Mental Health Model we are recommending is compatible with MTSS and in many cases both approaches are used together, the Five Cs (*Consciousness, Compassion, Courage, Confidence, and Community*), can create a strong foundation for efficiently and effectively addressing student needs on multiple levels. But there are also examples of screenings that are significantly more problematic, particularly in psychiatry, and especially for people outside of the white American "mainstream."

Screening tests have been used to marginalize and stigmatize "outsiders" or people from minority cultures or to pathologize normal aspects of human behavior, like sexuality. Screening has often served as a way to legitimize an "us" versus "them" attitude. For people from African American/Black or immigrant communities, social policies on "screening" people for disease have been used to perpetuate racism resulting in an understandable mistrust in the medical and scientific communities (Hollar, 2001; Williams et al., 2016). There are other cases where screening may have served a purpose at one point in our history—for example, rules against gay men donating blood during the early days of the AIDS crisis, which were quickly made obsolete with better understanding of risk—but remain as a screening policy thirty years later (Doheny, 2020). The instances of this are countless and well catalogued and must be considered when thinking about a universal screening program, and how the members of your school communities—especially students and their families—experience screening.

When considering a diagnostic and screening process, educators need to be alert to the potentially negative impact when students are screened for a particular risk or symptom, like depression or self-harm. We would argue that schools are not the place for diagnoses, even when they are sometimes the right places for screening and assessment unless there are dedicated and well-trained clinical staff, as in some school-based health centers. Most school staff are not qualified to diagnose and do not want to, so the purpose of screening is to establish whether a student needs a further assessment to determine a plan of action with a mental health and/or medical professional and how the school might assemble a team to address the needs of that student within the educational setting. Screening is not the same as a diagnosis, and yet, through screening there are many settings in which a student is labeled with a diagnostic label in a way that is inaccurate, unhelpful, and potentially damaging, sometimes for the rest of a student's school career.

Similarly, students may be labeled with a diagnosis because school staff are struggling with some aspect of a student's challenging behavior, such as being disruptive in class, disengaging from schoolwork, or having problems in relationships with other students. These are common behaviors for children who have experienced trauma, but who may receive a diagnosis or a label that does not account for or address the real issues that require attention. There are many cases, as Papert suggests in the quote above, where these "problem" behaviors indicate an actual *problem* in the way school staff are conducting classes or managing school culture rather than a symptom of individual deficit. Labeling a student or assigning a diagnosis can distract from real and systemic problems that need to be acknowledged and addressed by school staff and parents.

Labels and diagnoses are often not applied equitably, given that U.S. schools continue to struggle with institutionalized racism and sexism (Williams et al., 2016). This labeling is also commonly seen for students of color, who come from cultural contexts other than that of the often white cultural majority in schools and school leadership. As just one example, this has led to a large percentage of African American boys being labeled as having attention deficit hyperactivity disorder, because of behavior that does not meet the expectations of some

About Me: Thinking About Diagnosis and Labeling

Reading about screening and diagnosis, can you remember a time when a student in your school or class was labeled?

- What was the label that was used?

- Who did the labeling?

- Was that label used to help other members of the school community understand and support that student with compassion? Or was that diagnostic label used to stigmatize or problematize that student, explaining away "problem behaviors"?

- Did that diagnosis or label make you feel closer to or more alienated from that student? How might that label have obscured other aspects of this student, including their gifts and goals, challenges at home, or cultural context?

- How did the label affect how the student felt about themself?

Now, think about these questions in the context of yourself if you have ever been labeled or diagnosed with something that other people knew about. If you are lucky enough not to have been labeled, perhaps you care about someone who has. If you are able, think about a time when you were a child who was labeled, perhaps because of aspects of your personality or your family life or because of a real or perceived disability. Review the following questions in this context.

Were you called a "troublemaker" or diagnosed with "ADHD"? Maybe you were told you were "gifted" or "dyslexic." As an adult, were you diagnosed as "bipolar," labeled as someone who was "bossy," or did you receive another diagnosis?

When you think about your own experience in the context of a label or diagnosis, what do you notice?

educators (Morgan et al., 2013). Other examples are when girls are called "bossy" when standing up for themselves or asserting an opinion in class (Grant, 2014).

There may often be no right or wrong answers to these questions of diagnosis; a diagnosis can give us more insight into the next steps and possible treatments or interventions, or it may help us to feel part of a community of people who are similar to us. But these labels also have the power to dehumanize us, to make us think differently about ourselves, and to obscure the rest of our identities and lives beyond the label.

Universal Screening With Consciousness

For many schools, particularly during the recovery from the COVID-19 pandemic, universal screening may be an expectation. Done thoughtfully, this can be a powerful and important tool. We have reviewed some of the ways universal screening might be problematic, but we think it is even more important to identify ways we can implement universal screening in a way that benefits students and schools, in keeping with the goals of MTSS.

Programs implemented with thoughtful rigor can help identify students most in need of services more quickly and thus be a critical element of programs aiming to reduce student self-injurious and suicidal behavior (Miller, 2018). Moreover, they can be useful in helping to get funding for an array of supports to students who will benefit from extra services.

To begin, there are six elements of screening that need to be considered, shown in Figure 3.2, to implement universal screening consistent with our Compassionate School Mental Health Model. For example, it's not unusual to find that a school or district has identified that they want to screen for risk of suicide and are in the middle of implementing a screening intervention without fully thinking about the resources that may or may not be available for the follow-up that needs to occur quickly after students have been identified as at risk.

As you begin to consider screening and improving mental health programs in your school, it may be helpful to step back and assess what is working, what is not, and what is needed to find greater success. We have provided some

FIGURE 3.2   Essential Components of Conscious Universal Screening

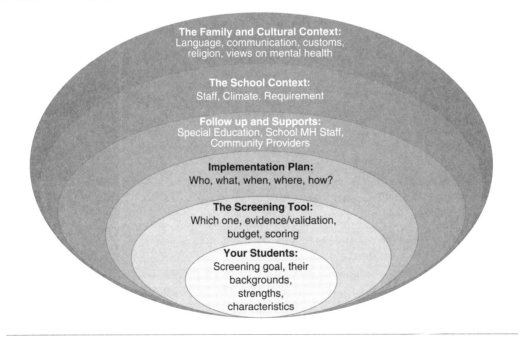

questions to frame this mini-needs assessment. We encourage you to think about these issues and answer the questions, on your own, and then with your colleagues. Any Tier I mental health intervention is dependent on engaging with your partners in a considerate and courageous way, students, staff, and beyond. Our aim is to present a high-level approach to best practices, using the lens of the Compassionate School Mental Health Model we have laid out and interweaving of the values and goals of creating a compassionate school climate.

School Climate and Culture Matters: Starting Discussion Guide

"School-Based Mental Health" is not an action or an end accomplished within a framework or through screening. Nor is it something that should only be accessible to the students who are struggling. The following questions are useful conversation guides for you and your colleagues to discuss together to create an environment where mental health is inexorably part of your compassionate school culture, to get a variety of perspectives, and to foster discussion:

- What is your school and classroom culture around mental health and screening? How is that fostered or impeded by school or district leadership?

- How does your school culture include and lend visibility to disabilities, mental health, and mental health problems? How can you deepen that inclusion?

- Are school personnel educated about screening goals and logistics? Can you find ways to educate all members of your staff?

- Do all members of the school community (teachers, staff, children, parents, other stakeholders) understand the expectations around screening, its intent and limitations, cultural considerations, concerns related to privacy and confidentiality, uses and misuses related to diversity and disabilities, the need for mental health literacy, and also the need to reduce its stigma and labeling?

- How can you incorporate facts/concepts/topics about mental health disorders into other aspects of your curriculum and culture rather than just as a stand-alone topic?

- How can you add mindful practices and strategies for improving student resiliency into your school climate? What resources can you draw on to do that?

If you could go to school tomorrow and find a culture that promotes school-based mental health and students with diverse experiences and needs, what would that look like?

Considerations Before Implementing Universal Screening

If you are making a decision about screening, consider the process that will be used for referral and services for students who are identified and make sure this is in place prior to beginning screening. Also, consider whether teachers are prepared to implement activities that may facilitate the well-being of students who are identified. It would be unconscionable to identify students and not follow through with some supports, but it happens, nonetheless.

> Educators also need to find out how invested other stakeholders such as parents, teachers, and the students themselves are in mental well-being. Asby (2019) explains, "It can be challenging to get parental consent due to the prevalent stigma around mental illness. Parents might worry that if their child is identified as potentially having a mental illness, they may be isolated or bullied by peers. This worry may not be unfounded as mental health labels can follow a child throughout their school career. In addition to peer isolation, educators may consciously or unconsciously treat children who have been identified differently.
>
> ***"Does your school have the staff, time, and funding capacity to screen all students and analyze the data?"***
>
> "While the earliest psychological assessments were largely developed from studies done on white, middle class populations, more recent research has attempted to look at how different populations of children demonstrate traits. Educators who work with diverse populations may find that they are getting a lot of 'false positives' or seeing students slip through the cracks without being identified because the language or concepts used in the screeners are not culturally appropriate for their population. Psychologists today are more aware of this issue and strive to study their instruments with populations that include youth with a variety of socio-economic, racial and ethnic, and cultural backgrounds.
>
> "Before a school makes the decision to administer surveys that give them an idea of which students are at-risk of or experiencing a mental health issue, they should ask themselves why they are screening. As neuropsychologist Larry Seidman told his mentees, 'If you are going to measure something, be prepared to do something about it. Screening students for risk of mental illness is a pointless endeavor if you don't do anything with the data you collect.'" (IPS Conference, 2019) (Asby, 2019 [October 15a])

The Dos and Don'ts: Screening Best Practices for Compassionate Schools

Before you Begin:

- Identify a clear goal in screening: What are you screening for? Who are you screening? By when?

- Carefully consider why you are screening: Is it because you are required, because it's a good idea, or because there are other members of the larger community who are advocating for it?

- Make sure that you are clear on the requirements for screening as set forth by your school, district, state, and in accordance with legal requirements and obligations.

- Assemble a team and make sure that the stakeholder groups in your environment are represented and feel empowered to contribute.

- Assess the resources available for this project: staff, subject matter/clinical experts, time, and budget.

- Carefully consider whether and how to conduct universal screenings if there are not appropriate and available follow-up supports for students.

Finding a Screening Tool:

Earlier in the chapter, we identified the School Health Assessment and Performance Evaluation (SHAPE) System as a terrific resource for helping you choose a screening tool, but it's important to think of the following factors:

- Ask if it is designed to accurately identify the problem your school is concerned about, which is described in two ways:
  - Does it identify "true positives"? Whether this test identifies every person who has the target disorder, which is called the test *sensitivity*.
  - Does it rule out "true negatives"? Whether the screening test correctly identifies every person who does not have the disorder, or the test *specificity*.

- Review the body of evidence that forms the background for the screening tool and the test's psychometrics. Does this assessment meet the statistical thresholds for demonstrating that it does what it says it does?

- Ensure that the screening tool is validated in populations that are like your schools, in terms of age and other demographic characteristics. Make sure that the screening tool you are using is appropriate for *your* students, and not just students in general.

(Continued)

(Continued)

- Make certain that the screening tool is available in the language your students speak, reflects the cultures of the children you work with, and is culturally appropriate for the community/families/ children in your school.

- Determine if this tool has been used often enough that it has face validity and legitimacy among educators, mental health professionals, pediatric primary care providers, and other important stakeholders.

- Establish if the cost for using the tool matches your budget. Verify that the requirements for administering this screening meet your resources and needs, in terms of administration, staffing, and scoring.

Choosing Which Tool Is Right for Your School

 Excerpted From Asby, 2019 (October 15b)

As discussed above, a number of evidence-based psychometric assessments indicate that someone might be at risk for a mental illness. However, a mental illness diagnosis *cannot* be given after a single screener. Rather, students must be given an individual comprehensive assessment by a licensed psychologist or psychiatrist. Yet, mental health screeners can help inform how your mental health support team offers assistance—such as special accommodations or peer support—and interventions for individual students or entire school populations. Some of the most widely used screening instruments include the following:

- Teacher's Report Form (TRF; Achenbach & Rescorla, 2001)

- *Behavior Assessment System for Children*, Third Edition (BASC-3; Reynolds & Kamphasu, 2015)

- Beck Youth Inventory (BYI; Beck et al., 2005)

- Behavioral Intervention Monitoring and Assessment System (BIMAS; McDougal et al., 2011)

- UCLA Post-Traumatic Stress Disorder (PTSD) Reaction Index (Steinberg et al., 2004)

These instruments take ten to twenty minutes to complete and have been developed for various ages (1.5–18). Please visit our companion website for more information: resources.corwin.com/compassionateschoolpractices.

Although these are some of the most utilized screeners that illuminate important mental health issues, this list is by no means complete. To explore more specific measures, visit the National Child Traumatic Stress Network's catalog of measure reviews.

More on the Tiers of Systems of Supports

In this chapter, we have focused largely on universal screening, an important part of Tier I supports. However, before leaving the realm of MTSS, it is essential to acknowledge the important contribution that can be made by practices such as

- implementing SEL programs, trauma-skilled approaches, and other universal procedures used with Tier I supports that are provided to all students in inclusive classroom settings.

- identifying students needing additional treatments and finding ways to deliver additional services with Tier II supports. Some of these students may receive services in specialized educational settings.

- providing more extensive supports to students most in need of those supports. These services are usually reserved for the 5 to 10 percent of students with the most serious needs and may include mental health treatments, services delivered in collaboration with mental health professionals, and other specialized programs.

We wholeheartedly agree with the value of many of the programs that are available to aid Tiers I, II, and III. Excellent reviews and insights into MTSS programs can be found at schoolmentalhealth.org and research by Averill, Rinaldi, and Collaborative (2011), Dillard (2017), and Eagle et al. (2015). However, over the years, what we have seen is that sometimes systems aren't ready for the level of complexity that MTSS provides; sometimes these services result in an additional time burden to schools; and sometimes these services are not delivered as planned. The reasons for nondelivery include the following: uncertainties about how to implement interventions; lack of commitment to the MTSS effort at the school level; unequal implementation that is dependent upon the willingness and readiness of the individual teacher to participate; and personnel shortages that may mean that the identified services provided by mental health providers are not available to a local community (Braun et al., 2018).

Making a Plan for Implementation

 Consider establishing a school-based mental health advisory group that can help guide your approach to screening and MTSS that includes members from each of the groups in your school. Some factors to consider include

- communications with students, parents, and families about the process, goals, consent, and results;

- how to involve students in screening and education about mental health;

- the mental health services that will be readily available to students and families; and

- how to inform and involve all school staff, including ancillary staff, around concerns about privacy, confidentiality, screening, and student supports.

Following Up and Fostering a Support System

What is the point of collecting data if the data don't inform practices? Do not fall into the trap of spending so much time and energy planning a comprehensive, universal screening procedure only to let the results sit and collect dust. *Before* screening, make a plan for what to do immediately following the screening when suspected risks become even more certain.

One of the most significant concerns that parents and educators have about MTSS and universal screening is about the dearth of community mental health providers for children, particularly for children who have public health insurance, or who are in rural areas. Students who need additional psychological assessment, psychiatric treatment, or a higher level of care, including residential care, can wait months to see a professional. These community providers may or may not accept the student's insurance, be a match for the student, or be trained in the types of intervention and assistance students need. Access and quality often depend on who you are, where you live, and what resources you have. Conducting universal screening to identify students who are at risk for a mental health problem without ensuring that those students have access to ongoing support is an injustice at best, and cruel and alienating at worst.

We are all heartbroken at this reality and are *still* in the position of accepting the real-world demands of the current educational system. So, we turn, again, to the framework we have developed, in order to approach every aspect of our educational practice.

Reflections on Student Mental Health and Well-Being

Start where you are. Use what you have. Do what you can.

—Arthur Ashe (2001)

This is a philosophy that underpins our approach to creating compassionate schools, and it includes extending compassion to ourselves when we are working in systems that are challenged by the suffering of our students and the stress of our teachers. Although we cannot fix many of the world's challenges on our own, we believe, and we have seen in practice, the profound differences that can be achieved when we orient our educational practice, our teaching, and our support of students toward curiosity and compassion. Our students who are struggling are children first and deserving of our courageous care. Whether these students are identified as requiring special education services, or screening positive for risk of mental health disorders, or for those who are flying under our radar, our students benefit when we model thoughtfulness and compassion, with ourselves, each other, and with them. Sometimes, that is the resource that is available, and those are the values and skills we hope to provide you with in this book. Rest assured that your compassion makes a difference in the lives of your students.

We urge you to "start where you are." However, we also remind you of some of the other contexts we have very briefly presented here. In our view, whether you use Tiers I, II, and III or not—whether you adopt universal screening or not—are not the most critical concerns. Beyond these concerns are questions such as the following: "Is this approach stigmatizing?" "Is the approach inclusive?" and "Does the approach consider the needs of the individual child?" We also ask, "Does the approach seem overly complex and difficult to implement?" If so, could it be that something more foundational is at your fingertips? Could it be that addressing the considerations for collaboration and the school environment that we presented in the tiered model of supports in Figure 3.1 could result in foundational assistance leading to greater success and effectiveness for your school and community?

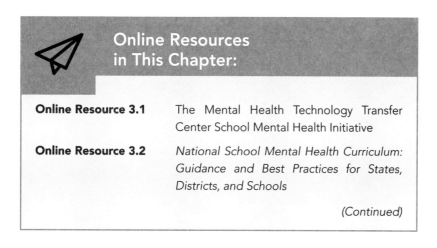

Online Resources in This Chapter:

Online Resource 3.1   The Mental Health Technology Transfer Center School Mental Health Initiative

Online Resource 3.2   *National School Mental Health Curriculum: Guidance and Best Practices for States, Districts, and Schools*

(Continued)

(Continued)

Online Resource 3.3	The University of Maryland National Center for School Mental Health
Online Resource 3.4	Orange County Department of Education MTSS Framework and Guides
Online Resource 3.5	Madison Metropolitan School District MTSS Toolkit
Online Resource 3.6	My School: School Climate and Culture Matters Starting Discussion Guide
Online Resource 3.7	Using Screening Data
Online Resource 3.8	Selecting the Right Screening Tool

Considerations for Staff Mental Health and Well-Being

4

> ## Key Principle #4
>
> *Teacher and staff stress is at an all-time high. However, both individual self-care and working conditions can be modified to alleviate stress and create a better sense of well-being.*

Uncertainty and Isolation

We live in stressful times—times of uncertainty and a "new normal." Consider lives transformed by a pandemic on a global scale not seen since the Spanish Flu virus in 1918, schools practicing lockdown drills replete with dramatizations of what to do if a shooter is at the classroom door, or populations scrambling to make sense of the impact of technological advances that are taking over many jobs. Until very recently, the threat of global warming may have been at the very top of our list of long-term stressors. That was before COVID-19. In 2020, our attention shifted to how we stay safe and healthy and continue living our lives as a community while in isolation. Experts warn that infectious diseases, climate events, and other tragedies may continue to occur as earth's resources are stressed. Educators have a responsibility to prepare for, work to prevent, and respond to these situations.

What do we say to children and families during these times? What advice do we give to the high school senior who had all remaining games for their last season canceled? Or to a single working parent who fears that he or she will bring disease home to their children? To parents who were counting on school breakfasts and lunches to feed their children? Our strength, kindness, compassion, competence, and resiliency are being tested by the many concerns we face today—many concerns that would not have made it onto our top ten list just a few months ago.

In the midst of these widespread concerns, behind virtual closed doors, school leaders are looking to peers, checking with health officials, and seeking guidance and direction from district and state education officials. Panaceas don't seem to be in sight for any of these or myriad other concerns.

Educators today, like all of us, are affected by global catastrophes. To help alleviate their stress and improve their well-being, we will be required to consciously consider these circumstances, even as we seek to understand more about their job-specific stresses. Fritzi Bryant, a 106-year old grandmother who remembers the Spanish Influenza had some sage advice, "There's no sense in playing it down. You have to look it square in the face . . . and do everything you can in your power to make it better" (Frame, 2020).

Staff Stress and Trauma Are at an All-Time High

Global conditions have a direct effect on the learning environment and academic and behavioral outcomes of students (University of Missouri-Columbia, 2020). Although teaching engaged students who are eager to learn can be rewarding, teaching is a physically, emotionally, and mentally taxing job, and today students who are disruptive, apathetic, or turned-off add to the burden that teachers shoulder.

Education and the school and administrative environment are strong predictors of teacher turnover (AFT, 2017). Unfortunately, too many teachers currently feel overwhelmed and under supported. Many schools struggle to create healthy and productive environments for educators and students. Districts that fail to recognize the importance of and invest in educator well-being may face higher turnover, more teacher and staff health issues, and greater burnout, all of which lead to higher costs, lower stability for students, and lower student achievement (AFT, 2017).

Although some administrators are incredibly supportive of teachers, and some teachers feel enormous encouragement from parents and their local communities, this is not always the case. Teachers want to feel that administrators have their best interests in mind and that they will stand behind them and support their actions. The overall rate of principal turnover is high, with most principals staying in a school an average of four years and 35 percent of principals being in a building less than two years. Schools with more students of color, living in poverty, or who are low-performing are more vulnerable to principal turnover. This in turn impacts trust, teacher morale, and attrition (Bradley & Levin, n.d.). With an ever-revolving door, with school administrators who come and go on an almost annual basis, the spirit of a school wavers. Each new administrator brings new dreams, ideas, and ambitions. Before long, teachers have lost any sense of trust and often find it easier to sit back and wait out the latest change.

In a recent study by the University of Missouri-Columbia (2020), 94 percent of middle school teachers reported experiencing high levels of stress. In 2017, the American Federation of Teachers (AFT) conducted a quality of life survey of 830 educators. Educators and school staff reported that they find their work "always" or "often" stressful 61 percent of the time, which is double the 30 percent of the time workers in the general population find their work "always" or "often" stressful. One teacher lamented, "This job is stressful, overwhelming and hard. I am overworked, underpaid, underappreciated, questioned, and blamed for things that are out of my control" (AFT, 2017).

Teachers reported having poor mental health for eleven or more days per month, twice the rate of the general U.S. workforce. They also reported lower-than-recommended levels of health outcomes and hours of sleep per night.

> "The stressful workload, the feeling of having to be 'always on,' the lack of resources, and the burden of ever-changing expectations take a toll on educators, and the health problems educators face are compounded by deficient building conditions, equipment and staff shortages, and insufficient time to prepare and collaborate with colleagues" (AFT, 2017).

Chronic stress and poor mental health impact teachers' job performance. Chronic stress compromises the immune system, increasing educators' susceptibility to illness, which may result in more teacher absences over time. This can disrupt student instruction, behavior management, and relationships with students, which all lead to lower student achievement (Ansley et al., 2018). Stress can also increase irritability, mood swings, exhaustion, depression, and anxiety. One teacher lamented, "For the past eight years, my blood pressure is consistently 20 points higher during the school year than in the summer" (AFT, 2017).

What Stressors Are Unique to Educators?

Although improvements have been seen in some areas, educators today are still impacted by the pressures to raise academic achievement (Feather, 2019). Perhaps one silver lining of COVID-19's impact was a temporary lifting of many expectations for student testing and meeting academic standards. However, leading up to COVID-19, during the No Child Left Behind and Common Core eras, teachers and schools found that their instruction and outcomes for students were heavily scrutinized. For many schools, that meant that instructional time was replaced by test-prep sessions, and that subjects of high interest to students were often sidelined. So, the pressure was on both teachers and students to perform at a high level.

Researchers from the National Education Association (NEA) surveyed fifteen hundred Pre-K-12 teachers about the effects of standardized testing. Seventy-two percent of teachers felt "moderate" or "extreme" pressure from both school and district administrators to improve test scores. Forty-two percent of teachers felt that the emphasis on improving standardized test scores had a "negative impact" on their classroom. The emphasis on high stakes testing has reduced time for more engaging, enriching, and creative learning opportunities, and 52 percent of teachers felt they spend too much time—roughly 30 percent—on testing and test prep. Many teachers are also stressed by education "reformers" who want to remove "bad" teachers and view standardized test scores as the main evaluation metric of success. Overall, nearly half (45 percent) of surveyed teachers considered quitting because of standardized testing (Walker, 2014).

A forty-three year veteran teacher in Michigan said the increased focus on standardized test results and uncertainty in school funding was one of her biggest stressors. "As the tests increased, the stress was put on the teachers because we're going to evaluate you on two days of testing, three days of testing with students that have no stake in it," Komar said. "Teachers really felt that, the impact of they're not engaged in what's going on here, yet my job hangs in the balance" (Feather, 2019).

Also, in recent years, educator stress has been heightened by factors (see Figure 4.1) such as the following:

- Expanding job descriptions, and vicarious or secondary traumatic stress (STS) (Minero, 2017)
- Lack of professional control and respect (AFT, 2017)
- Low pay and stagnant wages (AFT, 2017)
- Long hours and lack of resources (AFT, 2017)
- A tense political climate (Rogers et al., 2017)
- Increasing numbers of teens dying by suicide (Abbott, 2019)
- Fear of school shootings (Ansley et al., 2018)
- Health concerns

FIGURE 4.1   Teacher Stress

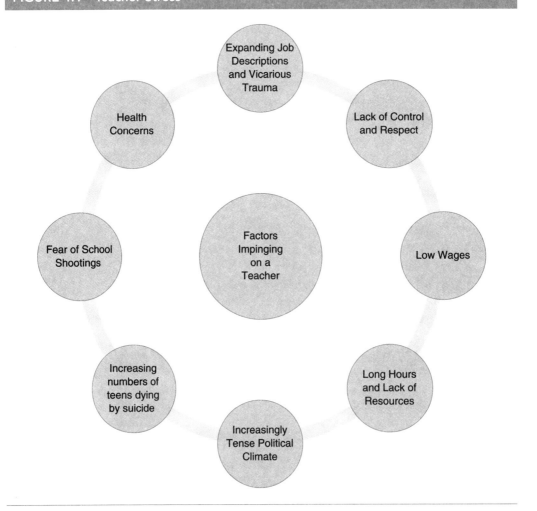

Expanding Job Descriptions and Vicarious Trauma

Teachers are incredibly motivated and caring individuals, who care about their students' success. They are also increasingly loaded with additional responsibilities, taking on roles such as mental health counselor, psychologist, and case worker. "Being a teacher is a stressful enough job, but teachers are now responsible for a lot more things than just providing education," says LeAnn Keck, a manager at Trauma Smart, an organization that assists children and adults in navigating trauma. "It seems like teachers have in some ways become case workers. They get to know about their students' lives and the needs of their families, and with that can come secondary trauma" (Minero, 2017).

Roughly half of American school children have experienced at least some form of trauma—from neglect, to abuse, to violence (Lander, 2018). Students cannot leave this trauma at home, so teachers often end up supporting their students' emotional healing in addition to their academic growth. Although normally we would expect that teachers should be able to address students' emotional needs as part of their regular classroom responsibilities, the extent of trauma and the recent upsurge in teens dying by suicide, for example, have both expanded expectations of teachers and increased their vicarious trauma.

Vicarious trauma, or secondary trauma, affects teachers' brains much as it affects their students'. "The brain emits a fear response, releasing excessive cortisol and adrenaline that can increase heart rate, blood pressure, and respiration, and release a flood of emotions" (Minero, 2017). Stress can manifest as anger, irritability, numbness, anxiety, social withdrawal, insomnia, headaches, sadness, or feeling hopeless, isolated, or guilty about not doing enough (Minero, 2017; Lander, 2018). Many teachers feel unprepared to help students who have experienced trauma, and many aren't equipped to address the toll it takes on their own health and personal lives (MHTTC, 2020, January 14; Minero, 2017). "Teachers, counselors, and administrators may recognize the cumulative stressors that they face, but they don't always realize that their symptoms are a common reaction to working with traumatized children—and that these symptoms have a name" (Lander, 2018).

Lack of Control and Respect

A teacher responding to the AFT's quality of life survey argued that the "majority of stress for teachers comes NOT from students, but from things outside the classroom like district bureaucracy, changing state mandates, and the constant flux in testing and other requirements" (AFT, 2017).

Educators report feeling some control over day-to-day classroom-level decisions such as teaching techniques, evaluating and grading students, homework levels, and student discipline; but they report having less influence over policy decisions such as curriculum selection, professional development, and budget decisions (AFT, 2017). Teachers' opinions on these matters that affect their day to day experience in the classroom are often not only disrespected or ignored but unsought. Although families' intimate experiences with home schooling

> The extent of trauma and the recent upsurge in teens dying by suicide have both expanded expectations of teachers and increased their vicarious trauma.

during the COVID-19 crisis has increased teachers' level of prestige in most communities, it remains to be seen whether that respect will be remembered and have any impact on whether teachers are invited into crucial decision-making conversations or whether their pay will be raised to match other professions that require comparable amounts of education and skill.

Long Hours and Low Wages

AFT's survey respondents averaged more than fifty hours of work per week (AFT, 2017). Despite long hours, important work, and demanding responsibilities, teachers receive woefully low wages. According to data from the NEA, teacher salaries fell 4.5 percent over the last decade when adjusting for inflation (Camera, 2019). According to the Economic Policy Institute, teachers receive 21 percent less pay than similarly educated and experienced professionals (Allegretto & Mishel, 2018). Pay is an important component of retention, recruitment, and satisfaction, so these real wage declines are particularly concerning. Teachers are increasingly striking to demand fairer wages, as we've seen in West Virginia, Kentucky, Oklahoma, and Arizona (Varathan, 2018).

Educators also face rising healthcare costs in addition to their stagnating wages. "My health suffers because I cannot afford the treatment that my physician would like. The cost of healthcare, for me and my wife, is too high. It causes a great deal of financial stress" (AFT, 2017). Many teachers even get second jobs during the weeknights, weekends, or summers to make ends meet.

Lack of Resources

> Educators also lack resources. One teacher noted, "In South Carolina, I never had enough novels to allow my kids to take them home and read them. We had to read everything in class. I had to pay out-of-pocket for items like tissues, hand sanitizer, and dry-erase markers. I was also only allowed a certain number of photocopies each semester. . . . I would play math games in my head: If I made the font smaller and reduced the spacing and margins, I could reduce the amount of copies per child to . . . have more copies left for another story on another day" (Amato, 2015). Rural schools in particular struggle with a lack of resources and have difficulty attracting and retaining teacher talent.

Schools also lack proper resources and training around mental health and behavioral management. One teacher noted in the AFT's survey, "What my school really needs is more social and emotional support for students (more counselors, social workers, etc.). We have students who have experienced trauma, and we struggle with behavior because of it; it causes a lot of stress for everyone" (AFT, 2017).

Increasingly Tense Political Climate

UCLA released a study showing that since the 2016 presidential inauguration, high school teachers across the country reported more stress, anxiety, and bullying among their students than before (Rogers et al., 2017). More than 20 percent of teachers reported heightened polarization on campus and increased incivility in their classrooms. A social studies teacher in North Carolina noted, "In my seventeen years I have never seen anger this blatant and raw over a political candidate or issue." Seventy-two point three percent of teachers surveyed agreed with the following: "My school leadership should provide more guidance, support, and professional development opportunities on how to promote civil exchange and greater understanding across lines of difference" (Rogers et al., 2017).

Fear of School Shootings

On top of everything else, we've entered a new, disturbing era where school shootings are increasing. Educators feel pressure to address the trauma their students have experienced and connect them to mental health resources as necessary. However, they don't feel properly trained or supported (MHTTC, 2020, January 14). "If teachers already face high levels of occupational stress, it's not hard to see how the recent spate of deadly school shootings—coupled with the idea that teachers should arm themselves to protect themselves and their students—can elevate their stress levels even higher" (Ansley et al., 2018).

Health-Related Concerns

Like others around the world, with the outbreak of COVID-19 in 2020, teachers were thrust into an era of uncertainty about their health, the health of their loved ones, and concern for their students and others around the world. COVID-19 created not only a new normal, but extraordinary levels of stress (CDC, 2020, March 23).

Stressors at My School

- What are the three greatest stressors at your school?
  _____

- What are the three greatest stressors you are currently facing?
  _____

- How are the stressors being addressed at your school and for you personally?
  _____

Teacher Attrition is at an All-Time High

As educators' jobs become increasingly taxing and stressful, more and more educators turn to other career opportunities. The number of teachers leaving after just one year has hit an all-time high (Morrison, 2019). Nearly half of all new teachers leave the field within the first five years. Among those who stay, nearly two-thirds admitted they were "not engaged," or mentally and emotionally disconnected from their role and students' needs (Ansley et al., 2018).

When turnover contributes to teacher shortages, schools often turn to inexperienced or unqualified teachers, increasing class sizes, or cutting class offerings, all of which negatively impact student learning. What's more, teacher turnover is far higher in poor districts and among teachers of color, who are more likely to have students of color. The biggest reason teachers leave is dissatisfaction—with the profession overall, the lack of advancement opportunities, the insufficient administrative support, or the challenging working conditions (Varathan, 2018).

The Relationship Between Student Trauma and Teacher Stress

Imagine a student comes to class with large bruises on her arms. She's quieter than usual and won't look you in the eye. While the other students are working, you quietly pull her into the hallway and ask what happened. She hesitates, but finally admits that her father hit her. You know you must report this incident. You're concerned for the safety of your student, as well as her overall well-being and family life. When you go home after school, you can't stop thinking about your student or shake your anxiety.

Imagine one of your students has fallen behind in school. You've been working with him, and he's showing progress, but suddenly his mother pulls him out of school. You're concerned for his future and wonder how he's going to continue his education and stay out of trouble. You notice your body is tense and you regularly worry about him.

Over time, the trauma that students experience affects teachers who see this trauma and deal with how it impacts students day after day. Over time, individuals who are surrounded by trauma also begin to feel its effects. They may become depressed, anxious, quick to anger. Teachers, like others, can find that their morale and job satisfaction is lessened. As they experience an urge to fight, flee, or freeze, they may also be less aware of the needs of students. In these cases, empathy may decrease, teachers may experience a sense of helplessness, and particularly without an understanding of the neurological impact of trauma, they may not even be aware of the secondary impact they are facing and their own need for greater self-care measures.

Secondary Trauma

- Are you experiencing secondary trauma?
- How is it manifesting?
- What steps are you taking to counteract it?

Understanding Current Needs and Concerns

Once you better understand the stressors facing teachers and other school staff, you can begin to address them. To start, consider conducting a needs assessment of your school. How do teachers and administrators feel? What are their biggest stressors? Concerns? Challenges? Once you collect some feedback, you can tailor a plan to address the most pressing issues. Once you have identified stressors, you can divide them into two categories: things where you likely have some control and areas out of your zone of control.

As indicated in the Degree of Control Example (Figure 4.2), perception regarding our ability to control various factors is not an either/or proposition. Some areas of concern clearly rest with how we live our lives, our values, and our practices. Other areas are governed primarily by outside factors. Even such factors as teacher wages, however, although being an area largely outside of individual control, may be impacted by collective actions such as union activity and teacher protests. In some cases, we may have some control over how we choose to address a concern. What we say and do can either contribute to or reduce student anxiety, so that even when we may not be able to address the underlying issue or cause, we can help build student confidence and resiliency through our guidance, attitudes, and instruction.

FIGURE 4.2 Degree of Control Example			
	IMMEDIATE ABILITY TO CONTROL		OUTSIDE ZONE OF IMMEDIATE CONTROL
	PERSONAL	COLLECTIVE	
Student Testing			x
Diet, Nutrition, Sleep, Exercise	x		
Teacher Wages			x
Student Attitudes/Interest	x	x	
Teacher Morale	x	x	
Societal Violence			x
Student Fears About Deportation	x	x	x
Fear About School Shootings	x	x	
Student Anxiety	x	x	x

Download a template of this tool from our companion website: resources.corwin.com/compassionateschool practices.

Sometimes when examining our lives and trying to make decisions about our priorities, it is useful to understand what is inside and outside our zone of immediate control. We may find greater immediate benefits and satisfaction in focusing on those things under our immediate control. For some of the items in the Degree of Control Example, further insights can be gained by realizing that for some events, such as student anxiety, teachers can take certain actions—for example, teaching about social emotional learning or mindfulness—to help students build resiliency.

Areas of Greatest Concern in New England MHTTC

In the New England MHTTC, when we asked Fellows about their areas of greatest concern, we learned that teacher stress was overwhelmingly the number-one concern, with 95 percent of surveyed Childhood-Trauma Learning Collaborative (C-TLC) Fellows wanting more information about how to reduce teacher and student stress (MHTTC, 2020). In conversations with Fellows, several administrators noted that they believe their high turnover rates are directly related to teacher stress. Some have even begun quietly encouraging mental health days (using paid sick leave) to reduce burnout. Administrators are listening to staff concerns and addressing those issues they have control over, but they want more tools. Our first piece of advice to them has been to start with themselves. If an administrator can find calm for themselves, they can be a model for their staff as they lead the way down a more peaceful path.

Practical Solutions to Improve Educator Mental Health and Well-Being

To create safe, welcoming, and beneficial learning environments for students, we—parents, educators, administrators, and communities—must work together to build supportive working environments for teachers and school staff (AFT, 2017). Jennifer Donohoo (2017), in her book *Collective Efficacy: How Educator Beliefs Impact Student Learning,* says, "Amazing things happen when a school staff shares the belief that they are able to achieve collective goals and they overcome challenges to impact student achievement" (p. 1). We believe that teacher collective efficacy has implications that expand beyond the boundaries of academic achievement. Sharing a sense that "we achieve collective goals and overcome challenges" can improve our outlook. Just to realize that we are a team, involved in a collective effort to make a difference, can increase our confidence, improve morale, and reduce feelings of alienation and isolation.

We view this as five-step process (see Figure 4.3).

As you read through the activities on the next few pages, consider which might be practical to implement in your school or your classroom. Here is a template to guide you with this planning.

FIGURE 4.3   A Five-Step Process to Develop Collective Efficacy

Practical Solutions to Improve Educator Mental Health and Well-Being

- Create Spaces for Educator Collaboration and Discussion
- Create Peer Groups
- Build Coping Strategies
- Practice Self-Care
- Practice Mindfulness and Infuse It Into the School Day
- Create a Timeline for Planned Discussions and Implementation of Initiatives

Create Spaces for Educator Collaboration and Discussion

Connecting with colleagues to share, talk through, and process experiences can be invaluable for teachers coping with secondary trauma, says Micere Keels, founder of the TREP Project, a trauma-informed curriculum for urban teachers. "Reducing professional isolation is critical," said Keels. "It allows educators to see that others are struggling with the same issues, prevents the feeling that one's struggles are due to incompetence, and makes one aware of alternative strategies for working with students exhibiting challenging behavior" (Minero, 2017). A wellness buddy program can help build community and foster well-being by pairing up educators who assist and hold each other accountable to their wellness goals. A professional learning community can also offer a place for teachers to check in with each other and share guidance, support, and practical learnings and advice.

Create Peer Groups

Setting aside time for teachers to work together, be it building curricula, sharing lesson ideas, or strategizing how to assist students, often results in improved student outcomes. Peer groups can be equally effective in addressing educators' mental health. Schools should create a regular space, perhaps once a month or even once a week, where teachers can come together and check in about how they are doing emotionally (Lander, 2018).

Build Coping Strategies

Students experiencing trauma may act out, becoming combative, disruptive, or aggressive. Once educators better understand trauma, its effects, and its symptoms, they are able to develop positive coping mechanisms and respond in a more productive way the next time they face a stressful situation.

When a student acts out in class, one teacher explains how she will take a few deep breaths, drink coffee, or go to a different part of the classroom to work with another student. Other positive coping strategies could be counting to five, visualizing a calming place, or responding with an opposite action—like talking to a student quietly when you want to yell. It can also be useful to review your day and note which times you felt most stressed, so you can be more aware and better prepare yourself (Minero, 2017).

> ## Considerations for Your Stress and Your Job
>
> Determine the positive and negative effects of your job by completing the Professional Quality of Life (ProQOL) assessment and exploring the toolkit created by Teaching Tolerance to learn self-care strategies. Learn how, as an educator, you can identify fatigue, burnout, and vicarious trauma as well as strategies for self-care through the tip sheet created by the National Child Traumatic Stress Network.

Practice Self-Care

Many teachers say they don't have time for self-care, but long-term self-care practices are vital to maintaining overall well-being and resilience. Educators can tailor these activities to their own interests and schedules, and they can pick from a range of activities such as going for a walk or run, hiking, reading, watching a movie, cooking, practicing mindfulness, taking a yoga class, meditating, or talking with a friend or family member—whatever feels right (Minero, 2017). Educators should also eat well, drink a lot of water, and do their best to get plenty of sleep.

> Long-term self-care practices are vital to maintaining overall well-being and resilience.

Practice Mindfulness and Infuse It Into the School Day

Picture yourself in the middle of a lesson: A student interrupts your lesson to make a rude and offensive remark. Your heart starts racing and you feel your insides begin to boil. Do you snap back angrily or take a deep breath to reset? Mindfulness will help you recognize your instinctive reaction, calm yourself down, and take a moment to determine the smart and productive response— calmly redirecting the students' attention to the task-at-hand.

Research on Mindfulness Training for Teachers

Flook, Goldberg, Pinger, Bonus, and Davidson (2013) studied the impact of an eight-week mindfulness training for teachers. They found that a mindfulness-based stress reduction course specifically adapted for teachers led to significant decreases in stress and burnout as well as improved self-compassion, attention, and classroom performance. Mindful Schools conducted a randomized controlled study on mindfulness during the 2012–2013 school year. They found that following a six-week mindfulness training, teachers reported greater job satisfaction, improved sense of teaching efficacy, reduced stress, greater self-compassion, and better relationships with students (Fernando, 2013).

Training teachers in mindfulness helps them manage and reduce their own stress and burnout while improving their compassion, attention, and job satisfaction. Teachers can then teach students about mindfulness and incorporate mindful practices in the classroom to reduce students' stress. This is a virtuous cycle, as reduced student stress leads to calmer and more productive classrooms, which further reduces teachers' stress and all of this can lead to a greater sense of equanimity and resiliency (see Figure 4.4).

FIGURE 4.4   Cycle for Calmer and More Productive Classrooms

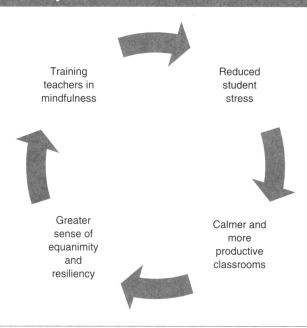

Try these practical exercises from *Mindfulness Practices: Cultivating Heart Centered Communities Where Students Focus and Flourish* (Mason et al., 2019):

Relaxing and breathing (p. 66-67)

1. Sit comfortably, with your back straight but relaxed.

2. Notice your breathing when you're relaxed.

3. Inhale fully through your nose, thinking "One, two, three, four."

4. Hold for a count of three.

5. Exhale fully through the side of your mouth, thinking "One, two, three, four, five, six."

6. Repeat four to six times.

7. Check to see how you feel.

Balloon Breathing (p. 67)

1. Get into a comfortable position.

2. Close your eyes.

3. Breathe in through your nose.

4. Breathe out through your mouth, with your lips slightly open.

5. As you inhale, imagine your abdomen is inflating with air, like a balloon.

6. As you exhale, imagine that the air is slowly leaving, like a deflating balloon.

Blow Out the Candles (p. 68)

1. Imagine a birthday cake.

2. Take in a deep breath through your nose.

3. Exhale through your mouth to blow out the candles.

Traditional Meditation (p. 85)

1. Rest the backs of your hands on your knees.

2. You can bring the tip of the thumb and index finger of each hand together and gently rest your wrists on your knees.

3. Close your eyes and focus on the area between your eyebrows.

4. Breathe deeply.

5. For any thought that comes, examine the thought briefly and then relax and let it go.

6. Continue for three to five minutes.

7.   Inhale deeply and exhale. Were you able to let your thoughts go and return to your breath?

8.   Open your eyes.

Do a Body Scan (p. 99)

1.   Lie down in a comfortable position.

2.   Close your eyes and be aware of your hands, feet, arms, and legs. Inhale. Then exhale, relax, and let go. Pause.

3.   Inhale and focus on your feet. Pause. Exhale, relax, let go.

4.   Inhale and focus on your legs. Pause. Notice the breath that occurs between every pause. Exhale, relax, and let go.

5.   Inhale and focus on your stomach. Pause. Exhale, relax, let go.

6.   Inhale and focus on your heart. Pause. Exhale, relax, let go.

7.   Inhale and focus on your lungs. Pause. Exhale, relax, let go.

8.   Inhale and focus on your arms. Pause. Exhale, relax, let go.

9.   Move up to your face (pause), scalp (pause), and the top of your head. Pause. Exhale, relax, let go.

10.   Inhale deeply. Relax, sinking down onto your mat or the ground beneath you.

11.   Remain in relaxation for three to five minutes.

Source: Used with permission. From *Mindful School Communities: The Five Cs of Nurturing Heart Centered Learning by Christine Mason, Michele M. Rivers Murphy, and Yvette Jackson.* Copyright 2020 by Solution Tree Press, 555 North Morton Street, Bloomington, IN 47404, 800.733.6786, SolutionTree.com. All rights reserved.

A Schoolwide Approach to Foster Well-Being

Build a Culture of Awareness

Having school leaders acknowledge that teachers might be experiencing vicarious trauma and stress is sometimes the first step. Teachers need to know that they are not alone. School leadership should find ways to recognize and appreciate staff both publicly and privately. Schools should also connect staff who may be experiencing vicarious trauma with resources and make it clear that asking for help is not a sign of weakness, but rather a sign of strength and self-awareness (Lander, 2018).

Become a Trauma-Skilled School

One way to foster a schoolwide approach and build a culture of awareness is to become a trauma-informed school. There is a movement around creating trauma-informed schools—schools that recognize and are prepared to assist community members affected by trauma and traumatic stress. We are advocates of going beyond a trauma-informed approach, toward becoming *trauma skilled*. Trauma-skilled schools deeply integrate social-emotional learning into their teaching, culture, and approach, understanding that the holistic health and well-being of students and teachers is essential for achieving academic success. To do this, trauma-skilled schools focus on fostering a supportive, caring culture and training their entire staff to recognize and support students suffering trauma (Lander, 2018).

Many of the practices, policies, and protocols that foster a holistic school response to youth mental health needs—such as a Comprehensive Behavioral Health Model like Boston Public Schools' Heart Centered Learning, and restorative practices—will assist schools on their journey in becoming trauma-skilled. Dr. Sandy Addis and his team at the National Dropout Prevention Center (NDPC) have been working since 1986 to figure out how to help more students graduate from high school. Over their decades of research, they came to the conclusion that the most important factor was that a school address students' trauma by going beyond merely educating staff about it (as a trauma-informed school does) or teaching them piecemeal strategies and practices to respond to trauma (as a trauma-responsive school does), but by truly integrating a multipronged approach to trauma prevention, recognition, and healing (as a trauma-skilled school does).

Over several years of working with fourteen staff, thirty consultants, and thirteen researchers in organizations, districts, and schools across the country, Addis and his team developed the Trauma-Skilled Schools Model, which explains the five steps schools take toward becoming the kind of compassionate school community that deeply understands how best to respond to the effects of trauma and severe mental illness while simultaneously preventing their occurrence.

The NDPC has an online program of five short courses that explain how school leaders can achieve each step on the journey toward becoming trauma-skilled. Schools that want more assistance can also contract with the NDPC to bring trainers into the school or district to provide more extensive supports.

In an edWeb Webinar, Dr. Addis (2020) said, "School solutions to the trauma issue must be Tier I, focused on behavior and learning, and focused on climate and educator practices." He cautioned that although twenty states do have mandates for schools to become trauma-informed, it is often little more than a single one-hour professional development session and a box to check. Instead, schools and districts need a plan that includes community stakeholder input, assigns specific roles and tasks to individuals, and sets up systems of accountability.

Teachers and other school staff want to make a difference in their students' lives. But they're battling stressors on all fronts, from long hours to low pay to vicarious trauma to school shootings, which can lead to high stress levels and burnout. Educators are facing more stress than ever before, and they need adequate resources, tools, and support so they can continue to excel in their jobs. Acknowledging educators' stress is the first step—it's important to validate their

Acknowledging educators' stress is the first step—it's important to validate their feelings and let them know they're not alone.

FIGURE 4.5 Trauma-Skilled Schools Model

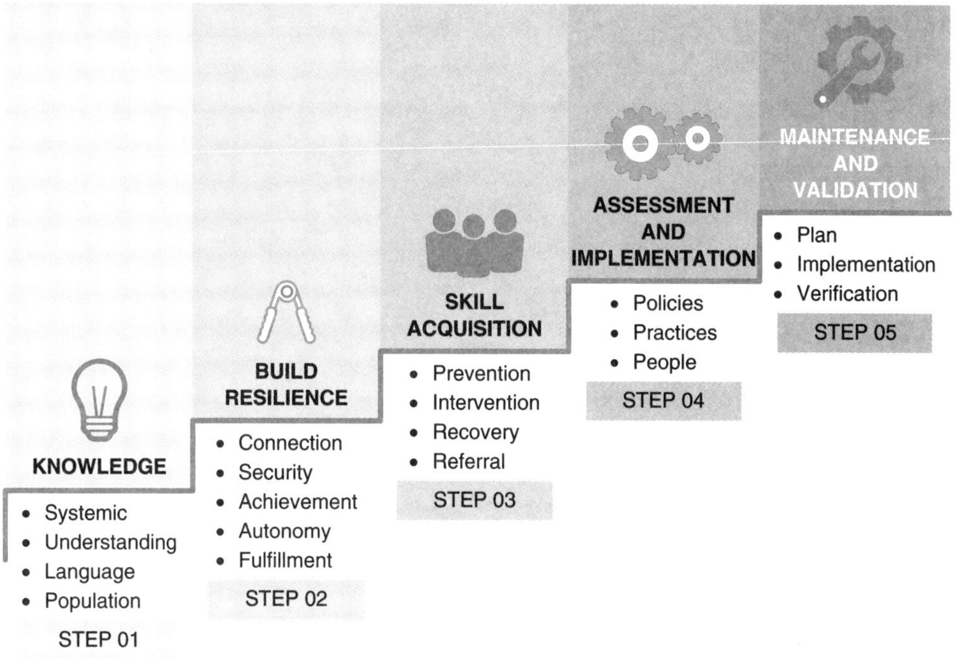

MAINTENANCE AND VALIDATION
- Plan
- Implementation
- Verification

STEP 05

ASSESSMENT AND IMPLEMENTATION
- Policies
- Practices
- People

STEP 04

SKILL ACQUISITION
- Prevention
- Intervention
- Recovery
- Referral

STEP 03

BUILD RESILIENCE
- Connection
- Security
- Achievement
- Autonomy
- Fulfillment

STEP 02

KNOWLEDGE
- Systemic
- Understanding
- Language
- Population

STEP 01

Source: National Dropout Prevention Center, 2018

feelings and let them know they're not alone. We need to build more compassionate and collaborative school communities where educators can come together to share and learn from one another. Additionally, when we teach educators about mindfulness, meditation, yoga, and deep breathing, they can then infuse these practices into their daily routines, increasing not only their own sense of well-being, but helping students gain valuable tools for use in their lives as well (see Figure 4.5).

Reflections on Strengthening Mental Health and Well-Being

Teacher attitudes are key. When a negative mindset accompanies us as we open the schoolhouse door, that mindset could influence most of our encounters throughout the day. In *Mindful School Communities: The Five Cs of Nurturing Heart Centered Learning,* Christine Mason and her colleagues state "conscious awareness takes time to develop; it does not happen overnight" (Mason, Rivers Murphy, & Jackson, 2020, p. 17). They provide close to two hundred pages of examples, activities, and insights into how to develop and sustain a nurturing community that will reduce stress and enhance student and staff compassion, resiliency, and competence. When we become mindfully aware, we can use that awareness to ease our own burden and the burdens of others. Although stress impacts all of us, if we have toolkits at our disposal, we can reduce our stress, even while wrestling with our own inner turmoil.

Online Resources in This Chapter:

Online Resource 4.1   National School Mental Health Curriculum

Online Resource 4.2   School Health Assessment and Performance Evaluation (SHAPE) System

Online Resource 4.3   Degree of Control Example

Online Resource 4.4   Implementation of Ideas to Alleviate Teacher Stress

Online Resource 4.5   30 Ways to Bring Self-Care and Mindfulness Into Your Classroom

Online Resource 4.6   Mindful Teachers' Self-Care Resources

Online Resource 4.7   Free, Guided Meditation Recordings From UCLA

Online Resource 4.8   Online Mindfulness and Implementation Courses From Mindful Schools

Online Resource 4.9   Trauma and Learning Policy Initiative's Resources

Online Resource 4.10   Trauma Responsive Schools Implementation Assessment

Part 2

Leadership

Adaptive Leadership Within the Childhood-Trauma Learning Collaborative

5

In social communities that experience extreme challenges, those with high levels of trust and cooperation fare better (Zolli, 2012). When challenges hit these communities, people quickly move into cooperation with each other. (p. 203)

—Elena Aguilar (2018)

Resiliency and Finding Hope

School leaders have tremendous responsibilities for children's well-being. As Patricia Ullman, author of *Eight Steps to an Authentic Life: Ancient Wisdom for Modern Times* (2018) states, "Only by actually feeling and understanding the suffering of another can we be fully engaged in compassion" (2018, p. 11). Effective school leaders not only need skills, they need dispositions, insights, compassion—and routines for their own self-care. Principals and other school leaders are called upon to render many decisions each day—to handle the small fires that erupt and also to find time for deep, serious planning, to motivate and inspire others, to take time to care, and to be thoughtful as they guide others through the fog, over the mountains, and on journeys that can seem endless.

Trauma can be one of the biggest obstacles to individual and communal well-being and our journey to success. It sometimes takes tremendous insight and patience to help staff work their way through trauma. One administrator,

Effective school leaders not only need skills, they need dispositions, insights, compassion— and routines for their own self-care.

a C-TLC Fellow in Rhode Island, described how she is working with her staff after a suicide in her community:

> There was unspeakable trauma in my school last year (with a young child who chose to die by suicide) and consequently, the school culture is suffering as a whole because of this tragedy. My goal is to increase the capacity of staff's understanding and response to trauma. One of the first steps is to learn where staff strengths and areas of need are in relation to the affect this tragedy has had on school culture (New England Mental Health Technology Transfer Center, 2020).

What leadership skills are demanded in such situations? For many of the most serious situations, there are no quick fixes. Instead, plans need to be put in place to systematically prepare staff to transform a school culture and climate.

 Joelle Brookner, a C-TLC Fellow in rural Massachusetts, explained how over the course of the year there was a shift in the consciousness and the compassionate actions of her staff:

Everything is so much better this year than last year. The main shift is a difference in adults' approach to children's behavior. Patience and empathy are so much higher. Child study groups are meeting twice a week. Around the holidays, some kids lost it and haven't gotten it back, however, everyone around the table had the vocabulary to talk about it, plan, and make an intervention.

Additionally, office referrals are down 25 percent since last year. We implemented schoolwide values, including monthly assemblies where 6th graders teach the rest of the school about different values. There is also more support among peers, and the social worker has made a huge difference in education for adults and support for kids. My staff's capacity to handle problems is so much better.

In order to enhance staff readiness to address student trauma, Principal Stacy Bachelder-Giles, a C-TLC Fellow in New Hampshire, brought her staff to a virtual book study of *Mindfulness Practices: Cultivating Heart Centered School Communities where Students Focus and Flourish* (Mason et al., 2019). Over the course of four months, they were part of a group that met every three weeks to discuss chapters, compare notes on their needs, and practice mindfulness exercises.

As Stacy explains it, during the book study, her staff strengthened their understanding of their students' needs for mindfulness practices while cultivating their own personal practices.

We held focus groups about stress several months after the conclusion of the *Mindfulness Practices* book study during the COVID-19 pandemic. Stacy's staff comprised one of the groups. It was beautiful to see how their mindfulness practices had been supporting them through this crisis. After each staff member shared their stressors, they—unprompted—concluded their answer with a positive change in their life. Because of Stacy's mindful leadership in cultivating a heart centered community, her staff had the resiliency to find hope within themselves and each other in the darkest moments.

In this chapter, we offer insights into the dispositions, knowledge, and skills that help leaders to be not only trauma-informed but trauma-skilled implementers of evidenced-based practices that make a difference during both ordinary and also extraordinary times.

In New England, we are seeing evidence of an expanded interest in helping staff learn about trauma, toxic stress, and how to use mindfulness to prevent and alleviate their negative effects. We are also seeing the impact in terms of staff who are feeling more confident of their ability and better able to implement programs that address compassion and students' well-being.

Others throughout the United States who are using a heart centered approach are also reporting significant changes. Usually these changes begin with changes for adults, who as they learn mindfulness and stress reduction techniques, also begin incorporating these in their classrooms.

Examples From Virginia and Maryland

 Richard Hang, a school psychologist at Mantua Elementary School in Fairfax, Virginia, has been working with teachers over the past six years to integrate social emotional learning in his classrooms. Teachers are using *Mind-Up*, a social emotional learning curriculum, and colorful puppets to teach kids about different parts of the brain. Hang reports that teachers, even during COVID-19, "aren't just doing lessons, they are connecting with kids."

(Continued)

(Continued)

Jeff Donald, the mindfulness coordinator in Montgomery County School District in Maryland, is teaching teachers and students about yoga, mindfulness, meditation, and restorative justice. During COVID-19, he is offering virtual training, and conducting restorative justice through online community circles. He is also working with teachers to ensure that each student is matched with a trusted adult with responsibilities for simply checking in with that student each day. Jeff, in a recent discussion, said, "There are kids who have no problem asking for love and attention. The ones we worry about are those who say nothing" (Center for Educational Improvement, Focus Group, April 30, 2020).

Leading in a Time of Fear and Uncertainty

With the COVID-19 Pandemic, the New England C-TLC Fellows, like thousands of educational leaders, were handling extreme stress. The C-TLC staff examined their stress, their actions, and their needs with a series of three focus groups in April 2020. Fellows shared with each other and our staff some of the situations they are facing, their own fears and anxieties, and the actions they are taking (Mason, Asby, et al., 2020).

When the pandemic struck, principals and educators shifted gears overnight. As one Fellow explained, "This is a traumatic event for everybody, but it's not equal for everyone. You have vulnerable families who were already at risk and now the parents have no job and no food and the students who look to the school for consistency and safety have nowhere to turn." She is "connecting with teachers every day. Academic success isn't the priority right now. Connecting with kids and families is." She recognizes that there are competing and sometimes contradictory messages coming from the district and state right now and that "It's important to be grounded in what we know is right in terms of being human."

With COVID-19, people around the world are experiencing reoccurring trauma and stress from their distant and recent pasts. As leaders, school principals have opportunities and responsibilities to assist their communities. They must help teachers, staff, students, and families brace for not only those moments when the waves of stress violently strike, but also for the apprehension of what might be. These leaders did this by saying something to brighten a child's day, providing a sense of calmness and security by just being there, or aiding a parent who is overloaded by all of the daily precautions we all are taking.

School Leadership and Mental Health During a Time of Crisis

 Mary Woods, an award-winning principal and principal mentor (Greenville, SC) explains some of the steps that leaders need to take during any disruptive crisis.

- Have a systemic transition plan

- Continue to provide nutritious food supplements

- Have appropriate protocols in place that address emotional needs

- Prepare all auxiliary staff on ways to interact compassionately with students

- Provide a safe group setting for staff to debrief and process

- Ensure that classroom are safe havens for students

- Develop a task force to address and meet the needs of the mental health issues that arise

Moving forward, school teachers and administrators need a systematic transition plan to minimize potential life-long effects of social, educational and cultural experiences exacerbated by school closures, economic family challenges, and social isolations. It is essential that the mental health cultures within schools are predicated on humanitarian behavioral best practices. (M. Woods, personal communication, April 2020)

Action Informed by Assessment

To identify and plan for the changes that were made at her school, principal Stacy Bachelder-Giles, like many effective leaders, began with a needs assessment (see Chapter 2, Using Heart Centered Learning to Build Compassionate School Communities in New England). C-TLC Fellows also turned to S-CCATE (see Chapters 1 and 2). These data gave them information on staff perceptions of their own leadership as well as student competencies and actions. With S-CCATE they also received specific recommendations for what they might do to improve their practice.

Alternatives to S-CCATE

Dana Asby and Danielle Rueda have described approaches to evaluating school climate in an article for the Center for Educational Improvement.

Measures of school climate and culture such as the Classroom Community Scale (CCS; Barnard-Brak & Shiu, 2010) that address important concerns such as equity, safety, and justice are beneficial for an administrator's broad understanding of the emotional environment within their building; however, this and most other classroom and school climate/culture scales fail to address such essential components of SEL as student understanding of emotions, how to build confidence and courage, and other factors measured by the S-CCATE that give a more detailed understanding of a school's culture (Baker et al., 2016).

Scales that measure individual aspects of SEL abound; however, some of these scales measure only a single component of SEL, falling short of the power of S-CCATE to assess multiple aspects of SEL. Student protection and trauma support for example, can be measured in the *Attitudes Related to Trauma-Informed Care Scale* (ARTIC; Baker et al., 2016). Additionally, compassionate school policies are assessed in *The Professional Quality of Life* Scale (ProQOL; Stamm, 2010) through a thirty-item self-report measure of the positive and negative effects that come with working with people who have undergone stressful events. Novel scales are also available to measure such forgotten components of SEL as students' attitudes toward human rights and violence prevention, which is measured in the *Human Rights Attitude Scale* (HRAS; Ercan & Yaman, 2015). *Excerpted from edimprovement.org* "S-CCATE: A More Effective School Culture Measurement" Tool (Asby & Rueda, 2018).

The Importance of Professional Development

The C-TLC Fellows made considerable advances with their school communities to become more heart centered and more focused on student well-being. They did this by assessing strengths and needs, zeroing in on the information they learned in the C-TLC that would be most relevant to their staff, and connecting with experts in their region to deliver effective professional development.

Leadership Development With New England Fellows

In a report on the activities and progress of the C-TLC Fellows in New England (New England MHTTC, 2020), Fellows indicated that they gained significant knowledge regarding trauma and brain development and are actively implementing innovative programs and sharing information with local educators. Their knowledge increased regarding trauma and brain development, implementing yoga, meditation, and mindfulness (95 percent reported an increase), early intervention (89 percent reported an increase), student self-regulation, needs and concerns of families, mental health concerns, and compassionate discipline (84 percent reported an increase).

Leading District-Wide Efforts

 C-TLC Fellows are leading district-wide efforts, reaching Pre-K-12 teachers, para-educators, and others, to secure professional development. A Vermont Fellow explained her actions to move toward becoming a trauma-skilled school:

I led the effort to create a three-year training and implementation plan for my school district that includes all staff Pre-K through grade 12. We initiated the plan in the fall with differentiated training based on participants' past experiences and knowledge. We have continued our training and support through quarterly teacher leader meetings and monthly faculty meetings.

- Paraeducators will receive opportunities to further their learning during the summer of 2020.

- Next year, professional staff will continue to have learning opportunities and are expected to implement trauma-informed practices, which will be connected to their supervision and evaluation reports.

- Additionally, during the summer of 2020, teams from each of our buildings will engage in a graduate level course focused on integrating trauma-informed practices in our Multi-Tiered Systems of Support.

Most C-TLC Fellows also want more information on compassionate practices in the school building. Fellows report that not only are attitudes of staff changing as they begin to more fully understand their students, but students are also gaining skills—they are showing less impulsivity and better self-regulation of their own emotions, better decision making and memory skills, and improved academic learning (Asby & Mason, 2020).

What Is Effective School Leadership?

For students who are most at risk, a leader's ability to cultivate a sense of safety and security; build student self-regulation, decision making, resiliency and confidence; and further individual growth and development are foremost.

Building a sense of agency, trust, and well-being among students, teachers, principals, and families supports students' learning and development, the implementation of innovations within schools, and school preparedness to address emerging societal needs (Toom, 2018). For students who are most at-risk, this sense of trust and agency is not easily gained. Students who feel betrayed, isolated, or alienated are often overwhelmed with a desire to escape, shut down, or lash out at those around them.

To be most relevant, schools must consider the learning and well-being of all of their members (students, teachers, staff, and administrators) and their relationships with families and the surrounding community. Effective school leaders are able to motivate others, build a strong sense of community, and contribute to an overall sense of well-being. Michael Bunting in *The Mindful Leader* (2016) puts it this way: "Leadership is not a solo act" (p. 111). Leaders foster collaboration by building trust, strengthening self-determination, and developing competence in themselves and others.

Reflect on the following questions in regard to your school and check those that apply (Hebert et al., 2019):

How Collaborative Is Our Leadership?

☐ Leaders participate side by side with teachers in professional development and in collaborative teams.

☐ Leaders share and nurture leadership in others, not just within the principal's office.

☐ Leaders establish a culture of trust and safety rather than a carrot-and-stick model of accountability.

Leaders are aware of the larger system of policies, structures, and protocols impacting efforts to implement trauma-informed practices. When policies and protocols get in the way of efforts to try new things, leaders recognize these barriers and adequately address them.

Barriers

Fellows in New England experienced barriers—they understood that teachers needed specific professional development that may not be in the district's plan, that policies they may not have complete authority over needed to be changed, and that many external factors made their job of breaking down these barriers more difficult. Yet, they persevered.

The most effective school leaders will build a strong sense of community, empowerment, and resiliency, where teachers, staff, students, and families feel a sense of belonging and trust. As we will expand upon in Chapter 6, one of the clearest signs of an effective leader is that they do not lead alone. If a mindful leader is to be successful in creating a sense of belonging for all in their school community, they start by inviting everyone's voice to be heard and using stakeholders' valuable opinions to vision together with others to create collaborations and coalitions to make dreams a reality.

What Are Our Barriers to Trust?

Barriers that diminish empowerment, a sense of belonging, and trust at my school include the following:

- ☐ Socioeconomic inequity within our community
- ☐ Prejudice or racism against certain groups, like immigrants
- ☐ Violence within the community or beyond
- ☐ Principal turnover
- ☐ Staff attrition
- ☐ Student attitudes
- ☐ Teacher/staff attitudes (morale)
- ☐ Bullying
- ☐ Mental health stigma
- ☐ Pressures with high-stakes assessment
- ☐ Other: _____

 Elena Aguilar (2018) in her book *Onward* describes how leaders can make school environments more supportive of students' emotional needs, suggesting that leaders:

- **Create opportunities for teachers to reflect on why they do what they do.** Teachers need to recognize that we do what we do because of the resources and skill sets that we have.

- **Humanize the need for change.** Invite current and former students (and their parents) to talk about their experiences in school.

- **Set up structures for listening.** We all need to refine our ability to listen to others.

- **Talk about and normalize emotions, especially fear.** Create an environment where staff, students, and families feel safe being vulnerable.

- **Collectively envision new realities.** Guide people in creating alternate futures to see how things could be different for themselves and kids. (p. 283)

Create Supportive Environments That Meet the Needs of Students

Review and reflect on these ideas from Aguilar (2018):

- How do we create opportunities for teachers to reflect on why they do what they do?

- How do we communicate with current and former students (and their parents) about their experiences in school?

- How do we refine our ability to listen to others and implement improved practices?

- How do we talk about and normalize emotions, especially fear?

Characteristics of Transformational School Leaders

To meet the needs of our most vulnerable students, whether it be a teen contemplating suicide, a youth depressed and feeling a sense of hopelessness, or an adolescent escaping through drugs or alcohol, school leaders need to develop transformational leadership skills. Transformational school leaders are inspirational and motivational visionaries, focusing on their impact on the school culture and climate. They are also change agents, interested in making a substantial difference to enhance not only the lives of the students they serve, but systems at the local, state, and national level that *should* serve these students.

- School leaders who are transformational tend to be people-oriented, considering the needs of staff and students while providing guidance, empathy, compassion, and mentoring.

- Their leadership inspires trust and commitment through a shared vision and their own enthusiasm, as well as their ability to create buy-in and support.

- Transformational leaders tend to build on the strengths of their staff, sharing responsibility and building morale.

- Transformational school leaders are systems thinkers who work with their teams to design intentional, compassionate policies, protocols, and practices that are trauma-informed and aid the growth of individuals and the entire school community.

- School leaders who enact lasting, transformational change are adaptable; they are constantly learning and visioning new ways to meet the ever-shifting needs of their community.

- These leaders also are great communicators who are active listeners and sensitive to the needs and concerns of those around them (Bryant et al. 2016; Burns, 1978; Elmore 2004; Sergiovanni, 2007).

A Compassionate, Transformational School Leader

 Andrea Elliot, a C-TLC Fellow and principal of Bishop Brady High School in New Hampshire, is an inspiring leader.

"Bishop Brady High School: A Caring Community" is on the sign outside this Concord, New Hampshire high school. Andrea Elliot, the principal of this small Catholic school that serves about three hundred students, thinks her school's foundational belief in the importance of loving one another—brother and stranger—is why hers is a compassionate school community.

Principal Elliot has a caring staff who seek to ensure that each student has someone to check in on them and connect with. There are always three to four adults during free time searching out the kids who have no one to talk to. Principal Elliot's background as a school counselor has helped her look at the whole child to see what's standing in the way of success—far too often the answer is trauma.

Compassionate action is key at BBHS, with its requirement that each student complete one hundred hours of community service before graduation. In addition to the work of the twenty-three student organizations, many of which focus on service learning, BBHS has several schoolwide initiatives that demonstrate compassionate action:

- *The Thanksgiving Food Drive* is an annual event where students take the lead in collecting food, creating around twenty-five baskets, and delivering them to neighborhood families in need.

- *Operation Santa* is a yearly program that staff, students, and parents participate in to bring Christmas gifts to 130 families from around the state who otherwise might not get a gift.

- *A Day of Dignity*, an event where students spent the entire day in conversations about bridging differences between students and coping with difficulties with positivity, was recently piloted at BBHS.

Principal Elliot is not only passionate about bringing compassionate practices to her own school, but New Hampshire as a state, New England as a region, and beyond.

(Excerpted from Asby, 2020, April 4)

Many transformational leaders are also mindful, focused on the present without judgment, and are able to instill a sense of well-being among their staff and students (Kabat-Zinn, 2012). They are generous with their time and attention, sharing resources and credit for gains that are made.

School Leaders as Change Agents

As transformational leaders, each of the twenty-four Fellows in New England committed to being agents of change, not only for their own schools but also for their communities and beyond. One goal of the C-TLC program is to foster relationships between school leaders and state or regional government officials to discuss the importance of providing appropriate levels of attention, funding, and staffing to support school mental health services. Doing this has allowed these transformational school leaders to share powerful personal stories about how trauma and mental illness are directly affecting their students and staff with officials who are often far removed from what happens in the classrooms.

The Journey of Addressing Trauma at St. Albans City School

Joan Cavallo, Principal of St. Albans City School (Vermont)

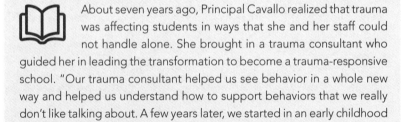 About seven years ago, Principal Cavallo realized that trauma was affecting students in ways that she and her staff could not handle alone. She brought in a trauma consultant who guided her in leading the transformation to become a trauma-responsive school. "Our trauma consultant helped us see behavior in a whole new way and helped us understand how to support behaviors that we really don't like talking about. A few years later, we started in an early childhood expansion pilot with First School, where we learned about Conscious Discipline. We are now in our fourth year of implementation."

Principal Cavallo has learned that the most effective response to trauma is to address both its underlying causes in the community and how teachers can appropriately respond to its effects on students. St. Albans City School now has a comprehensive set of initiatives to enhance both student and staff wellness, including equity and justice, Conscious Discipline, and resiliency training for all school staff and a Resiliency Leadership Team.

St. Albans City School also takes the time to celebrate successes, "to notice each other and when people are really making things work." Principal Cavallo has learned through this process that "to take care of children, we also need to take care of each other."

Personalized Support. At a reflection session at the end of the last school year, Principal Cavallo and her staff realized that there was still a missing puzzle piece in their delivery of trauma-responsive education. Staff came together to create *Raider Learns to Own It, Fix It, and Move On*. Using characters, locations, and situations familiar to each student in the school, Principal Cavallo and her staff wrote and illustrated a story that made all of the great work they'd been doing concrete for students. Students and staff now had a common language to use when a problem arose, "Have you owned it? Fixed it? Moved on?"

Leadership Outside the School Building. Principal Cavallo is part of a collaboration between the Vermont Principal's Association and Prevent Child Abuse Vermont to help schools become better at identifying and addressing the social emotional needs of children. She's also been in meetings with the Vermont Governor's Liaison, who she's lobbying to bring Vermont's Agency of Education and Agency of Human Services together to bridge the divide between the two in an effort to better address the needs of students, especially those who have adverse childhood experiences (Asby, 2019, November 11).

The Substance Abuse and Mental Health Services Administration: National Leaders in Mental Health Support

The C-TLC is one project of the New England Mental Health Technology Transfer Center (MHTTC), a five-year Substance Abuse and Mental Health Services Administration (SAMHSA) grant-funded project. "SAMHSA is the agency within the U.S. Department of Health and Human Services that leads public health efforts to advance the behavioral health of the nation" (SAMHSA, n.d.).

SAMSHA funds myriad connected public health campaigns to advance evidence-based best practices for clinicians, peers, school mental health support providers, and the general public. They provide specific technical assistance and training tailored to the needs of individual mental and behavioral health service providers or agencies in the United States. SAMHSA partners with universities, nonprofits, and other organizations that are already experts in a variety of areas of mental health and substance misuse. The School Mental Health Initiative of the MHTTC network—of which the C-TLC is one of many projects around the nation—releases high quality products to guide our country's school

(Continued)

(Continued)

mental health practices and keep practitioners up to date on new research-informed best practices.

The work SAMHSA funds fosters alliances and relationships with key stakeholders. From these relationships comes creative problem solving, systems-building through the creation of new centers or programs, and public policy changes.

Evolving Leadership: Being Inclusive and Visionary

To implement change, effective transformational leadership often begins with an inclusive vision, a vision that is formed with input from many stakeholders (Mason, Liabenow, & Patschke, 2020; Senge et al., 2012). Howard Adelman and Linda Taylor in *Mental Health in Schools* (2010) describe the role of leaders as change agents:

> Every school can foster staff and student resilience and create a school climate that encourages mutual support, caring, and sense of community. In a real sense, efforts to enhance school climate focus not just on mental health in schools but on the mental health *of* schools. (p. 80)

In *Schools That Learn*, Senge and colleagues (2012) describe the opportunities for schools to continuously evolve. For students who are most at-risk or already experiencing extreme emotional distress, schools have not yet reached their apex. Administrators, teachers, and other leaders in the school community often have limited experience and understanding about mental health issues, which negatively affects how well our school communities serve students with the greatest needs.

What Kind of Leader Are You?

- What kind of leader are you in your most desired future?
- How do your students see you?
- What impact do your efforts have?
- What future do you want to create together? (Senge et al., 2012)

Peter Senge and colleagues (2012) have also described the inclusive nature of school settings that consider the needs of *all* students. Tim Lucas (2012), one of Senge's coauthors, writes, "A learning classroom embodies not just the understanding that all children can learn, but that students learn in multiple ways, that their abilities are not fixed at birth. . . . In such a class, students recognize that part of their purpose is making sure that everyone succeeds" (p. 162).

Lucas goes on to say that "The best educators I know focus a great deal of attention on getting to know kids. . . . Once you have knowledge about the children— once you really see what they care about—then you can do a great deal more for them" (p. 180).

In *Visioning Onward,* Mason, Liabenow, and Patschke (2020) explain how teachers and students can create a shared vision of a classroom with goals to improve "(1) conscious awareness of self, including emotions and the impact of one's actions and attitudes on others, (2) compassionate thoughts and actions, (3) the EF [executive functions] involved in academic learning, and (4) building a nurturing, compassionate culture supportive of a students' readiness to learn" (p. 180). The school principal's attitudes and actions will be instrumental in determining whether a shared vision is developed, whether teachers and students collaborate to further compassion, and whether a compassionate school environment becomes the backdrop for learning and development. The principal's attitudes and actions will impact teachers' understanding of all students—including those whose trauma has resulted in externalizing or internalizing behaviors (see Chapter 3).

However, creating a vision needs to begin from the inside out. Mindful school leaders start with their own self-assessment. In *Visioning Onward*, Mason, Liabenow, and Patschke (2020) suggest that leaders begin by gaining a deeper understanding of themselves—"Who are you, what do you believe, and what are your guiding principles?" (p. 23).

Visioning at My School

- Does my school have a shared vision? What is it?

- Do I understand who I am as an individual, what I believe, and the guiding principles I follow in my practice? What are my guiding principles?

- Do the leaders within my school understand who they are as individuals, what they believe, and what their guiding principles are?

- What evidence of shared vision and underlying understanding of self, beliefs, and principles at my school can I point to?

Transactional School Leadership Management Practices

Although the value of transformational leadership is clear, we must also recognize the value of strong management and select transactional school leadership practices within transformational leadership. The importance of visionary leaders who are agents of change and who are compassionate, enthusiastic, and supportive is undeniable, but transactional leadership focuses on supervision, organization, and performance. It is task-oriented and uses rewards and consequences as compliance and motivational tools to reach goals (Rosenbach, 2018).

Others have described transactional leadership as "utilitarian," underscoring the value of clear goals and expectations (Bell & Bolam, 2010). However, ethics is a major consideration and the use of rewards and consequences associated with transactional leadership has been criticized as a short-term substitute for the more important work that may be needed and ultimately more valuable. Additionally, the authoritarian, top-down approach of traditional transactional leadership has many downfalls. The emphasis on tasks rather than people often leads to lower levels of staff satisfaction, decreased morale, and reduced creativity, and furthermore, transactional leadership can keep leaders and followers from reaching their full potential (Faraz et al., 2018; Kark et al., 2018).

When asking others to be on the cutting edge of change, to go beyond ordinary steps to give students a sense of security and safety, school leaders need to be "practical" visionaries. Targeted transactional school leadership practices and strong management furthers productivity—that is whether our ideals actually result in measurable changes, whether changes result in a decrease in deaths by suicide, drug abuse, teenage pregnancies, or gang involvement, for example. Such practical outcomes spring from a leadership mindset that understands systematic planning and organizing basic school operations, setting expectations, efficiently managing budgets, and establishing and maintaining routines (Kotter, 1996). When safety is critical, transactional leader practices such as correcting errors and active monitoring of safety behavior may be particularly needed (Adams et al., 2018; Willis et al., 2017).

Strong Management Skills

Although we are not recommending carte blanche adoption of transactional leadership practices, we see the value of incorporating a few elements from transactional leadership in implementing change in schools (Adams et al., 2018; Arenas, 2019; Baškarada et al., 2017; MacNeill et al., 2018).

When crises hit, a sense of order and preparedness is crucial. Leaders who already have developed crisis response teams and are able to deploy strategies with decisive action are vital. In a similar vein, leaders who have already built relationships with others and have systems in place for referrals, procedures for coordinating services with mental health providers, and strategies in mind for students not only during an individual crisis, but as they return to school, help to ensure a sense of trust and safety, thus providing much needed security during difficult times.

Balancing Transformational and Transactional Leadership

"Though transformational and transactional leadership are often presented as being at opposing ends of a spectrum, a combination of select elements from both leadership styles may yield the best results" (Lai, 2011, p. 4). For example, a new assistant principal might be more of a transactional, rather than transformational leader. Mindful school leaders who are focused on the big vision may choose to use a transactional approach to give their new colleagues duties where they thrive while mentoring them in the art of visioning, collaboration, and compassionate community-building. In this way, transformational leaders can raise a new generation of emerging leaders that will maintain growth even after they have left their schools.

Research on transactional leadership confirms that many of the traits or attributes of a transactional leader really fall under the category of management. Transformational principals who have certain strong transactional leadership skills can guide their schools to be more effective and to achieve more positive outcomes for all students, for those with whom we must exert more effort and care and have a willingness to negotiate and to take risks in being earlier adopters (Pepper, 2010). As you review Figure 5.1 below, consider the implications for your leadership and addressing the needs of students who are most vulnerable, as well as their families and your staff.

FIGURE 5.1   Attributes of Transactional (Management) and Transformational Leadership

	TRANSACTIONAL (MANAGEMENT)	TRANSFORMATIONAL
Staff motivation	Manages through rewards and consequences to reach goals and objectives	Manages through inspiring and motivating staff intrinsically
Focus	Task Completion	Improving school culture and climate
Culture	Rule-oriented	Facilitates a culture and climate of mutuality and interdependence (teaming)
Leads through	Policies, expectations, and measuring performance	Fostering autonomy with guidance, empathy, compassion, and mentoring to create buy-in and support

(Continued)

FIGURE 5.1   (Continued)

	TRANSACTIONAL (MANAGEMENT)	TRANSFORMATIONAL
Vision	Top down	Shared vision – a collective vision developed with input from many in the school community
View of Leadership	Leader is a director	Leader is a role-model and facilitator
Expectations	Expect staff to complete tasks	Assists staff in trying new ideas and finding creative solutions
Attitude toward risk	Reactive: risk-adverse and hesitant to try new, unproven solutions	Proactive: encourages experiments and risk-taking
Communication	Relies on their authority and tends to provide feedback primarily as a corrective action	Great listener; communication reflects sensitivity to others and conveys understanding and caring
Who leads?	Only one leader	Distributed leadership
Considerations for school settings	External pressures support this leadership style – principals operate to meet expectations of district and state leaders. In this style the principal is the "mid-level" manager tasked with implementation.	Sensitive to potential contradictions between policies and needs of students and staff. Strives to balance student and staff needs with district and state expectations.
Consideration for addressing mental health challenges in schools	Although an authoritarian approach can present numerous barriers to effective schools, this style can be important in establishing routines, order, and predictability, which contribute to a sense of safety.	Strong communication skills and the ability to inspire and motivate others tend to uplift staff and students and contribute to a climate that is welcoming and supportive of individual needs.

When trying to find the balance between transactional and transformational leadership, we urge you to lean into transformative leadership, but there may be times when you must turn to a transactional approach when there is a sense of urgency, or a need to maintain order or compliance with a prescribed protocol.

During times of rapid change, uncertainty, and a need to tackle tough challenges, adaptive leadership is critical to mobilize, engage, and motivate followers.

Adaptive Leadership

Nana Arthur-Mensah and Jeffrey Zimmerman (2017), in their article on change during turbulent times, stress the impact of adaptive leadership:

> A unique feature of the adaptive leadership process is the creation of a holding environment: a safe place with the right amount of tension whereby followers can actively debate issues and share their fears and frustrations without penalty, thereby generating new ideas and solutions that help followers adapt to complex change. (p. 10)

During times of rapid change, uncertainty, and a need to tackle tough challenges, adaptive leadership is critical to mobilize, engage, and motivate followers. With adaptive leadership, leaders consider not only the task at hand but also the emotional toll and need to help others regulate distress, as attention is turned toward solutions, new expectations, and new practices.

Transactional and Transformational Leadership at My School

Refer to Figure 5.1 and complete this from your perspective as a school leader, teacher, or other staff position.

- My school leader has strengths in these areas:

  _____
  _____
  _____
  _____
  _____
  _____

- These are areas for potential growth for my school leader:

  _____
  _____
  _____
  _____
  _____

- The strengths and areas of growth of my school leader have an impact on school climate and the school's collective sense of security in the following ways:

  _____
  _____
  _____
  _____
  _____
  _____

Effective school leaders have a toolbox of strategies available to uplift, motivate, and guide staff and others in their school communities. When we examine student well-being, certainly visions, strategies to support those on the front line, and practices that generate trust and a sense of security, even as risks are made, are beneficial. Strong leadership is critical.

Reflections on Mental Health and Well-Being

Consider your own reactions to leadership.

- How does leadership help to reduce your stress?

- As a leader, what do you do that assists in reducing the stress of others?

- None of us is perfect. Can you envision a time when you could have been a more, caring, effective leader?

- What lessons have you learned?

- When you examine your school, how supported are students who are most at risk? Do they feel a sense of trust and security?

The most successful leaders have insight into their own mental health and well-being, including when they need to ask for additional help, and they know this has a direct impact on their ability to be adaptive in challenging circumstances, and to inspire the trust of their staff. This trust can often be cultivated using the techniques and concepts we discuss above but can also further be enriched when leaders are transparent about their process, their needs, and their mistakes. These things allow leaders to build school climates that help teachers and other staff feel supported and able to take risks, including being vulnerable about their own stress and mental health. This modeling of stress management, compassion, and adaptive transparency is likely to allow teachers to pass those elements along to their students and their families, knowing they have the full support of their leadership, and creating a shared culture furthering the mental health of all members of the school community.

In the next chapter we will explore how caring and competent school leaders set the stage for a compassionate response to students' well-being.

Caring and Competent Leadership for Children's Mental Health and Well-Being

6

Understanding Our Vulnerabilities: Leading With Care, Love, and Acceptance

Caring and love may well begin with an understanding of our own vulnerabilities. Although most people are ashamed of their vulnerabilities, Brené Brown sees the power in accepting them and choosing to love ourselves and others in spite of them: "Vulnerability is the core of belonging, love, creativity, and joy" (Brown, 2010).

Brown argues we need to confront our vulnerabilities head on, instead of living in fear of them. Leaders need to recognize their own vulnerabilities, accept them, and share them with others. Leading by example, they can demonstrate that it's ok to be vulnerable—it can actually make us stronger and more connected with those around us. Sharing when we feel anxious, overwhelmed, or uncertain can be empowering as we accept support from others.

When the stigma of mental health is reduced, educators can create a more compassionate, inclusive, and authentic culture to meet the needs of the most at-risk students. With more trust and transparency, we can better identify and quickly address student needs. Thus, we can better treat the whole child—ensuring they're mentally, physically, and emotionally healthy.

When we consider vulnerabilities, the stigma of mental illness, and school leadership's capacity for a compassionate response, Larry Davidson's (2003) comments related to schizophrenia seem pertinent to many people experiencing trauma and/or at-risk for mental illness. Davidson explains that individuals

> may feel at times that there is no place for them, at least not among the community of human beings into which they were born. *The one thing that appears to be the most effective antidote to such an extreme sense of isolation and estrangement is the care, acceptance, or love of another person* (emphasis is ours). Having some place where the person feels that he or she belongs is predicated on there being at least one other person who views him or her, and accepts him or her, not as "a schizophrenic" or as a mental patient, but as a fellow human being, as a peer. (p. 163)

Mental Health Stigma

- At my school do we have open dialogues about mental health?

  _____

  _____

- If so, what's working well?

  _____

  _____

- If not, what is holding us back?

  _____

  _____

- Is there a stigma about mental health that hampers some of these dialogues?

  _____

  _____

- What practices can we put in place to remove that stigma to allow for more open dialogues?

  _____

  _____

By embracing vulnerability, we can both have more open dialogues about mental health and also reduce its stigma:

One of the best ways of reducing the stigma is to talk openly about mental health. Determine your level of comfort . . . . You can normalize the idea of getting help for mental health issues. . . . If you encourage open discussion about mental health, students will feel more comfortable telling you about a parent's struggle, which in turn can help you support your student. (Burch, 2018)

The School Leader as an Antidote to Isolation and Alienation

- How can a school leader address the needs of students who may be feeling an extreme sense of isolation and alienation?

- What can school leaders do to prepare themselves and staff at their schools to be responsive to needs of these children?

- How can school leaders conduct efforts to create tidal waves of caring at their schools?

Three Overlapping Lenses to Develop Positive School Leadership and Improve Children's Well-Being

Caring School Leadership, Heart Centered Mindful School Leadership, and Compassionate School Mental Health are three interrelated approaches to improving children's well-being. Although they are complementary, Caring School Leadership provides an overall frame for competent school leadership, Heart Centered Mindful Leadership emphasizes the value of calmness and self-care, and the Compassionate School Mental Health Model we present throughout this book targets specific skills and attitudes that are most responsive to the needs of students who are most at risk. *Note that this section of this chapter includes three ways of viewing leadership, with exercises to guide you as you consider your school's strengths and needs. These do not need to be completed in sequence, or even at the same time. You may find it valuable to begin with one practice and later go back and dive into the analysis of another approach.*

Caring School Leadership

In their book *Caring School Leadership,* Mark Smylie, Joseph Murphy, and Karen Seashore Louis (2020) explain that "caring" is not only what someone does but also an action that is *dependent on the why and how as well*. Our underlying motivations and how we demonstrate our caring affect whether our caring makes a difference. As Smylie and his colleagues say, it is "not something that can be defined as a specific set of actions and interactions . . . [but rather] as a quality of a relationship—the manner, matter, and motivation of personal and professional action and interaction" (p. 18). They also describe the differences that caring school leadership makes to students, reporting that it is key to their success in school. Students say that "when they feel cared for, they are more likely to engage in school and work harder academically . . . [and] less likely to behave in ways that might jeopardize their success" (p. 11).

When we reflect on our caring, it is good to reflect on how it affects the person's (the student's) perception. According to Smylie, the effects of caring are dependent on how our actions and interactions are interpreted by the other. They elaborate on these factors in Chapter 2 of their book. We have summarized key components of their analysis of caring in Figure 6.1. (Summary of elements in Figure 6.1 developed by authors Mason, Asby, Wenzel, Volk, & Staeheli [2020] for this book.)

Smylie's analysis (with our interpretation of it in Figure 6.1) could provide a template (see Figure 6.2) for both assessing areas of need within our schools as well as a leader's areas of strength and areas for potential focus as they plan and implement programs to enhance caring. **You can access downloadable and printable copies of Figure 6.1 and Figure 6.2 from the book's companion website: resources.corwin.com/compassionateschoolpractices**.

Heart Centered Mindful School Leadership

In our chapter on Heart Centered Leadership in *Mindful School Communities* (Mason, Rivers Murhpy, & Jackson, 2020), we highlight the following aspects of leadership. In the list below, we show the relationship to components of Smylie et al.'s Caring Leadership framework:

- Leading by example with an awareness of our impact on others (Emotional Intelligence)

- Showing gratitude and recognition (Emotional Intelligence)

- Leading with humility and kindness (Mindset & Competencies)

- Communicating with compassion and a conscious awareness of their own thoughts and feelings (Mindset & Competencies)

- Having the confidence and courage to be catalysts for change (Virtues & Competencies)

- Showing equanimity of emotions (clarity of thought and calmness) (Emotional Intelligence)

- Creating a community of connectedness and belonging (Emotional Intelligence)

FIGURE 6.1 Elements of Caring Leadership

ELEMENTS OF CARING LEADERSHIP

Aims	To address the particular **needs, problems, and concerns** of individuals or groups	To promote certain benefits—social, emotional, psychological, and behavioral—of being in a relationship and being cared for	To promote further caring

Positive virtues and mindsets	**Virtues** include compassion, empathy, patience, sympathy, kindness, fairness, justice, humility, equity, authenticity, humility, vulnerability, prudence, transparency, honesty, trustworthiness, and respect for others	**Mindsets** include attentiveness to others and understanding their situation; motivation to act on the behalf of others rather than acting in one's own self-interest; how we view ourselves personally and professionally; the mindset of playfulness which is manifested by creativity, inventive thinking, flexibility, and adaptability.

Competencies	Our **skill in learning about the needs of others.**	To act **strategically.**	Knowledge of self and our ability. Recognition of	**Knowledge and skills for developing** caring among **others:**
	Our ability to • inquire • listen and hear • observe and see • assess and understand	• Our understanding of the relative effectiveness of strategies to further the well-being of others • Our effective action on another's behalf • Our engagement with the ethical and practical dilemmas that arise	• Our orientation, strengths, limitations, predispositions, and prejudice • Our sources of fear and joy • Our ability to deepen and strengthen our capacity for caring	• Our knowledge of how our classroom and school organizations consider caring • Our knowledge and skill related to professional development • Our skills to increase supportive structures and to develop organizational mindset

FIGURE 6.1 (Continued)

ELEMENTS OF CARING LEADERSHIP

Emotional Intelligence (Goleman, Boyatis, & McKee, 2013)	Self-awareness *Attunement to*	Self-management	Social Awareness	Relationship Management *Competency and ability to*
	• Our feelings and how our feelings affect us and our job performance	• Self-control and ability to self-regulate our emotions and impulses and channel them	• Our attunement to the emotional signals of others	• Inspire others and guide and motivate them to a compelling vision
	• Our guiding values and how we intuit best courses of action	• An authentic openness with others about our feelings, beliefs, and actions	• Our empathy and ability to listen attentively and understand others' perspectives	• Model that vision in our own actions
	• Our need for self-improvement and how to proceed with that self-improvement	• Our adaptability	• Our organizational awareness – being socially and politically astute	• Influence others, be engaging and persuasive, and build support
	• The accuracy of our self-assessment	• Our optimism	• Our service competence: our ability to foster an emotional climate to maintain customer and client satisfaction, including being available to customers and clients	• Develop others
				• Show a genuine interest in those we are assisting and understand their needs, goals, strengths, and weaknesses
				• Manage conflict
				• Promote teamwork, collegiality, and collaboration
				• Model respect, thoughtfulness, and cooperation
				• Build commitment to collective efforts
				• Build spirit and identity

Adapted from *Caring Leadership* by Smylie, Murphy, & Seashore Louis (2020).

FIGURE 6.2 Elements of Caring Leadership Template

Elements of Caring Leadership Template

Date _____

Aims	To address the particular needs, problems, and concerns	To promote certain benefits		To promote further caring
Positive virtues and mindsets	Virtues	Mindsets		
Competencies	Skill in learning about the needs of others.	To act strategically	Knowledge of self and our ability.	Knowledge and skills for developing caring among others:
Emotional Intelligence (Goleman, Boyatis & McKee, 2013)	**Self-awareness** *Attunement to:*	**Self-management**	**Social Awareness**	**Relationship Management**

In the *Mindful School Communities* chapter on Heart Centered Leadership, we also discuss the importance of listening, reflecting, positive feedback, learning from mistakes, problem solving, addressing biases, mindfulness, and inspiring equity (Competencies, Emotional Intelligence). We encourage leaders to create an atmosphere of psychological safety and encourage educators and students to take risks in order to inspire innovation and creativity. We recommend that leaders learn and practice mindfulness both to improve the accuracy of their perceptions as well as for their own self-care (Emotional Intelligence).

Heart Centered Mindful School Leadership at My School

Another way to cultivate students' social emotional learning is to consider your leader's heart centered leadership skills (Mason, Rivers Murphy, & Jackson, 2020, p. 163–164) by asking yourself the following:

- Do you or your leaders listen attentively and think about how others feel? _____

- Are you or your leaders attuned to others' moods? _____

- Do you or your leaders coach and mentor others with compassion and personally invest time and energy in mentoring? _____

- Do you or your leaders articulate a compelling vision, build group pride, and foster positive emotional tone? Do you or your leaders lead by bringing out the best in people? _____

- What are your or your leader's strengths as a conscious leader? _____

- How confident are you in your own or your leader's abilities? _____

- What courageous steps have you or your school leader taken to improve the lives of students, families, and staff? _____ _____

- Do you or your leaders have your/their own stress-relief or mindfulness practice? _____

- How compassionate are your school politics? _____

Addressing Mental Health Concerns With the Compassionate School Mental Health Model

To address mental health concerns, educators need to consider additional leadership components, some of which go beyond recommendations for caring and heart centered leadership, by specifically responding to factors that present barriers to mental health and well-being. Examine your leadership skills and dispositions for addressing mental health concerns as presented in the Compassionate School Mental Health Model (see the preface).

Leadership for Prevention

Leaders who value actions that alleviate stress and prevent mental illness will integrate and align programs for social emotional development with academic learning; seek to enhance mental health of students, families, and school staff; build the capacity of teachers to reduce barriers to learning and healthy development; and address systemic matters that affect mental health (such as high stakes testing, substance misuse, trauma, bullying, and use of mindfulness to address these issues). They will also further screening and assessment, implementation of Tier I universal interventions of MTSS; address cultural concerns that are barriers to learning and well-being; reduce stress; create calm and safe school environments; and develop crisis response teams and suicide intervention plans.

Leadership for Supporting the Child

To develop and implement programs for serving children who have been identified with mental health needs, school leaders will facilitate relationships with mental health service providers and implement programs such as aggression replacement training and programs for substance misuse treatment. They will also develop the schools' capacity to respond to crises; mobilize teams for recovery and support; intervene early after onset of emotional, behavioral, and learning problems; develop programs for family support; establish and monitor programs for home visitations; implement Tiers I, II, and III of MTSS; and assure that individual treatment plans are developed and implemented. Leaders will also establish programs and protocol for recovery and a student's return to school after hospitalization.

Leadership to Build Resiliency

Great leaders understand the importance of resiliency and focus on students' holistic development and integrate curricula to teach resiliency, growth mindsets, and problem solving; build student confidence and success; and teach students self-regulation, metacognitive skills, and coping mechanisms. They recognize and accommodate diversity, reengage disengaged students, and honor student strengths, views, cultures, and values in order to create stimulating, caring, and positive classrooms. Additionally, they promote student agency and self-determination by engaging students in planning and decision making and sponsoring service learning projects and peer support programs.

Leadership to Develop Protective Factors

Great Leaders do the following:

- Build resiliency

- Build community

- Foster connectedness and strong relationships

- Are sensitive to their students' and staff members' needs

- Support staff by
  - reducing environmental stressors
  - increasing personal capabilities
  - enhancing job assistance

- Shift from a deficits-remedial model to one of collective, shared responsibility that is strength-based

- Support
  - after-school programs
  - programs for safe and drug-free schools
  - positive peer and staff relationships

- Promote self-care and mental health

- Foster social emotional development

- Integrate positive behavioral supports

- Champion restorative practices

- Develop a comprehensive, multifaceted, and cohesive continuum of school-community interventions

- Enhance collaboration among schools, communities, and homes

- Recruit families to strengthen these connections

- Reach out to families of students who do not come to school regularly

- Confront equity considerations

- Address marginalization, discrimination, bullying, and harassment

- Develop and implement policies that reduce punitive discipline such as suspensions and expulsions.

The 2013 Texas Youth Risk Behavior Survey (n = 2,560) found that a sense of belonging reduced youth's suicidal tendencies (Olcoń et al., 2017). Ways to increase feelings of belonging include the following:

- *Develop collective efficacy*—create a shared belief that through collective action, educators can positively influence student outcomes. Encourage persistence, trying new teaching approaches, setting more challenging goals, and attending more closely to the needs of students who require an extra assist.

- *Create an inviting environment*—learn students' names, assign peer partners, hold pep rallies and collective activities, display student work on the walls, and post signs in multiple languages.

- *Foster communication*—hold class meetings, design schoolwide service-learning projects, use project-based learning.

School Safety

In *A Framework for Successful Schools*, The National Association of School Psychologists (NASP, 2013) provides a checklist of standards for school leaders to create and maintain safe and healthy schools. This excerpt from the Framework reinforces the need for effective management of funding and policies that are responsive to students' mental health needs.

Policy Recommendations to Support Effective School Safety (NASP, 2013)

1. Allow for blended, flexible use of funding streams in education and mental health services;

2. Improve staffing ratios to allow for the delivery of a full range of services and effective school-community partnerships;

3. Develop evidence-based standards for district-level policies to promote effective school discipline and positive behavior;

4. Fund continuous and sustainable crisis and emergency preparedness, response, and recovery planning and training that uses evidence-based models;

5. Provide incentives for intra- and interagency collaboration; and

6. Assist Multi-Tiered Systems of Support (MTSS).

(NASP, 2013, p. 1)

When designing crisis prevention and response plans, make sure they are context-appropriate, minimally disruptive, and efficient in their use of available resources. Be sure to regularly review and practice these plans. Engage all relevant stakeholders in discussing, determining, and reviewing appropriate protocols. Think about needs, strengths, and gaps in existing services and supports (e.g., availability of school and community resources, unmet student mental health needs) that address the physical and psychological safety of the school community. Additionally, invite mental health professionals to train teachers and support staff on trauma, resiliency, and risk factors. (For more about crisis response teams, see Chapter 5, Strong Management Skills.)

For a comparison of Caring Leadership (Smylie et al., 2020), Heart Centered Mindful Leadership (Mason, Rivers Murphy, & Jackson, 2020), and Leadership for Compassionate School Mental Health, see Figure 6.2, How to Provide Compassionate School Mental Health, which is also available as Online Resource 6.2 on the book's companion website: resources.corwin.com/compassionateschoolpractices.

Use Figure 6.2 (or Online Resource 6.2) to make notes on areas of strength (+) and needs (-) at your school.

FIGURE 6.2   How to Provide Compassionate School Mental Health

CARING LEADERSHIP (SEE TABLE 6.1)	PREVENTION	SUPPORT THE CHILD	BUILD RESILIENCY	DEVELOP PROTECTIVE FACTORS
Has Clear Aims				
Has Positive Virtues and Mindsets				
Meets Competencies				
Has High Emotional Intelligence				

HEART CENTERED LEADERSHIP (SEE CHAPTER 1)	PREVENTION	SUPPORT THE CHILD	BUILD RESILIENCY	DEVELOP PROTECTIVE FACTORS
Leads by Example				
Communicates with Compassion and Consciousness				
Shows Equanimity of Emotions				
Creates Community				
Shares a Compelling Vision				
Is Confident				
Shows Courage				
Develops Compassionate School Policies				
Uses Self-Care Practices				

Principals Set Policies and Protocols

Whether we are considering prevention, treatment, building resiliency, or strengthening protective factors, consistency and fairness are important. The most effective principals realize that children and youth benefit from fairness and that sometimes school policies are outdated and in need of change. They strive to update policies, working with others in their schools and also within their district and beyond to implement policies such as restorative justice, considering the best protocol for handling emergencies, and knowing when and how to make exceptions that are in the best interest of students, their families, and their staff. For additional resources on how to set policies and protocols, see resources at the end of this chapter as well as the companion website.

Monitoring Progress

Just as great leadership starts with informal and formal assessments to aid leaders in determining needed action, effective leaders realize the value of formative, ongoing assessment to measure progress, evaluate the impact, and refine actions and interventions to strengthen outcomes. Similarly, students, teachers, and leaders alike all benefit from periodic self-assessments to explore their individual progress, set individual goals, and monitor their actions. Such self-assessment can lead to better self-regulation, renewed determination and commitment to specific actions, and also to a better sense of self—including a more realistic appraisal of our needs, strengths, and areas for self-improvement. We encourage you to further your staff's ability to use metacognitive skills to better understand themselves and to strengthen their competence and sense of well-being.

Self-Care: Mindful School Leadership

Leaders set the emotional tone of the school by how they convey their own emotions and how they interact with others. Mindful leaders are highly self-aware and have clear goals and values that shape a culture where others can develop these same characteristics. Aware of their own vulnerabilities, mindful school leaders seek out healthy practices to improve their own well-being. With this foundation, they create a culture where teachers feel passionate about their work, where fear and anxiety are reduced, and where everyone feels motivated to persist through difficulties with flexibility and an ability to cope with changing circumstances.

Leaders may struggle with compassion fatigue or "vicarious traumatization." When school leaders learn of suffering or injustice experienced by their students or teachers, many try to step in and become entangled with the distress of living these stressful experiences. One teacher explained how difficult it can be: "We can get kids in a good place, but it's limited. They go home to chaos, dysfunction, drinking, drugs, a parent in jail, and they have to come back in the morning to start all over again. Those things are hard and frustrating. And my heart is broken over these students; it is emotionally draining" (Mahfouz, 2018b). Time management can be a challenge, and leaders sometimes sacrifice family time for the sake of their professions.

The Impact of Mindfulness Training for Administrators in Pennsylvania

Julia Mahfouz (2018a) examined the impact of mindfulness training for thirteen school administrators in a school district in rural Pennsylvania. The program used for training, *CARE* (Jennings et al., 2013), included exploration of bodily awareness of emotions and practicing mindful awareness, reflection, mindful movements, mindful listening, breathwork, and acceptance. Some of the findings reported included the following:

- An increased awareness of one's reactions, including anger, to events throughout their school day

- An increased understanding of the physical impact of their emotions, including an awareness of when they felt increased tension

- An improved ability to be calm, regulate their own emotions, and be less emotionally reactive to the tensions and many concerns that others bring to them

An improved awareness of others leading to greater sensitivity, better listening, and greater reflectivity.

Mindfulness can be an important part of a leader's toolkit. Linda Lantieri, who has implemented the Inner Resiliency Program in New York City and studied its impact, reports that mindfulness *improves self-awareness, understanding, concentration, the ability to relax your body and release tension, the ability to handle stressful situations, the ability to control one's thoughts, and deeper communication among adults and children* (Lantieri et al., 2016, p.121). Principals who participated in the Inner Resiliency program reported that they made several changes in their schools, including taking these steps:

- Starting staff meetings with ice-breakers, breathing and relaxation techniques, and acknowledgements

- Having monthly agendaless meetings (with snacks, watercolors)

- Instituting a day of meditation and relaxation as part of a regularly scheduled professional development

- Providing funds to facilitate a social skills study started by teachers

- Adding yoga and calmness/focus building activities

- Approaching each situation in their school with the intent of being positive, caring, and encouraging (p. 128)

Self-Care Exercises

Try out the mindfulness exercises below for self-care and see what works best for you—and share them with others in your school and community.

Tara Brach, an expert in mindfulness and meditation, has developed RAIN, an easy-to-remember tool for bringing mindfulness and compassion to emotional difficulty. RAIN stands for the following:

- **R**ecognize what is happening

- **A**llow things to be as they are

- **I**nvestigate inner feelings with interest and care

- **N**urture with self-compassion (Brach, 2020)

With RAIN, at each step along the way, practitioners take time to fully experience feelings and emotions. In life we tend to rush through the "allowing"—often we feel such a strong urge to move beyond the unpleasant that we rush toward solutions without fully appreciating what our hearts, minds, and bodies are telling us. Leaders can practice RAIN and integrate it into their daily routine, taking a few minutes with each step before considering not only self-compassion in the moment, but additionally steps to further self-compassion (Neff & Germer, 2018).

In *Hardwiring Happiness: The New Brain Science of Contentment, Calm, and Confidence*, Rick Hanson, a neuroscientist and renowned author and speaker, explains how inner strengths such as a positive mood, common sense, integrity, inner peace, determination, and a warm heart will assist you in overcoming any obstacles (p. 4). Hanson's technique has several things in common with the RAIN steps. Hanson's HEAL approach also requires some quiet, meditative time. As with rushing past the negative, we find that often we rush through our positive experiences as well. HEAL includes four steps for "taking in the good" or purposefully internalizing positive experiences:

- **H**ave a positive experience

- **E**nrich it

- **A**bsorb it

- **L**ink it to the positive (Hanson, 2013, p. 60)

In his books, Hanson explains the neuroscience behind taking time to HEAL. As we contemplate the good things—whether they are major milestones, or the small things such as our breath, a beautiful flower, or a glass of cold water—we strengthen neural pathways that tell us that all is well. As Hanson says, it is fine to start with small things, but it is important to take time to enrich the experience—to draw a vivid mental picture, by using our five senses to embellish upon the experience—and then to simply sit with the experience. While we meditate on the beauty of the rise and fall of our abdomen as we take in and release air, we allow the fullness of our breath to be absorbed in our systems. And then the final step, "link," allows us to connect our positive experiences. We may think, "I am here, sitting in the warmth of the sun on my porch, breathing in fresh air, hearing a mourning dove cooing, and listening to the beat of my heart. I am surrounded by beauty, I feel healthy, I give thanks." In his books, Hanson offers similar meditations for feeling a sense of contentment, connection, compassion, and love.

My Self-Care

- Try some of the self-care exercises from the prior two pages—RAIN and HEAL—or other suggestions for self-care. Which ones resonated with you? _____

- Do you need more information or guidance to fully implement these? _____

(If so, we suggest you look online for a wealth of additional information.)

- Are you ready to share one or more of these with teachers, students, or families? ____

Anchor of Awareness Meditation

For those of you who are experimenting with meditations, we suggest that you give yourself time and practice without anticipating results, but rather to practice the practice. Over time, you will find that you are less distracted and that your focus improves. This repeated centering will train your brain to come back to and fully experience the present moment. Here is an awareness meditation exercise from *Mindfulness Practices* (Mason et al., 2019):

1. Close your eyes and begin long, deep breathing. Keep the focus on your breath.

2. Every time your mind begins to wander, refocus on the inhale and exhale of your breath. Let go and re-center your thoughts on the here and now.

3. Repeat for three to fifteen minutes.

Be Mindful of Others (Mason et al., 2019). We can use mindfulness not only to enhance our own sense of well-being, but also to increase our consciousness regarding the needs of others.

1. Consider people in your environment. Depending on where you are, it could be someone in the classroom, a friend, or a family member. Focus on one person.

2. Consider the person's general nature (happy, friendly, angry, fearful) and how the person appears in your imagination right at the moment.

3. Look at the person's face and imagine him or her speaking to you.

   a. What is he or she saying?

   b. What kind of voice is the person using?

   c. How do you feel around this person?

   d. Does the person need anything from you?

When children are hurting, more than anything they need someone who cares. Effective school leaders deliver caring in ways that are contagious—motivating others to care as well. Their schools become centers for healing—centers where compassion is central and even the most vulnerable children and youth feel connected. As they establish a culture of safety and trust, those in their schools awake to an understanding that being vulnerable is powerful. As they promote mental health, they dedicate the necessary resources and funding to make it a priority.

Reflections on Strengthening Mental Health and Well-Being

Effective leaders also are implementers of care, love, and acceptance. Their impact can be significant. They lead by example, with humility, kindness, calmness, and competence. As they practice self-care, caring leaders also expand their own skills and abilities to be mindful, to be rooted in a sense of calmness, and to stay the course, inspiring others to move beyond trauma and stress with a fearlessness that strengthens their own resolve and transforms their schools to better care for staff and create opportunities for all to learn, to grow, and to heal.

Online Resources in This Chapter:

Online Resource 6.1	Elements of Caring Leadership Template
Online Resource 6.2	How to Provide Compassionate School Mental Health Exercise
Online Resource 6.3	Handbook of Mindfulness in Education
Online Resource 6.4	How Trauma-Informed Schools Help Every Child Succeed
Online Resource 6.5	Guide to Trauma-Informed Organizational Development

Online Resource 6.6	Trauma-Informed Social Policy: A Conceptual Framework for Policy Analysis and Advocacy
Online Resource 6.7	Trauma Sensitive Schools Training Package
Online Resource 6.8	Measuring Progress Toward Becoming a Trauma-Informed School
Online Resource 6.9	Restorative Practices: Approaches at the Intersection of School Discipline and School Mental Health
Online Resource 6.10	COVID-19 Symptoms and Testing
	Older Adults
	Pregnant Women
	Schools and Childcare Programs
	First Responders and Law Enforcement
	Resources for Your Home
	Community- and Faith-Based Leaders
	Resources for Businesses and Employers
Online Resource 6.11	COVID-19 Stress and Coping

Part 3

Child and Family Supports

Belonging and Building Community

7

The Drive to Belong

Everyone wants to belong. It's why most us who look back at our junior high yearbook ask, "What were we wearing?!" and give knowing smiles to our children or students as they enter the room in this year's ridiculous trend. But where does this deep-seated need to be a part of some group come from? Why are so many of us looking for our squads, teams, family, people?

A drive for belonging is a part of our survival instinct. From an evolutionary perspective, bonding with others in our community kept us alive. In the times of hunter-gatherers, being ostracized from the group meant a lower chance of securing food and escaping predators. In the twenty-first century, we may have smart devices and apps that manage our everyday struggles, but we still rely on human connection to thrive. It is easier to meet the needs of the community when everyone works together.

Over the years, schools have been given more and more responsibilities. In addition to teaching common core subjects and social emotional skills, they are also providing an array of services including essential medical screenings, extensive food programs, and specialized mental health supports. When teachers across the country went on strike during the 2018–2019 school year, they weren't just striking for higher salaries. They were demanding "full-time nurses, social workers and librarians in all city schools; expanded counseling services; and recruitment of more Black and Hispanic teachers" (Smith & Davey, 2019). Teachers, principals, and mental health professionals are all stretched so thin, doing extraordinarily emotionally—and sometimes physically—taxing work for long hours and low pay.

To help teachers support student mental health, counties and school districts in cities around the nation have implemented wraparound services to varying degrees. To learn more about how the Boston Public School (BPS) District has done this, see Chapters 1 and 2. When schools understand how to communicate and collaborate with community organizations, they can ease the burden on teachers who don too many caps by bringing qualified professionals into the school building to address youth mental health needs. Although many teachers are warm, caring individuals who have only the best interests of students at heart, they usually aren't equipped with the specific knowledge and tools needed to recognize or address serious mental health challenges or risks.

Creative Funding to Bring Professional Mental Health Service Providers Into the School Building

Kathleen Sullivan, principal at Haley Pilot School, a K–8 all-inclusion school in BPS's Comprehensive Behavioral Health Model (CBHM) program, knew that her most vulnerable students needed more than sporadic visits with an array of part-time mental health support staff, but she wasn't sure if the funding was there. Alexander Freeman, a school psychology intern from a nearby college, was one of many adults providing mental health services for students. Alexander was in and out of the building regularly, and understanding that students would benefit from him being there consistently, Kathleen decided that no matter what the budget looked like she would find room for him to come on full time.

She also realized that she had five different clinicians from the same agency visiting with a variety of students in her building. Teachers hadn't taken the time to form relationships with these staff members, because they weren't there enough. There wasn't any room in the budget to hire a second full-time school psychologist from the district. However, she did some creative accounting and found that if she worked with the agency that provided in-school clinicians for student counseling sessions, she could get one adult to be dedicated to Haley full time with that clinician's salary funded 100 percent by families' Medicaid or private insurance co-pays. Now, that staff member has been able to form closer relationships with students, families, and staff, increasing the chance that collaboration around expectations and progress will lead to greater success.

Belonging: A Psychological Need

A sense of belonging is essential for a human being to thrive. Since Maslow (1968) defined the hierarchy of needs, we've understood that merely having enough food to eat, warm clothes, and a safe home is not enough for humans to realize their full potential. Before we can access the parts of ourselves that make us unique and lead to ideas that transform the world, before we build esteem from completing works that define us, before we transcend the need for that esteem as we realize our greater purpose, we must feel loved. We must feel as though we belong to some community. We must feel that we are wanted and our ideas are valuable to those in our circle.

Isolation, Mental Health, and Well-Being: The Numbers

According to the U.S. Department of Health and Human Services (2019), "Two in five Americans report that they sometimes or always feel their social relationships are not meaningful, and one in five say they feel lonely or socially isolated." Isolation does not just affect mental health; there are a variety of additional consequences of loneliness, including impaired executive function, increased cognitive decline, poor sleep quality and cardiovascular functioning, and impaired immunity at every stage of life (Hawkley & Capitano, 2015). In fact, research shows that loneliness is just as damaging to health as smoking fifteen cigarettes a day (HHS, 2019). Half of the twenty thousand Americans surveyed by Cigna in 2018 reported that they sometimes or always feel alone; only 53 percent reported having meaningful in-person interactions on a daily basis. Cigna (2018) concluded "that most American adults are considered lonely, and that the youngest generation of adults is the loneliest of all."

Many have speculated about the effect of social media, smartphones, and constant streaming content on the mental health of America's youth, but research has remained inconclusive as to the root cause of the loneliness. In the mid-1990s, around 50 percent of teens reported meeting up with friends "almost every day," but in 2016, only around 25 percent of teens met up with friends that frequently (Twenge, 2019). The reality is that teens are spending less time face to face and more time interacting with screens. Although some marginalized groups, such as LGBTQ youth in rural areas where there may not be another queer teen in their town, may find a sense of belonging among their online peers, teens are experiencing alarming rates of cyberbullying online, too.

Cyberbullying: More Than Just Online Teasing

Cyberbullying is a serious issue for many young people, especially teen girls. DoSomething.org, a global digital platform for youth well-being, has compiled the following statistics about online bullying:

- About 37 percent of young people between the ages of twelve and seventeen have been bullied online. Thirty percent have had it happen more than once.

- Ninety-five percent of teens in the United States are online, and the vast majority access the Internet on their mobile device, making it the most common medium for cyberbullying.

- Twenty-three percent of students reported that they've said or done something mean or cruel to another person online. Twenty-seven percent reported that they've experienced the same from someone else.

- Girls are more likely than boys to be both victims and perpetrators of cyberbullying. Fifteen percent of teen girls have been the target of at least four different kinds of abusive online behaviors, compared with 6 percent of boys.

- About half of LGBTQ+ students experience online harassment—a rate higher than average.

Four out of five students (81 percent) say they would be more likely to intervene in instances of cyberbullying if they could do it anonymously.

Many young people who have trouble "fitting in" struggle because they have not yet developed the interpersonal skills necessary to navigate the complex social worlds of playgrounds and cafeterias. A student who has been impacted by trauma may have a "hair trigger" response; an accidental bump in the hallway may lead to a reflexive instinct to punch someone. In other cases, the world may be so overstimulating that they do the opposite: withdraw, "numb out," freeze, or avoid. Behavior like this and some of the other behavior responses some-times demonstrated by students who have experienced trauma when they feel threatened—throwing objects, being verbally combative, destroying property, spitting, screaming, or crying—can lead to social isolation as these students are otherized and often segregated from the classroom when their behavior disrupts learning.

Students who are currently experiencing or who have experienced abusive or neglectful home environments may not have formed any secure attachments.

If parents and caregivers, many of whom experienced abuse or neglect themselves, are unable or unwilling to provide young children with positive models of soothing extreme emotions, these children will look to peers and other adults in their lives as examples. Teachers, coaches, and administrators often must be their students' example of calm, so that students can learn how to regulate their own emotions and develop a sense of safety and belonging that enables them to learn and grow.

To best serve children whose trauma has resulted in some type of externalizing (disruptive, aggressive) behavior, educators will need to take a two-pronged approach: (1) directly teach self-regulation skills through evidence-based practices (see Chapters 1 and 2) and (2) develop a compassionate school culture and climate in which all students have secure attachments with at least one staff member—which we will discuss below.

School Connection: Loving the Challenging Kids

When I taught second grade in Athens, Georgia, one student in particular, who I'll call Matthew, age nine, hated everything—math, science, P.E., lunch, recess. Matthew got suspended multiple times in the first three months of school for fighting, throwing chairs, and threatening to bomb the school. I talked to his mother, who was a single mom in and out of the hospital with chronic health problems, and his fifteen-year-old sister, who was practically raising Matthew on her own. I got him into regular counseling and connected him with a Black male mentor to provide the positive role model that Matthew was seeking. I started only choosing books that related to his greatest interest (sports) to read with him. I stayed after school with him when no one came to pick him up. I tried to form a closer relationship, but each time I was met with silence and defiance.

I knew that what Matthew really needed was a connection and I wasn't it. I started to pay attention to Matthew during times when I was not in charge of his class. I peeked into the music room to see him pouting in a chair alone against the wall. I watched him throw a basketball out the gym door and stomp off to sit under the bleachers. But then, I watched him doing a hand-clapping game with one of the other second-grade teachers at recess. I started to notice that when this teacher passed by Matthew, he winked—and Matthew winked back! I even caught the glimmer of a smile once or twice. Pretty soon, after a successful trial run

(Continued)

(Continued)

doing guided reading in this teacher's classroom, we (the administration, the second-grade team, and I) made the difficult but necessary decision to move Matthew across the hall to spend more time with the one adult in the building he'd been able to connect with. I looked outside my classroom and to the wider school community for resources that would serve my student best when I was unable to serve him as an individual teacher. I understood that Matthew's life had been disrupted with unspeakable traumas and what he needed was a consistent, positive male role model who he felt comfortable opening up to. By the end of the school year, Matthew had made good progress and was beginning to form meaningful relationships with his peers and those smiles appeared more and more frequently.

Dana Asby

Finding That One Caring Adult

The safest place for many students impacted by trauma may be in the counselor's room. This can become a warm, inviting space where they are able to practice mindfulness and learn the emotional regulation skills to cope with stress and heal from trauma. But the most important element of the room is the counselor him- or herself. When administrators hire new mental health support staff like counselors, social workers, and school psychologists, they have an opportunity to bring a strong source of assistance to students experiencing mental health challenges. During the interview process, an important question might be, "How do you plan on ensuring that every student has a connection to at least one adult in the school building?"

> How do you plan on ensuring that every student has a connection to at least one adult in the school building?

During the early months of the COVID-19 pandemic, we held focus groups with educators to better understand how the virus had affected the school community's stress levels and how they were able to apply some of the strategies and tools we'd been teaching them to their current situations. We learned that, overwhelmingly, the biggest stressor was the sense of disconnection, especially around the most vulnerable children who relied on that school connection for stability and safety.

These school leaders sprang into action and developed an array of systems to ensure that each and every student was making contact with an adult in the school each day or week, depending on the needs of the family. We heard stories of elaborate phone trees, Google Sheets, and food delivery systems all developed to get eyes and ears on kids to make sure they were emotionally and physically ok.

By taking the advice of the educators on the ground actually implementing the systems of care, school leaders were able to come back to the plan they developed and make revisions that provided a more effective way of ensuring that each student got a chance at connection with adults in the school community in a way that reduced rather than exacerbated teacher stress.

With our Compassionate School Mental Health Model (see the preface), therapy and counseling are two primary ways to *provide treatment* that children need. Connecting with therapists in meaningful ways can be critical to *developing protective factors and building resiliency*.

However, *resiliency and protective factors* are also strengthened when schools, agencies, and families work together to reinforce the same self-regulation, cognitive reframing, and self-confidence skills, students will see quicker and longer-lasting success, because they will get to practice these new skills in many environments. When teachers and other school staff practice mindfulness and self-care and when they teach students these important tools, they can uplift emotional well-being. Students and families experiencing a mental health challenge may benefit most from such resources, but all members of the school community will be gaining important coping skills to use in the future. Together these protocols also form a network of supports that alleviate stress and interrupt cycles of toxicity, thus helping to intervene early and *prevent* serious mental health challenges.

> Together these protocols also form a network of supports to alleviate stress and interrupt cycles of toxicity, thus helping to intervene early and *prevent* serious mental health challenges.

Protective Factors During COVID-19 and During Reunification

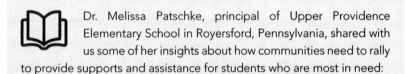

Dr. Melissa Patschke, principal of Upper Providence Elementary School in Royersford, Pennsylvania, shared with us some of her insights about how communities need to rally to provide supports and assistance for students who are most in need:

Many of our students have experienced the impact of re-traumatization by losing the safety of their community supports. Schools, churches, civic groups, and mental health resources are called to not only stay connected with those we know are high risk, but also intentionally look for children and families that have first time trauma impacts due to a high potential of resource deprivation, emotional instability, substance misuse, homelessness, or mental health concerns. We need communities to become protective, nurturing sources of encouragement for children who are the most vulnerable.

All reunification plans for schools following the distance learning experiences of 2020 must also prioritize relationships and place an emphasis on the social/emotional security of students. Our time together will be best served by listening, supporting, and reteaching individual learners. *Only after we've created this safe space*, will *growth and healing begin to transpire*.

School and Agency Collaboration

One way for schools to foster a sense of community and belonging is through collaboration. To collaborate means to work together *in service of a common goal;* so to begin a collaboration, we must ensure that everyone at the table does indeed have common goals. True collaboration is built on mutual trust and strong relationships built over time. As schools move from being purely academic in function to playing a wider role in both educating the whole child and in belonging to the wider community, the role of collaboration is essential. Collaborations happen on multiple levels. They can be informal or formal, and they can happen both internally (inside the school) or externally (outside the school, with community partners).

No matter the type of collaboration, the target audience and goals must always remain at the center. That may be the student, establishing a culture of compassion, or something else.

Key Players

Mental health issues can affect all parts of a person's life. A child with anxiety may have trouble sleeping. Drowsy, they wait at the bus stop, feeling nauseous from a bad night of sleep and little breakfast. Arriving at school, they grab breakfast from the cafeteria. They feel a little better, but paying attention in class is a struggle. Everything feels disorganized. Grades suffer. At the end of the day, though, their coach sees a different perspective: strength and perseverance at the mental toughness and physicality it takes to excel on the soccer field. Heading home, parents wonder why the child no longer reaches out to

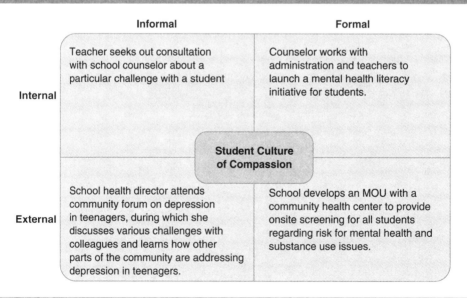

FIGURE 7.1   Types of Collaboration to Build School Cultures of Compassion

	Informal	Formal
Internal	Teacher seeks out consultation with school counselor about a particular challenge with a student	Counselor works with administration and teachers to launch a mental health literacy initiative for students.
External	School health director attends community forum on depression in teenagers, during which she discusses various challenges with colleagues and learns how other parts of the community are addressing depression in teenagers.	School develops an MOU with a community health center to provide onsite screening for all students regarding risk for mental health and substance use issues.

Student Culture of Compassion

their friends. In just this small example, we see cognitive, emotional, physical, and academic impacts of mental health—and also resilience, coping strategies, and caring adults (see Figure 7.1).

Because of the complex and deep influence of mental health on all aspects of our lives, it can be beneficial to identify who the "key players" may be when working with children in school systems. Teachers, administrators, nurses, bus drivers, support staff, and coaches may all interact with students daily. In addition, there are a host of mental health professionals who are embedded in schools. **School psychologists** are licensed professionals who work with students, teachers, and school systems. They conduct a range of assessments (e.g., behavioral, developmental); help to develop plans for students to succeed academically, socially, behaviorally, and emotionally; and work to strengthen the connection between school and community. Similarly, **mental health counselors** and **social workers** also work with students and school communities. They may run support groups for students, provide individual counseling, and/or be a part of teams that support students. Counselors typically spend most of their time working directly with students, while social workers and psychologists may also have roles that extend to the wider community. For more information on each of these professions, check out the resources at the end of this chapter.

School mental health professionals are often the first "go to" when a student seems to be struggling. Teachers with concerns about a student may refer the student to the school psychologist, mental health counselor, or social worker— or they may seek out one of these to get professional guidance about how best to proceed with a particular student or situation. Access to mental health professionals in schools is uneven. Poor districts may not have the resources to employ counselors. Rural districts may not have any qualified candidates to fill positions. Districts facing budget cuts often have to sacrifice mental health professionals in favor of other priorities, leaving existing teams with unsustainable caseloads. While legislation has tried to address these issues, our country has much work to do in ensuring equitable access to school mental health resources (Menas, 2018; Osher et al., 2019).

Unfortunately, most school districts in the United States have limited access to school counselors, with the median ratio at 411 students for each counselor versus the American School Counselor Association's recommended ratio of 250:1 or lower. The schools with the highest student-to-counselor ratios are in the poor, diverse, and urban school districts (Gagnon & Mattingly, 2016).

Counselors and Other Mental Health Support Staff in Schools

In addition to making sure no kids are slipping through the cracks, the mental health support staff are integral in building a sense of belonging for students who feel they have no one who understands them. For students who have exhibited signs of anxiety, depression, eating disorders, or another mental illness, counselors can form group therapy sessions where students can meet others struggling with similar issues.

Pairing Mindfulness and Cognitive Behavioral Therapy

Some schools have found success pairing mindfulness with cognitive behavioral therapy focused on specific topics. For example, the University of Georgia offered its college students one-hour yoga and anxiety classes that included thirty minutes of yoga to strengthen the mind-body connection, twenty-five minutes of group therapy to share members' experience of anxiety over the past week and how the exercises presented in the group helped or didn't help them, and five minutes to introduce a new cognitive behavioral strategy for anxiety-relief. Such structures can be adapted for elementary, middle, and high school students. Group therapy sessions can sometimes be the first time a young person has met anyone else who understands the specific problems they are experiencing. It can be empowering and comforting to realize that others share your pain. This one hour in the week can be a powerful tool in creating a sense of belonging for students who have never felt it before.

Counselors, administrators, and educators can also inspire students to feel a greater sense of belonging by introducing them to real-life and fictional people who have experienced similar struggles in life and with their mental health. Bibliotherapy can help students connect with people who have overcome trauma, depression, fear, and other challenges that may resonate. Biographies, poetry, nonfiction articles about neuroscience or growth mindset, and even fiction can offer students a better understanding of why they are experiencing the emotions they feel and normalize them rather than pathologize them. For example, it can aid in removing the stigma of bipolar disorder to know that Carrie Fisher, the actress who played Princess Leia in the Star Wars films, not only had bipolar disorder but was an outspoken advocate for mental health.

For younger children, it's important to recognize the role of **Early Interventionists (EI)**. EI professionals are a part of the Early Intervention Program for Infants and Toddlers with Disabilities (also known as Part C, from IDEA), which consists of federally funded programs for infants and toddlers who show signs of developmental delays. EI providers work with children from birth through age two and may provide assistance that includes occupational therapy, speech therapy, and other developmental supports. When a child turns three, they "age out" of EI and often parents then work with the school system to develop plans for the child to prepare for and succeed in their educational career (Parlakian, 2018). The school system's director of special education is often the liaison for EI, parents, and school-based services. To best aid students, all of these entities can work together to ease transition periods, which can be stressful for both children and parents.

While they do not often work in school systems, it is worth mentioning that psychiatrists also may play a role in the lives of children, particularly when they have significant mental health struggles. Psychiatrists are physicians who specialize "in the diagnosis and the treatment of disorders of thinking, feeling, and/or behavior affecting children, adolescents, and their families" (AACAP, n.d.). Usually, a referral to a psychiatrist comes from a child's pediatrician or occurs during a hospital visit. Psychiatrists can prescribe medication and may work with students who have eating disorders, anxiety or depressive disorders, and so forth. In the context of schools, psychiatrists may work with the school mental health provider or a community liaison, provided that the student/parent provide consent.

Collaboration Within the School System

In the context of school systems, collaboration ideally happens both inside the school system and externally. In most schools, internal collaboration happens every day, both formally and informally. Second-grade teachers may collaborate with one another to ensure that curriculum is unified across classrooms. Science teachers may work together with social studies teachers to design a particular lesson from multiple perspectives. Counselors may work with the school nurse, particular teachers, and administrators to develop a plan for an individual child or to address a building-wide issue. For example, when the community experiences a loss, counselors may work intensively to provide ways for students, as well as the school community, to grieve. They may provide professional development sessions for teachers, as a way to help them understand the behaviors that may show up in the classroom as developmentally specific ways of showing grief. They may work with administrators and others to organize memorial services and/or community rituals that help to process grief and find healing.

Common Understanding of School Culture

Within a school building, it is far easier to collaborate if everyone has a common understanding of the school culture that they want to promote. Throughout this book, we have advocated for a compassionate and collaborative school culture, a school community that is driven by a common vision of hope, healing, and positive change. Each school will be built on a foundation of unique values and beliefs, but if the foundation of those beliefs is compassion, whatever culture blossoms will support aid the well-being for students and staff.

For example, a school may say that it is "trauma informed," but if teachers and staff do not have a clear vision of what that means and how it is operationalized in their day-to-day work and in school policies/procedures, it will make collaboration more difficult. For a vision to be crystal clear to the educators who will be turning that vision into a reality, include their voices in the early stages of visioning. To learn more about how to intentionally create compassionate school culture, read about the Five Cs of Heart Centered Learning and visioning in Chapters 1 and 2.

Describe your ideal school culture. What words come to mind?

Now imagine you are a student in your school. Picture yourself walking through the door, down the hallway, and into the classroom. What is your experience like? How does it feel?

What are the differences in the culture you imagined in both scenarios? Do they match? If you could change one thing, what would it be?

When reflecting on your school's culture in the context of compassionate responses to mental health, think about the following elements:

- How is student discipline handled? Are responses uniform across classrooms, school buildings, and the system? Are disciplinary policies set up to teach skills and problem solve or are they shaming of students?

- Are educators and staff equipped with the knowledge and skills to respond to big emotions? Do they have mental health literacy skills?

- Does the school have data on key issues related to mental health? (e.g., bullying, student fights, reports from school-based mental health professionals)

- How does the school actively work to promote resilience among children and staff alike? How does the school care for the well-being of its staff—including educators and non-classroom personnel?

Collaboration Beyond the School Walls

Ideally, collaboration should extend beyond the school walls. External collaboration takes many forms. For the purposes of this chapter, we will highlight examples relevant to mental health and well-being in the context of creating compassionate school cultures.

Advantages of Collaborating Externally

Effective collaborations can lead to meaningful changes for students, educators, and families.

- *Educators gain a deeper understanding and appreciation of the lives that their students are leading.* The more educators understand the various places and institutions where their students spend time, the more holistic a picture they will have of those students. For example, when educators partner with the local 4H Club, they may see a side of their students that would otherwise not be revealed in the classroom.

- *Students and their families see the school system as a more integrated part of their community and daily life.* For example, when educators participate in important community events (e.g., Pride parade, Town Day, holiday parades), students and families come to recognize that the school is a part of the community, rather than just a building that sits outside of the rest of community life.

- *Local organizations, agencies, and service providers gain insight into the educational lives of children.* When community members come into the school building to interact with students by sharing their knowledge and resources, they may not realize that the needs of their community's children were as great as they are or that there is a wealth of talent that could support a project they hope to achieve.

- *Schools access funding sources only available to school-community partnerships.* Many grant projects or private funding come with a requirement to collaborate with a community organization. This can be a powerful incentive to find a like-minded partner in a nonprofit or small business in your town.

Think of a time when you formed a partnership or collaboration. Maybe you worked with another teacher, an outside agency, or a part of your school system with which you don't typically work.

- What worked about the collaboration?
- What was challenging?
- What might you do differently next time?
- How did it aid (or hinder) student or educator well-being?

Wraparound Services

Compassionate schools embrace collaboration and a common understanding of trauma-skilled culture. They also recognize the need to go "beyond the school's walls" to truly assist their students. More and more, schools are adopting various models of wraparound services to meet the nonacademic needs of students and communities. Wraparound services provide "a process of planning and coordinating school, home, and community resources in order to improve academic, social, and emotional outcomes of at-risk students" (Hill, 2020). Wraparound services may include mental and physical health, food access, housing coordination, and access to other social services.

Additionally, adopting a wraparound model does not mean that schools actually provide all these services; rather, it means that they form relationships with outside agencies, co-locate services, and think holistically about how to meet the learning needs of their students.

To describe this differently, consider student needs as concentric circles (see Figure 7.2):

- *Individual.* Students work one on one with teachers, mental health providers, and caregivers to address mental health issues.

- *Mental Health Team.* Students have their mental health needs addressed by a team of people. This may include IEP meetings, internal and external collaborations, and coordination with caregivers.

- *Wraparound Services.* Wraparound services literally "wrap around" the students, addressing their needs holistically. They include but are not limited to mental health. They may address material needs like food and shelter, physical health, mental health, or other social service needs.

FIGURE 7.2   Wraparound Services

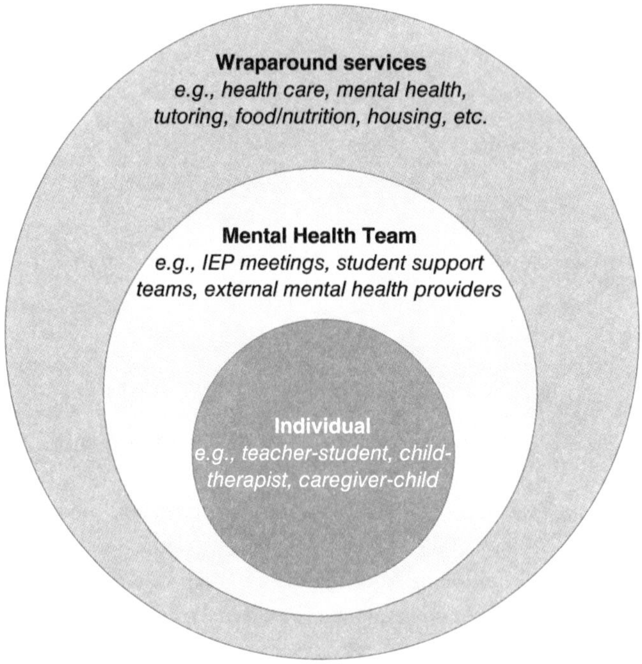

AmeriCorp Evaluation of Whole School Whole Child Model

City Year's AmeriCorp evaluated its *Whole School Whole Child* model, which embeds team members in K–12 schools, particularly in high-poverty districts. They focus on building relationships with students and supporting teachers—all in service of improving both academic and social-emotional outcomes. Across six hundred schools in twenty-two cities, the evaluation demonstrated that City Year's students are less likely to drop out of high school or be chronically absent. Schools that partnered with City Year were twice as likely to improve English language arts and math proficiency rates (Meredith & Anderson, 2015). More information about both of these models can be found in the Resources section of this chapter.

McKenny-Vento Homelessness Liaisons Provide Wraparound Service

One clear example of how wraparound services have worked is the case of the McKinney-Vento Homelessness Liaisons. Established in 1996, the McKinney-Vento Act legislated that students who are homeless have a right to the "same free and appropriate education as provided to other children and youths" (42 USC Chapter 119, Subchapter VI, Part B). Children who are homeless face extensive barriers to school attendance and academic success, including but not limited to transportation, frequent moves, violence and chaos in the home, and higher rates of illness than their housed peers (Bassuk et al., 2014). The McKinney-Vento Act requires that every school district in the United States has an appointed "liaison" to work to remove barriers for these children. Additionally, each state has a coordinator of homeless education, typically situated in the Department of Education. In locations with large numbers of children who are homeless, the McKinney-Vento liaison may actually be an office with several staff. Smaller systems may have administrators (e.g., principal, superintendent, counselor) who perform these duties along with their other responsibilities.

McKinney-Vento liaisons identify students who need help. They train educators and others in schools to recognize signs that a student may not

(Continued)

(Continued)

be adequately housed. They work with shelter systems, food pantries, transportation systems, tutoring services, and mental health counselors—all in service of ensuring that students receive a quality education. They network with local organizations and businesses, attend key community meetings, participate on cross-sector task forces and policy committees, and form relationships in and across sectors (e.g., housing, child welfare, mental health). To learn more, check out *Homelessness and Education Cross-System Collaboration: Applied Research Summary and Tools*, listed in the reference section of this chapter (McGah & Saavedra, 2015).

Strategies for Getting Started

As you are getting started on a new collaboration, it may be useful to assess your readiness (or your school's). Consider:

- What collaborations do you already have? List them and identify if they are internal or external. _____
  _____

- What collaborations would you like to develop? List them below and identify if they are internal or external. _____
  _____

- Do you have the time and resources to commit to developing a relationship right now?

- Do you have buy-in from your supervisors and team to develop a collaboration?

- What would be your first step in developing a new collaboration? Does it seem straightforward? Daunting?

- Is your school or the potential collaborator going through a transition in leadership? Sometimes, this means collaborations will be welcome and other times, it means that collaborating is particularly difficult.

- Conducting this kind of assessment will aid you in identifying opportunities and challenges and planning how you proceed.

Find Common Goals

Whether you're collaborating with internal or external partners, developing and codifying a common set of expectations is helpful. Consider the following example:

Josie is in seventh grade and is struggling both academically and emotionally. The school administrators convene a meeting that includes her mother, two of her teachers, the school social worker, and the principal. Prior to the meeting, each person reflects on their goals for the meeting:

Josie's mother: "I need strategies to help me get Josie out of bed and onto the school bus every day. If I can just get her to school, then she'd be successful. That is my goal for this meeting."

The counselor: "My goal in this meeting is to help everyone understand that Josie's emotional health must come first."

The teachers: "Josie is one of seventeen students on our team that is struggling academically. She's a bright girl but doesn't apply herself. Our goal is to focus on study skills—once she feels some academic success, she will feel better about coming to school."

The administrator: "I don't really know Josie. My goal is to facilitate this meeting and make sure everyone leaves here with a clear plan to help the student."

If these goals remain unarticulated, then collaboration will be a challenge because everyone will be working toward something different.

Consider: How would you facilitate this meeting? What questions would you ask? Who else should be at the table? What would change if Josie were participating?

Write It Down

As you set common goals, it may be useful to articulate them in writing. This is especially important when partnerships are more formal. For informal partnerships, you may consider simply asking a few questions and facilitating a discussion about common goals. Writing them down in the form of meeting notes may suffice. For more formal collaborations, you may consider developing a memorandum of understanding (MOU). MOUs articulate the goals of the collaboration, and the responsibilities of each party. They often include a time frame for activities, desired outcomes, cost sharing, and key players. We've included a link to sample MOUs in the resources section of this chapter.

Identify Roles and Responsibilities

Whether internal or external, identifying roles and responsibilities is often a crucial step. For internal collaborations, this may be as simple as concluding conversations and meetings with "Action Steps" that are then reiterated via email or meeting minutes. For external collaborations, it is essential to identify one person who serves as a liaison between the school and the external collaborator. For example, school psychologists often conduct assessments with students that may be useful to other people involved in the student's care outside of the school system. The psychologist may be a key part of the student's care team (sometimes called Student Support Team), which could include parents, teachers, outside mental health professionals, and so forth. The school psychologist could be appointed as the liaison between the school team and the external team. This may include sharing assessment data, working with a hospital team to develop a plan for the student to transition back to school, and/or working with the child's caregivers to address any concerns they may have (NASP, 2010).

Account for Confidentiality and Data Sharing

Parents, students, and professionals must work closely together to understand what can and cannot be shared and with whom. These issues should be articulated in consent forms, MOUs, and other documents so that all parties are clear on data sharing agreements.

Evaluate Collaborations

We are at our best when we understand what is working and what is not. From time to time, all collaborations should be evaluated. This may be an informal check-in ("How's this working for you and your team?") or more formal (e.g., codified in an MOU). Use feedback from all stakeholders—including parents and students—to improve your work, identify areas for growth, and develop creative solutions.

Collaborating Across the State of Massachusetts to Bring Mental Health Best Practices to Schools

In January 2018, three years after the inception of the mental health initiative in Methuen, efforts were undertaken to establish the Massachusetts School Mental Health Consortium (MASMHC). The purpose and intent of the MASMHC was to share resources and provide training and technical assistance in order to further school mental health implementation across the Commonwealth. In many ways, the efforts of the MASMHC were an attempt to replicate the lessons learned and collaboration that was fostered during Methuen's engagement in the NQI CoIIN facilitated by the National Center for School Mental Health.

What began as a meeting with thirty districts has, in two years, grown into a statewide, coordinated effort to foster school mental health implementation. The MASMHC's membership now exceeds 130 districts in eastern and western Massachusetts, and sponsorship of the consortium has grown to include institutions of higher education, regional mental health advocacy agencies, and community-based service providers. Monthly meetings showcase best practices across all tiers of support and highlight innovative, local examples of implementation and partner agency presentations that foster a greater connection with community-based mental health advocacy groups and service providers. Hundreds of school mental health staff and educators alike have received training and resources from the MASMHC, and efforts at providing training, coaching, and technical assistance have advanced over time, allowing for deeper work to be conducted with individual districts.

Early sponsorship of the consortium by Representative Linda Dean Campbell translated into a legislative earmark, also supported by former Massachusetts Senator Kathleen O'Connor Ives, that assisted the MASMHC during the 2018–2019 school year in designing programs to foster school mental health implementation. One such example, the MASMHC Mini-grant Program, was an attempt at providing a small amount of funding to foster school mental health implementation, which ultimately benefited the larger membership owing to the sharing out of best practices and lessons learned through project presentations required of grantees. Through continued advocacy of promising school mental health policies and practices, support for direct implementation, and providing reliable opportunities to convene and network, the MASMHC is working to ensure students across the state get the help they need to find success.

John Crocker, MEd
Director of School Mental Health & Behavioral Services
Methuen Public Schools

Belonging and building community happen in both formal and informal ways. Compassionate schools should strive for both. No matter where you are in your journey to create a more compassionate culture, find a way to continue. This may be a small gesture, a conversation with colleagues, an initiative to address a particular issue in your community, or a new collaboration entirely.

Thoughts for Strengthening Mental Health and Well-Being: Leverage Parent Resources to Fulfill Needs, Wants, and Dreams

Students' mental health is directly connected to their families' mental health, and both can be furthered through counseling, communication, and effective partnerships with the school community. Once positive relationships have been established with families, school leaders and educators can strategize to make the most of their talents, resources, and connections within students' families. For example, consider creating a digital database of the types of resources, gifts, and volunteer offers for students' parents and families, which can be gathered during the beginning of the year via parent contact forms. Likewise, if you use a survey platform like Google Forms or Survey Monkey to gather information about families, the program can automatically create spreadsheets that educators can easily use to search for particular words or phrases. Seeing parents as diverse sources of culture, experience, skills, and connections is an important part of developing relationships with families and learning more about your students, in addition to enriching your school activities and community connections. An understanding of these family resources and potential volunteers can be especially valuable in times of crisis and need when communities pull together.

The manner in which you communicate with families matters, too, and can have a profound effect on whether families want to partner with their children's school. Ensure that your communication is in the language(s) your families speak and attentive to the cultural context of your community. When you frame a request, it's essential to show respect for the many demands on parents and gratitude for their past contributions, being respectful of their time, energy, and central importance in school. Asking for concrete assistance that directly connects their actions to their child's success is a powerful motivator for parents to get involved. Instead of scrambling to do the best you can with a small budget or staff, parents' support can turn a mediocre program or event into a rich, memorable, and exciting one. To garner more support from parents, build positive relationships and be intentional with how and when you ask for help.

Building a positive relationship with families can make it easier to facilitate positive connections with services to benefit youth mental health inside and outside the school building. Beyond that, searching for and finding ways to connect the culture within the school to the culture *outside* it demonstrates that you see your students as people, and their parents as partners, and demonstrates that teachers and staff have the resources needed to do the same.

Online Resources for This Chapter:

Online Resource 7.1	American Academy of Child and Adolescent Psychiatry
Online Resource 7.2	American School Counselor Association
Online Resource 7.3	Developing Memorandum of Understanding: Guidance from the American Psychological Association
Online Resource 7.4	Child Development and Early Intervention
Online Resource 7.5	National Association of School Psychologists
Online Resource 7.6	National Center for Homeless Education
Online Resource 7.7	School Social Work Association of America

How Schools Can Help Families

8

Key Principle #8

Families and educators working together as a team can convey consistent, collaborative, and responsive efforts to better support the mental health and well-being of students. However, this will take understanding, time, patience, sensitivity, and effective communication.

A Sense of Urgency

Today, families are facing numerous challenges that create a great sense of urgency to help improve parent-child relationships. Bullying (including cyberbullying), anxiety over global health crises and global warming, the increase in teen suicides and school shootings, along with concerns over the impact of technology and a generation of children whose friendships are largely virtual, have exponentially increased our anxiety and stress. As we assist schools in crafting compassionate responses to children's mental health concerns, we celebrate the many schools that are already implementing positive, proactive practices. There are many caring teachers and staff who are making a difference for children and families. We also celebrate the many families who have spent countless hours with therapists, negotiating their way through a maze of protocols and options, to strengthen the care they are providing their children. Yet, we realize that many families and children need greater support.

To feel a sense of security, students need healthy relationships with their caregivers—in and out of the classroom. However, many parents don't have a lot of time to engage in the school community because they must juggle work, household chores, children's extracurricular activities, and more. Even though they may be stressed out and short on time, parents are still interested in learning more about child development and how to be a good parent. In fact, one study found that 79 percent of parents want more information about raising children, yet 65 percent of them never attend a single parenting class (Zepeda et al., 2004).

In her book, *Preventative Mental Health in Schools* (2014), Gayle Macklem, author and educational psychologist, highlights the importance of home-school interactions, stating, "Parent support has more impact on children's and adolescents' school success than income or demographic variables" (p. 69). However, when we consider well-being, it is our belief that parent education and involvement furthers not only success in school, but beyond, impacting a child's overall well-being, sense of security and self-esteem, and happiness.

To further parent involvement, educators must consider specific family and community needs and strive to make schools welcoming to a diverse range of parents, considering specific cultural and ethnic factors and communicating to parents about their role as partners. For parent communication to be effective, it should give parents materials they need to implement the strategies, be digestible, and not take up too much of a parent's time (Magnuson & Schindler, 2016). During COVID-19, many schools used trial and error to discover the best way to deliver important messages to parents at a distance. Many parent education programs moved their work online and those that were already online saw a huge jump in participation.

This approach can help improve emotional intelligence and home-school relationships. "When school leaders are mindful and responsive to school community members' needs and concerns, more positive and trusting relationships are cultivated" (Mason, Rivers Murphy, & Jackson, 2020, p. 150). Relationships and relationship building are key. This takes time, understanding, and compassion.

Although parents may be anxious about connecting with schools, educators may be equally uncertain of how best to communicate with and collaborate with parents. As educators, it is helpful to consider how to communicate effectively with the child and the family by first discovering how each feels, what they have experienced, their likely pain-points, and what, under the circumstances, is most important to say. Sometimes, enlisting the assistance of a school counselor, administrator, social worker, or mental health service provider will give educators additional insights to further positive communication.

Of course, educators will also want to be active, engaged listeners. Sometimes listening is the most important thing an educator can do.

Communication Is a Two-Way Street

Both educators and parents have myriad reasons to make effective communication a high priority. Parents may be intimidated, embarrassed, lack the time, be stressed out about the stigma and the situation, not be aware of the seriousness of the need, or feel that they have tried and were not heard.

Educators may feel unprepared, not realize the importance of the communication, find that parents are unresponsive to their outreach, or even believe that such communication really is beyond their area of responsibility. Communicating about children who exhibit the most serious emotional and behavioral challenges can be difficult for all, because of home-school boundaries and things shared in confidence.

Talking to Parents About Their Child's Mental Health Challenges

Sometimes, parents will be the ones to bring a mental health concern to the attention of teachers. However, at other times, unaware that their child is experiencing a mental health struggle and lacking knowledge about the specific problem or diagnosis, parents either may not understand or accept the situation. Parents who have experienced trauma themselves or have been let down by their educational institutions as a youth sometimes approach anything delivered by the school or school leaders with skepticism or defiance. The tone and language with which you convey information will make the difference between whether it is absorbed or ignored.

Communicating With Parents: Three Key Steps

 Recommendations From ZerotoThree.Org *For more information about these strategies please visit their website.*

Early childhood education advocates Zero to Three promote evidence-based practices for optimal brain development during children's earliest years when brains are growing most rapidly and are most vulnerable to toxic stress and trauma. Here are three steps schools can take to enhance home-school communication:

Step 1: Notice how you are feeling.

Step 2: Look at the interaction from the child's point of view.

Step 3: Partner with parents.

- Use "I" statements.

- Ask for the parent's perspective.

- Most important: Look for a place to compromise.

- Finally, don't forget to check in.

Consider parents' perspective. If you discovered that your own child's teachers and principals suspected that they had a mental illness that may affect them and follow them for the rest of their life, how would you want that shocking news delivered?

With a strengths-based approach, educators will have already connected in positive ways with parents before issues arise:

- Consider how to best communicate a sense of support to the parents.

- Develop a pattern of meaningful communication about the small things, versus all communication being about difficult issues and decisions. Texting parents to say that Stephen had a good day at school or that their child won a "kindness award" can establish a meaningful basis for collaboration and trust.

- Texting may work well with one parent, but others may prefer phone or email. Ask what works best for each parent and use that communication mode to enhance your messaging.

- Follow-up and stay in touch with parents who may themselves be experiencing anxiety about their children's mental health challenges.

- Avoid labels. Although teachers and administrators can describe outbursts or a child's apparent sadness, formal diagnoses are made by school psychologists.

- Use a log to document your communications. This is standard best practice for home-school communications.

The Power of a Newsletter

 If you want to soften difficult news, have a stock of good news to balance it. A weekly classroom newsletter helps parents feel proud of their child's performance at school and like they are part of a classroom family.

You can also communicate reminders, important curriculum updates, social emotional learning (SEL) and mindfulness tips, needs, and successes. Celebrate each and every student in your classroom within the first month of school for a variety of accomplishments, such as Top Five Math Whizzes, Five Kindest Hearts, and so forth. Convey to your parents that SEL is just as important as academic learning by showcasing both.

Get students involved as well. Older students could write sections of the newsletter. Students could write a weekly piece reviewing what they learned in each subject, providing an informal assessment, a chance for review, and an opportunity for reflection.

When parents get consistent, positive communication from their child's teacher, they feel a stronger connection and sense that they, too, are a part of the classroom community. The trust that is built between parent and teacher may assist teachers when they need to discuss challenging topics like mental health.

As more difficult issues arise, educators, mental health providers and school psychologists must be careful not to refer to a child as having a certain mental health challenge before they receive a proper diagnosis. It is important to put the parents' minds at ease by explaining that many people experience anxiety or depression throughout a lifetime, and that even when the present moment seems grim, recovery and resiliency are possible. However, educators need to let mental health professionals discuss mental health. Administrators and teachers may not have adequate knowledge, training, or the proper language to discuss mental health conditions and should leave this step to school psychologists, therapists, counselors, and social workers. However, when meeting with parents, if no mental health professional is able to be present, administrators and teachers may be able to describe the behaviors they have observed and their concerns, perhaps by saying something such as the following:

> Although John is often happy and cheerful, there have been more and more days when his mood shifts quickly, and he becomes angry or agitated suddenly. He reacts to that anger by throwing things, yelling, or hitting other students. His behavior has become a safety issue, so we wanted to discuss some possible solutions with you.

After a teacher or other educator has conveyed their direct experience with the student's behavior, a mental health professional may be able to follow up by conveying suggested next steps:

> We have many options for how we might be able to help John build the skills he needs to express his anger more healthily. We're going to start working with him tomorrow to put some more tools in his toolbox. However, he may be able to get some additional services if we screen him for anxiety and depression.

Parent and Family Supports at My School

☐ A mental health provider is available to assist with children's stress and well-being.

☐ Parent-school communication is generally effective.

☐ We have successfully partnered with parents to handle children's mental health crises.

☐ We have the backing of counselors and others to aid in addressing mental health challenges and home-school communication and collaboration.

☐ We have significant needs, including _____.

A home visit can be an opportunity for a new teacher to meet not just a parent but an entire family including siblings and any extended family living in the home. Teachers can model best practices during visits and provide parent education in a more casual and authentic way. Families who live in rural areas far from school and lack transportation can be reached by having teachers ride home on the bus with students at the beginning, middle, and end of the school year, perhaps to deliver missed assignments or a small holiday gift.

Teachers, counselors, and principals were brought into family's homes in more intimate ways than ever before during COVID-19 as students carried their tablets around the house introducing their class to pets and family members. School staff saw unsafe living conditions, domestic violence, and other concerning insights to students' family lives during the quarantine. Having a more complete picture of a students' environment enables staff to respond more effectively to the students' needs.

The earlier a school attempts to connect with parents, the stronger the relationships will become. Reaching out to parents before students begin their first day of their new grade in a new building can be a tool to initiate a relationship with families that will immediately convey a sense of belonging. School leaders can use the time at the beginning of the school year to host events that allow families and educators to casually get to know each other, learn more about the school mission and vision, or contribute to a project together. Although these efforts are most effective when started at the beginning of the school year and continued consistently throughout the year, any scheduled event will increase the bond of your school community.

If you make a digital parent survey, you can easily compile the responses into a database which can be consulted any time there is a particular challenge or need. For example, if you are looking for a parent volunteer to come into the school to discuss the effects of vaping on one's health, you could search for the term "doctor" on this database.

Parent Communication Throughout the School Year

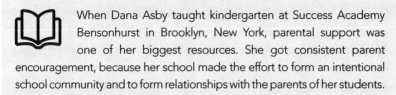

When Dana Asby taught kindergarten at Success Academy Bensonhurst in Brooklyn, New York, parental support was one of her biggest resources. She got consistent parent encouragement, because her school made the effort to form an intentional school community and to form relationships with the parents of her students.

Two weeks before school, Success Academy Bensonhurst had a school picnic in a park across the street from the school. Students got to meet their new teachers and classmates. The principal was able to pump up the parents for the coming year and deliver important reminders. And everyone had fun and got excited about school before it even begun. Parents were required to attend one of several parent orientation sessions, held morning, midday, and after school to accommodate different schedules. Parents were given a presentation about the school's mission, values, and commitment to their children. After getting an explanation of the importance of parent-school partnership, parents were asked to sign a contract that the principal had already signed himself stating that they would work together to educate their child.

Teachers sent a postcard welcoming each child into their class, letting them know how much they were looking forward to getting to know them better. Each parent got an introductory phone call or voice message. Investing just five minutes with parents can save you a wealth of time for the rest of the year, because now you have a partner in each child's future.

Throughout the school year, the positive parent-school relationship was enhanced by monthly school community assemblies, curriculum-themed family fun nights, education activism, and holiday gatherings. Teachers maintained regular contact with parents, texting or e-mailing them pictures of their children in a positive context as often as possible and having phone conversations to discuss more difficult topics that can sometimes be misunderstood through written communication.

By the end of the year, despite some really challenging situations that required a lot of courageous conversations, Dana had the support of all of her parents.

Parents can also contribute valuable assets to schools in numerous ways. Parents who own restaurants can donate food for certain events. Parents who work at nonprofits might be able to serve as liaisons for community service projects or collaborative programs. To put together a low-cost school festival, you could reach out to parents who own party rental equipment companies, parents with connections to the local movie theater who can donate popcorn, or parents who are artists willing to man the face painting station. With enthusiastic parents, a sign-up sheet might draw a large number of volunteers, but when parents are hesitant to write their name on the line, don't assume they don't want to be an active member of the community. They may just be overwhelmed with the choices, feel like others have it covered, or not be comfortable with jumping in. Sometimes, a personal message with a direct "ask" can be more effective at engaging parents.

The tone of your message to parents can also have a large impact on their desire to partner. When you frame a request as a team effort, showing gratitude for their past contributions coupled with a plea for help that directly connects their actions to their child's success, you have a powerful motivator for parents to become involved.

Increasing Mental Health Literacy

Although mental health knowledge is becoming more ubiquitous, many populations exist in the United States and around the world that do not have the language to talk about mental health. They do not have a basis of understanding for best practices when there is a mental health challenge. Mental health stigma is prevalent in many cultures. This discourages youth and their families from speaking openly about their own mental health challenges, otherizing an ordeal that is actually common.

Reducing the Stigma

The biggest hurdle when talking to families about mental health—after they've gotten them through the door—is knocking down the stigma. Although therapy, social emotional learning, and mental well-being are becoming more popular in America—especially in urban areas—mental illnesses still carry a lot of stigma in many communities. Communities of color, rural communities, certain religious or ethnic groups, and immigrant populations are all more likely to face stigma around mental health. This leads to members of these communities talking about mental health less often, getting screened or diagnosed for mental illnesses less frequently, and having lower levels of access to and receiving less treatment for mental health challenges (Office of the Surgeon General, 2001). Overcoming this stigma and putting families at ease about the topic of mental health is a necessary precursor to any serious discussion about a specific mental health challenge.

When educators acknowledge the difficulty of the topic and convey the importance of talking about these needs at home with their child by connecting emotional difficulties with observable behavior and academic challenges, parents have a more concrete understanding of why you must discuss mental health.

Stigma is often the result of fear of not being like everyone else. Reassure parents that these are normal emotional reactions that many children experience. Keep a positive stance and solutions-oriented focus. Offer to facilitate a conversation between the family, student, and a mental health staff member. Fostering healthy conversation skills about mental health furthers positive family relationships.

As mental health advocate and author Michelle Yang (2019), who lives with bipolar disorder, writes,

> Unpacking pain and these deep scars so many of us have been taught to bury deep within is not a sign of weakness nor is it shameful. It is healthy and makes us stronger. . . . With stronger communication, both children and parents are able to express and understand what one another is feeling. With this understanding, there is decreased frustration and will ultimately provide a nurturing and stable family environment that set a child up for healing rather than falling deeper into the stigma.

Once families have the tools to talk to their children about mental health, they may begin to see their own levels of stress and disease lower as communication and connection are enhanced. Starting the conversation is only the beginning. Once parents feel comfortable talking about mental health, they may still resist complete acceptance of their child's diagnosis. Many parents may also feel a sense of shame or blame, so be nonjudgmental as you broach these topics. Reassure parents that this is not their fault.

Overcoming stigma with a strong community can be less intimidating. There are networks of parents whose children have mental illnesses or have experienced trauma that offer help groups online and in person. The National Alliance on Mental Illness (Meadows, 2016) provides the following guidelines for working together with others to serve a child with serious mental health challenges:

1. Accept the diagnosis.

2. Get educated and start networking.

3. Listen without judgment.

4. Call a crisis line or contact other counseling services when needed.

5. Don't allow shame or stigma to prevent you from getting help.

6. Empower the youth who is struggling by providing tools and resources.

7. Start a conversation about suicide and mental health (as developmentally appropriate).

8. Have hope.

Creating a Safe Environment

It's important for schools to create a safe environment where everyone feels comfortable confiding in one another about their challenges and seeking assistance, security, and healing.

Sharing fact- and evidence-based information about mental health with parents, especially when that data can be directly related to their own child's life, starts the conversation about mental health. Parents of teenagers need to understand how the rising rate of anxiety and depression can affect their children, how to recognize symptoms of mental illnesses, and who they can contact if they need resources. It can be useful for parents of younger children to learn the connection between behavior and emotions and how intervening with self-regulation strategies can reduce the risk for later mental illness. This information can be conveyed to parents in a number of ways:

- In a Health and Well-Being Corner in the school newsletter
- In skits during school events like sports games or family events
- In handouts included in take-home folders
- As social media posts on the school page
- In town halls or small group meetings
- During a Mental Health First Aid training for parents
- During parent-teacher conferences
- On posters throughout the school building

Tips for Educators and Parents About Talking With Children and Teens

Educators may be able to reach more students and their families if they partner with parents to increase parent mental health literacy by giving them tips on how to talk to their children about their well-being, challenges they face, and needs that may be unmet. Youth of different ages need information tailored to their level of development; parents often need guidance to understand what language to use and how or when to talk to their children. Schools can offer that kind of advice. Facial gestures, body language, and tone are an important part of communication. Sometimes teachers and parents will need to slow down the communication process to reflect on their own feelings and emotions as well as the child's needs prior to beginning a conversation. Depending upon the child's age and the issue, it may be best to directly say to the child, "Let me think about this," or "I didn't realize you were so unhappy. I want to help. I want your thoughts about what we might do."

Educators can model positive attitudes and mindsets about mental health in front of students and their families. To further parents' awareness of their child's needs, the American Academy of Child and Adolescent Psychiatry (2017) recommends that educators discuss the student's mental health challenges with the child and their parents using the following considerations:

- Be sure the child feels safe and comfortable before the discussion begins.

- Use straightforward communication.

- Communicate at a developmental level that is appropriate to the child's age.

- Carefully monitor the child's reaction during the discussion.

- If the child shows confusion or looks upset, slow down or repeat parts of the discussion.

- Parents can replicate this method in their homes. Developing positive communication between a parent and child can make it easier when difficult subjects such as divorce, death of a loved one, or an upcoming move need to be addressed.

Younger Children

With younger children, make sure you have the child's attention, eliminate distractions, and gain eye contact. This means putting aside a cell phone or turning off the TV and getting down to the level of the child. Young children often focus on visual stimuli, so they may be aware that a family member is crying or upset. Use positive, encouraging words, which will help build the child's sense of safety and self-esteem. Smile if appropriate, use a gentle tone, and cuddle the child.

Older Children

Find a good time to talk—not when the child is playing a videogame or watching TV. The American Academy of Child Psychiatry (2017) provided an example of the kinds of questions that parents may expect from older children, "Older children have more information needs and may ask straightforward questions i.e. 'Why is Mommy crying? Why does Daddy drink and talk to himself? Why does Mommy cry when Daddy drinks?' Children worry about their safety and the safety of their family and friends. Parents should answer their questions directly and honestly to reassure them and validate their feelings."

Teenagers

Communication can become even more challenging as children become teenagers who value privacy to explore their new feelings and changing bodies. When educators and parents work together to keep lines of communication open while respecting new boundaries, they allow teens the autonomy necessary to grow. Adolescents who regularly engage with their parents and caregivers are less likely to participate in risky behaviors or experience violence in relationships, even as they go to college (HHS, 2019).

Schools and families can benefit from key strategies:

- **Demonstrate love and kindness**. Be responsive, encouraging, and supportive even when they make mistakes; love them no matter what.

- **Don't wait for them to come to you**. Look for or create opportunities when adolescents feel comfortable talking. At home, this could be watching TV together, playing sports with them, or cooking. At school, it could be striking up a conversation at recess, as they enter the building, or during lunch. Choose topics they are interested in, including popular movies, musicians, current events, or shared family memories.

- **Talk less, listen more.** Do not interrupt, but do ask follow-up questions. This may encourage teenagers to seek advice. Share how you felt in certain situations when you were their age.

- **Avoid lecturing.** Teens will respond more positively to a dialogue and are more apt both to listen and to share information when they feel you are interested and willing to hear what they have to say.

- **Let them decide.** Guide teenagers in thinking through decisions by explaining the different outcomes of different decisions. Show them how to weigh costs and benefits of their decisions.

Communicating With Teens

- Realize that teens may be more open with friends and peers; this could lead to misinformation about topics such as mental illness.

- Stay calm and explain your concerns if they disagree with you, so they open up to you in the future. If necessary, take a pause in conversation and come back to the discussion later.

- Discussing sensitive issues like substance use, sexuality, and peer expectations can be intimidating but beneficial. If you do not engage your teenagers, they will find other sources for information which may lead to misinformation and negative influences. If some topics are too hard to tackle head on, start texting with your teen or take a ride in the car together.

Parents and children learning together about mental illness leads to improved recognition, earlier and better treatment, increased understanding, greater compassion, and decreased stigma if the child *and* their family are part of the process.

Cultural Considerations

Macklem (2014) describes the challenges of home-school communication and collaboration with parents from various cultural and ethnic groups, cautioning not to overgeneralize about any one ethnic group, saying "Not all families from the same background are alike" (p. 81). Yet, there are cultural differences that will impact both the conditions leading to trauma and mental illness, and also a family's understanding and acceptance of a child's mental illness.

Suicide is an example of an area of concern affected by cultural, ethnic, and racial differences. In their research, David Goldston and colleagues (2008) point out differences not only in the events that may precipitate attempted teen suicides, but also cultural differences in beliefs and attitudes about suicide, and a typical family's response, including stages of help-seeking behaviors. For example, suicide may be a more common response to feelings of shame or loss of face in some East Asian (Korean, Chinese, and Japanese) cultures. Native Americans are greatly impacted by long-standing discrimination, alcoholism and drug abuse, lack of economic opportunities, and a sense of isolation and hopelessness. Latinx families have recently experienced renewed discrimination in their efforts to immigrate to America to overcome hardships in their home countries and the increase in U.S. Immigration and Customs Enforcement (ICE) raids in local communities in the United States. These experiences increase both their sense of despair and also their reluctance to openly seek mental health assistance. For many Black and African Americans, systemic racism and discrimination also work against a family's comfort in acknowledging concerns or seeking professional guidance.

One reason some families don't feel comfortable discussing mental health is the deeply held beliefs passed down from one family member to another about the origin of mental well-being and its relationship to spirituality. For example, Elizabeth Wolfe, a therapist in Washington, DC, found that many of the Latinx clients she sees visit a *curandero*, or spiritual healer, before seeking her advice about mental health. Because her clients receive "a lot of support and strength from their faith," Wolfe says that is "something I try to bring into the therapy consciously, to help support that person" (Schatell, 2017).

In the Asian-American and Pacific Islander community, seeking help outside the immediate family goes against one of their most deeply held cultural values of interdependence, relying on the strength of your community. Children fear revealing their challenges to their parents because they may assume that you are "crazy" because of "their poor parenting or a hereditary flaw" (Mechammil et al., 2019). In a qualitative study by Molly Mechammil and colleagues (2019), researchers found that "the family would say, 'This is our problem, we have to solve this together. You are not on your own. We're together in this.'" Participants emphasized that families made it their duty to care for each other as the first avenue of recourse. One of the respondents in that study elaborated, "You don't go out of your family for an issue, I mean, everything is a family thing. And if it can't be resolved in the family then it's irresolvable." In cultures with such strong family connections, heads of households can be seen as strong authority figures. If mental health professionals can bring those members of the family into the conversation and show them the value of working together to achieve mental well-being for a youth in their family, they have made a powerful ally.

Families of color may also experience mental health stigma because the mental health professionals they interact with do not look like and/or speak the same language as they do. In case of a language barrier, it will be important to secure a translator for any conversations about mental health or other important school issues. It may be difficult and unnecessary to match the race of a counselor to a student, but when recruiting mental health service providers, school leaders can be mindful of their student population and attempt to recruit qualified candidates from a variety of backgrounds, especially those that align with the student population.

Cultural Considerations

☐ We have experienced/are experiencing cultural challenges.

☐ Cultural considerations are impacting the effectiveness of counseling programs and other services for students most at risk for behavioral and emotional challenges.

☐ We are addressing concerns by _____.

Discussing Sexuality

Many families and cultures who have high stigma for mental health also have high stigma for issues of the queer community. For youth who are not heterosexual who grow up in largely heteronormative families and cultures, they may feel outcast and experience isolation, depression, or anxiety related to the questioning of their sexuality or the conviction that they are queer.

Lesbian, gay, bisexual, transgender, and queer (or questioning) (LGBTQ) youth have a high risk of engaging in non-suicidal self-injury (NSSI), attempting suicide, experiencing peer victimization, and having low levels of self-compassion and well-being compared to their cisgender peers. In a recent survey, 56 percent of LGBTQ youth reported having suicidal thoughts within the past thirty days, and 53 percent experienced peer victimization. Schools and parents can buffer against the increased risk of mental health challenges for LGBTQ youth by working together to increase parental and non-parental adult advocacy, along with feelings of safety and belonging in school, which serve as protective factors for the well-being of LGBTQ youth. A feeling of connectedness reduces

LGBTQ youths' risk of suicidal behavior and increases their sense of well-being (Espelage et al., 2018; Taliaferro et al., 2019).

LGBTQ youth have a more difficult time discussing bullying with parents, often due to a fear of revealing their sexual orientation (Espelage et al., 2018). Indeed, youth are more likely to suffer from depression or experience suicidality if their parents reject their gender identity or sexual orientation (Ryan et al., 2009). Schools can offer safe spaces for LGBTQ youth to discuss their challenges in counselor's offices, peer support networks, or pride clubs.

If parents are accepting, they can still face difficulty with adjusting to a new gender identity or sexual orientation and may require additional counseling or peer support. Parents of teens transitioning to a new gender identify who attended a support group reported receiving high levels of emotional support, describing the group as a source of knowledge and "a space we could let our guard down. Knowing we wouldn't be judged because of the decisions we made as parents to listen to what our child was telling us" (Hillier & Torg, 2019). Schools can encourage parents to create these safe spaces to strengthen home-school and parent-child communication and collaboration.

When a Mental Health Diagnosis Is Part of the Equation

After a formal diagnosis has been delivered or discussed, leave the conversation on a positive note by talking about the array of treatment options available. Educators can even send the parent home with some tips and strategies and encourage them to try them out at home.

It is essential that any information about a specific mental health diagnosis be given only by a qualified mental health professional. Parents' worries and concerns can be lessened by providing them with information that normalizes what their child is experiencing, evidence-based strategies to address and lessen the emotions and behaviors the child is struggling with, and words of hope.

Resources for Parents About Specific Mental Health Diagnoses

Many nonprofit organizations and government agencies offer valuable information to assist parents in navigating the overwhelming world of youth mental health.

- **Child Mind Institute: childmind.org** This research and advocacy nonprofit focuses on strengths-based solutions to youth mental health challenges that are bolstered by evidence.

(Continued)

(Continued)

Resources include articles, guides, a symptom checker, and an opportunity to "Ask an Expert."

- **National Alliance on Mental Illness: nami.org** This grassroots mental health organization connects families with service providers and peer advocacy in their states. They offer online and in-person support groups, help navigating local systems of care, and guidance on preventing and responding to mental health crises.

- **Youth.gov: youth.gov/youth-topics/youth-mental-health** This online federal initiative was created to bring free, evidence-based opportunities to promote positive youth mental health in more communities. Fact-based information as well as programs about specific diagnoses and topics related to youth mental health and well-being can be found on their site. If you can't find a program to meet your needs, there is also guidance for applying for funding for your unique program.

In the Midst of a Child's Crisis and Its Aftermath

Will Foley, in an article for the Center for Educational Improvement wrote,

> We are never traumatized alone. We are wounded together. Together, too, we heal. Relying on one another for support and love, we help each other through the darkest times. Those who inflict harm can become the same people that restore us. People and communities torn asunder by violence can heal together with the support of intentional practices brought to schools. (2019)

When a child has experienced a psychotic episode or has been admitted to an emergency ward because of a drug overdose or suicide attempt, some extra precautions and considerations are needed with home-school communication. Schools can be helpful by providing resource information, on such things as support and advocacy groups or crisis intervention centers. Schools can also be essential partners for families as they attempt to provide some sense of consistency and community amidst a mental health crisis.

When students are receiving in-patient care for a mental health crisis, teachers can provide community by making cards or art to decorate the student's room, have teachers or school mental health service providers visit the student, or have the student video chat with a friend or trusted adult in the building. If in-patient care is for an extended period of time, schools can work with therapists to slowly reintegrate schoolwork, especially work that allows for reflection and creativity, into the students' daily activities as they begin to transition from

What to Do During a Mental Health Crisis

 NAMI (2018) provides an excellent practical guide to navigate a mental health crisis. For a complete list of warning signs and advice, visit the companion website for this book: resources.corwin.com/compassionateschoolpractice.

Warning signs of a mental health crisis:

- Inability to perform basic tasks such as bathing, brushing teeth, brushing hair, changing clothes

- Rapid mood swings

- Abusive or violent behavior to the self or others

- Isolation from teachers, family, or friends

Warning signs of suicide:

- Talking as if they're saying goodbye or going away forever

- Dramatic changes in personality, mood, or behavior

- Withdrawal from family, friends, and normal activities

What to do in an actual crisis (NAMI, 2018):

- Listen, express concern, and reassure – "You're important to me, and we will get through this together."

- Focus on being understanding, caring, and nonjudgmental – "You're not alone in this. Your family, friends, and school all care about you and are here to support you."

- Call a psychiatrist, nurse, therapist, case worker, or family physician familiar with the student's history, or 911 as a last resort.

mental health facilities back into the home. Before students return to a full schedule at school, school leaders should work with families—including the student themselves—to make a plan to gradually increase the time spent at school. During the beginning stage of the transition, students will need extra encouragement, such as weekly or even daily one-on-one sessions with a trusted adult, peer support, or a special pass to take frequent breaks. These students may also need to spend more time building specific coping skills to address the triggers that led to their mental health crisis.

Counseling and Schools

When students experience mental health challenges or crises, schools can provide the consistent and caring environment students need to heal. Part of the healing process is gaining the skills necessary to cope with feelings of hopelessness, isolation, and fear. Another part of the process is understanding why they are having these feelings by creating a cohesive narrative for themselves. Both of these essential steps can be provided in the school building by a counselor, social worker, psychologist, or therapist during individual counseling sessions. Because parents usually have to sign off on their child's participation in these sessions, schools must help parents understand what counseling is and why it's important.

Group counseling can also be used in schools where groups of students share common challenges like anxiety, depression, eating disorders, and so forth. Learning and talking together with peers can be a powerful experience for a youth who has been carrying the burden of his or her mental illness in silence much of their life. Explaining this to parents can help convince them to allow their child to participate.

Individual vs. Family Counseling

Although there are many excellent family therapists seeing children, teens, and their parents individually and as a family, this highly effective resource is often only available to those with very good private insurance or to those able to pay for the services out of pocket. Individual sessions allow the therapist to work with a youth more one-on-one and focus on solving the individual's behavioral challenges. Family sessions allow the therapist to work with the family as a whole to improve communication, resolve conflict, and develop coping strategies. For families with a parent also struggling with a mental illness, family therapy can be especially beneficial.

School leaders can research what local options might be available to families who are struggling with mental health, trauma, or tragedy. Many universities have low cost or free group counseling programs. Support groups for specific mental health challenges can be comforting and empowering to parents and may assist them on their road to recovery.

Counseling Services at My School

☐ We have a strong counseling team at our school.

☐ Our counseling team collaborates with families around mental health support effectively.

☐ We are establishing a counseling team, but we need more backing and guidance.

☐ We do not have a mental health support team or it is ineffective. We need to improve _____.

Home School Collaboration

When schools and districts operate with consistency, all students and families, but especially children who have experienced trauma or struggle with a mental illness or emotional/behavioral disorder, feel more secure and trusting of their school community. If all stakeholders—particularly schools and families—can coordinate messaging to reinforce the same values, norms, and expectations, students will have a clear understanding of how to belong to their community as a valued member. Although it is important for messaging to remain clear, concise, and consistent, it must also be dynamic to accommodate new needs, challenges, and resources that present themselves.

It's Not Parents, It's Families

Educators need to consider not only parents but families. A *child's well-being is affected by the entire family* and a child's well-being impacts the entire family. Families with one child or adult struggling with mental illness, long-term chronic illness, substance use, or disabilities will be impacted as the entire family dynamic shifts to accommodate to the special needs of that child.

Similarly, *family structures strengthen families in various ways.* Some single parents rise to the occasion to demonstrate significant strength and resiliency, while others flounder as they try to bring in adequate income, provide for children, and meet their own emotional needs. Some two-parent families share responsibilities with an enlightened understanding of children's needs, yet others struggle with parental deficits or an inability to resolve marital conflict peacefully.

Children in "traditional families" may feel the impact of an abusive home; others may experience the trauma, instability, and uncertainty of being moved from one foster family to another; while others raised by extended families or single mothers may receive a high degree of assistance. It may be challenging for a parent in any family constellation to provide the nurturing and caring to meet a child's needs.

Nontraditional families, especially single parent families, experience an added layer of stress from a lack of social support and resources, potentially affecting their parenting (Gleeson et al., 2016; Taylor & Conger, 2017). However, increased social and emotional encouragement from extended family and friends increases single parents' well-being, parenting skills, and relationships with their child. Moreover, parents who are emotionally secure with a strong sense of self, self-efficacy, and optimism tend to have better parenting skills and a capability that serves as a buffer against parental stress and mental illness.

In families that are burdened by dysfunction, sometimes *extended families are available to ease the burden.* The presence of an extended family member is often higher in non-white populations as elders may live with Asian families, or live close by in Native American or Hispanic families. In families impacted by adult incarceration or drug abuse, a grandparent may assume primary responsibility for child rearing. Often the presence of a grandparent or another relative can be the protective buffer a child needs for a strong sense of self and well-being. Maternal and paternal involvement are both important for protecting adolescents from internalizing and externalizing problems and substance use; grandparent involvement further contributes to developing prosocial tendencies (Profe & Wild, 2016).

Given these varying circumstances, educators need to be alert to the potential for family strengths and the ways in which they need to consider not only the parent and the child, but the whole family. By modeling positive communications with students and their families, educators can serve as models for how parents can practice compassion with their own children, hopefully reducing instances of abuse and neglect.

Our Families

☐ School leaders and educators know which families have nontraditional compositions and provide an extra helping hand to those parents.

☐ There is a strong sense of deep connection among single parents, foster parents, and other nontraditional caregivers at our school.

☐ I'm unsure about the family make-up of most of my students.

☐ We are struggling to assist nontraditional caregivers. Specifically, we need _____ _____.

Connecting Parents' Past Experience of School to Their Child's Present

Parents' past childhood experience with their own schooling can impact how they view their child's present schooling. A parent may have had a negative school experience at the same age their child is now. For example, a mother may have been very bright, but she felt ignored and lost in a school system that was busy dealing with disruptive and struggling students. Perhaps a parent was suspended or expelled multiple times because his cries for help were misinterpreted as aggression or disruption. Perhaps he flew under the radar earning Cs, never making connections with adults, being quietly bullied by peers, and feeling invisible to his school community. These parents can often be distrustful and skeptical of schools, authority figures, and rules or regulations required by the school. Approaching these families with compassion can lead to a better understanding of how the school community can work together to meet the needs of its children and perhaps heal some parental wounds.

Challenging parents require school leaders and teachers to confront difficult situations with kindness, active listening (fully concentrating, understanding, responding to what is being said), and an open mind. It takes courage to have tough conversations, but a pattern of dysfunction can continue for years if it is not broken by mutual understanding and compromise. Instead of trying to impose a prescription for their child's success upon parents, invite the parents into the conversation as an equal participant as soon as possible. By hearing them out, you may discover a new perspective that leads to an improvement in school well-being.

There are many reasons for parents' lack of involvement, but one of the most important to understand and to heal is that many parents themselves experienced trauma. Schools may have failed to respond compassionately, letting them slip through the cracks unassisted or unintentionally making the trauma worse. School leaders who understand how intergenerational trauma affects not only students but their parents as well are better equipped to interact with parents who have experienced trauma and their children.

Stress, Trauma, and Domestic Violence

Stress, trauma, and violence is all too prevalent, inflicting visible and hidden scars. In the United States, more than one in three women (35.6 percent) and more than one in four men (28.5 percent) have experienced rape, physical violence, and/or stalking by an intimate partner in their lifetime. One reason why many women who are experiencing domestic violence live with their abusers for decades is because the constant abuse they endured resulted in a loss of agency (National Domestic Violence Hotline, n.d.). Over time, as their abusers isolated them more and more, the number of choices they were able to make diminished. This is also true for other forms of abuse—sexual abuse, emotional abuse, and neglect. To help students and their families leave traumatic home environments and to avoid getting into similar situations in the future, it is important to build confidence in one's own choices. Whenever possible, offer parents and students meaningful choices.

Parenting Through Intergenerational Trauma and Mental Illness

Because childhood trauma occurs within the family, it adds a layer of complexity for schools interacting with parents of children who have experienced the trauma. A majority of traumatic events that directly affect young people are enacted by an adult (SAMHSA, 2014). Abuse, neglect, and other forms of traumatizing parenting are often learned behavior. Infants learn how to regulate their emotions by looking to their adult caregivers' reactions to their cries of hunger, bubbling laughter, or pained expression at bumping an elbow. If their caregiver reacts inappropriately (e.g., laughing at a baby's cries of pain) or doesn't react, the child does not experience a healthy example of how to soothe their extreme emotions or how to mimic the correct response.

The Transmission of Trauma

Over time, dysfunctional parenting can lead to attachment disorders that cause difficulties in interpersonal relationships, mental health, and emotional regulation throughout the course of a child's life. In a study of fourteen thousand U.S. children, 40 percent lacked strong emotional bonds—secure attachment—with their caregivers. Insecure parental attachment is correlated with long-term educational and behavioral problems (Richardson, 2014). Once these children grow up and have children of their own, unless they formed healthy relationships with other adults who modeled positive interpersonal relationship skills, they will not have the necessary strategies and resources to navigate communication and compromise with others. This can lead to increased relationship conflict, often resulting in instances of domestic violence, aggression, and verbal fights, all of which are stressors on family relationships.

Parents who grew up in environments of trauma often do not have the necessary positive examples of loving, consistent caregiver-child relationships that allow infants to flourish. Although most new parents want information about raising their child, very few actually take a parent education class. Many parents who experienced childhood trauma continue to live in poverty or isolation and do not have the social equity needed to learn about, much less access, parent education classes or basic child development information. Often impoverished, younger parents living in high crime urban environments or rural areas with few resources find it difficult to learn from someone in their own community. They do not have access to experts who can visit or provide virtual parent education.

If these parents do not know about best practices or the negative consequences of certain parenting behavior, they are likely to fall back on the only model of parenting they received: their own, flawed past experience. For example, many parents continue to spank their children for minor infractions despite the American Pediatric Association, the American Psychology Association, and other reputable organizations releasing statements condemning the practice as being more harmful than prescriptive. It can sometimes be very difficult for adults who experienced negative parenting behaviors to identify them as such when they become parents. Consider a child born to a mother who experiences severe postpartum depression. For the mother who seeks treatment and is given the appropriate prescription medication and therapy, her own depression can be attended to and she will be able to be present and engaged with her infant. If a new mother does not recognize she is depressed or does not know who to turn to for assistance, she may fall into a deeper depression that may lead her to neglect her child. When a child repeatedly does not get their needs met, it may become a source of trauma that eventually leads to developing depression. The neurological channels that deliver dopamine and serotonin, the "feel good" brain chemicals, start to wither from underuse (see Figure 8.1).

FIGURE 8.1   This diagram illustrates several different ways depression can affect a child.

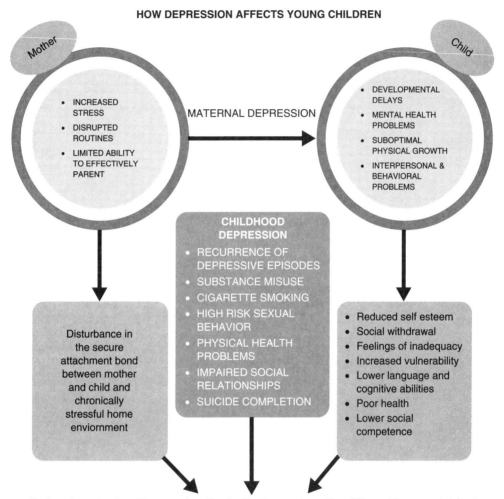

FIGURE 8.1   This diagram illustrates several different ways depression can affect a child.

"Based on research from Cuijpers et al., 2015; Horowitz & Garber, 2006; Lima et al., 2013; and Martins & Gaffan, 2006."

The Importance of Early Mother-Child Interactions

The disconnection between mother and child in the early stages of life leads to the mother looking at and speaking to the baby less often, resulting in developmental delays that later in life lead to lower language and cognitive abilities (National Research Council and Institute of Medicine Committee on Depression, 2009). Because of the lack of volley and serve interactions between mother and child, where the child would have learned how to respond to stressors and extreme emotions, the children of depressed mothers have more interpersonal and behavioral problems, which results in lower social competence and isolation (National Research Council and Institute of Medicine Committee on Depression, 2009). Over time, this can result in the development of a mental illness.

Parenting With Substance Misuse

Another topic that is important to acknowledge about the parent–child relationship—but inappropriate to discuss among staff or directly with parents—is substance misuse.

> In 2017, 19.7 million people, or 7.2 percent of adults, age twelve or older had a substance use disorder in the last year. About 3 percent of American adults suffered from both a mental health disorder and a substance use disorder, or co-occurring disorders (SAMHSA, 2018c). Often trauma, mental health disorders, and substance misuse are co-occurring, which means that people suffer from more than one affliction at the same time. For example, many people with mental health diagnoses misuse substances as a means of self-medicating because their culture looks down upon mental health treatment.

If educators suspect there is any drug use in the house that puts children in danger, it is their mandated duty to report these situations to their local and/or state child protective services agency. All staff should be briefed on these protocols on a yearly basis, including signs of substance use, abuse, and neglect in the home.

School leaders must take special care when they talk to staff about parental talk drug use, so it is done with compassion rather than judgment and blaming. Instead of discussing specific parents and passing blame, educators can talk about the effects of parental substance use on children in general. The stigma around substance use has caused many people around the world to turn their backs on people with the medical condition of addiction. If educators become aware that a parent is actively struggling with addiction or is recovering from addiction, practicing compassion for them in the same way you would with any parent recovering from an illness can encourage them to feel a sense of belonging in the school community. And we know that a strong sense of community is one of the most essential elements of recovery from substance misuse.

Working to Heal Intergenerational Trauma by Cultivating Compassionate School Communities

The first step a transformational leader can take to address intergenerational trauma in their school is to talk about it. Many teachers and administrators around the world are getting trained on the neurobiology of toxic stress and trauma, as a part of becoming trauma-skilled. This training often addresses how the hippocampus and amygdala get overwhelmed by stress and stop storing memories and regulating emotions efficiently while the decision-making and executive functioning skills start to shut down in the overwhelmed prefrontal cortex. Trainings connect this neuroscience to student behavior and to potential risks for mental illness. *But few delve into the larger picture of how this trauma is healed, not just for the student who is experiencing it, but for the adult in their home.* The adult might also be a victim of abuse, or sometimes be both a victim and perpetrator.

After a mental health disorder begins to affect their child's life, a parent may also begin to experience secondary trauma related to caregiving. We can teach youth who have experienced trauma resiliency, coping, and self-regulation strategies to help buffer against and address the trauma in their childhoods so they have the tools to parent their children compassionately one day. *Until parents have a mindset shift or communities start confronting the intergenerational nature of trauma, these students will go back to homes where they will be re-traumatized.*

Family Composition, Well-Being, and Resiliency

- What do I know about the mental health and intergenerational challenges of parents in my classroom and school?

  _____

- Where are there significant needs? _____

- What are the implications for me, as an educator? _____

Using the Compassionate School Mental Health Model at the School Community Level

As our model explains, a Compassionate School Mental Health support system has multiple approaches:

Prevention through reduction of the causes

Support the Child

Build resiliency

Develop protective factors

In Chapter 1, we explained how each of these is an essential piece of the puzzle of compassionate, school-based mental health. All are important for the well-being of the school community and if any one approach is missing, the others become strained (see also the preface).

Prevention: Reduce the Causes

Involving families at each step can strengthen the impact of a school's mental health services. For example, schools can alleviate or stop trauma by working with a mother experiencing domestic violence to help her get the resources she needs to safely leave that situation—for example, a domestic violence shelter, a social worker, and an escape plan. When the trauma is societal, bring affected family members into the conversation about how to respond to an injustice causing trauma for students, staff, and/or community members.

Support the Child

When deciding how to treat a student's mental health challenges, it is imperative that parents be involved from the very beginning. Many districts will not even allow a school to do screening for mental illnesses without parental consent. If your school or district is doing universal mental health screening, make sure it is communicated to parents clearly and that they have the choice to opt out. Some schools doing universal screening have discovered that they can screen more students if they ask parents to return a form saying their child is *not* to be screened rather than sending in a form that gives the school permission to do the screening.

Build Resiliency

Just as students who are unable to meet expectations are doing so because those expectations outstrip their skill set, parents who are missing the mark are usually doing so because they don't have the skills and/or resources to make it. We don't expect children to perform perfectly even after we've taught them a skill over and over. Why do we expect parents to know how to regulate their emotions, set goals, reflect on their actions nonjudgmentally, and perform a host of resiliency-building strategies without teaching them how to do so?

Schools can help families experiencing trauma by teaching parents about compassion, self-regulation, and growth mindset, which will help families bounce back from trauma. Include a short mindfulness exercise for families to do together at home that builds these skills or do a skit at half-time at the next basketball game that teaches families about the importance of regulating emotions. Schools have the responsibility of teaching not just the students in their building but also the families they go home to about how to protect and remove themselves from trauma.

Develop Protective Factors

Schools can create a safe space for students impacted by trauma at school, but they can also create safe spaces for families in the school building and introduce families to safe spaces throughout the community. School leaders can curate positive relationships between students and caring adults in the building, but they can also connect parents in need with parents enthusiastic about nurturing others. Schools can use messaging, events, and norms—such as the tone and language used during class discussions—to convey the idea that they are a compassionate school environment, but they can also work with the community to extend that idea into hospitals, community centers, grocery stores, and other places where families gather. One way to do that would be to have a Community Cares Day where students partner with local businesses to raise money for a charity.

Offering Parent Education to Foster Compassionate Parenting

One way that schools have traditionally aided parents was to offer courses or training to parents on such topics as discipline and positive parenting practices. Although parent education has been piloted and studied since the 1970s, few programs have been found successful enough to scale up, promote, and fund widely. There are many reasons for this, the primary one being that there is a trade-off in programs between effectively teaching essential parenting skills, especially responsiveness, and retaining parents throughout the duration of a program that lasts weeks or months. Parent educators also have a difficult time disrupting established family routines without extensive time in the home. There is also often a cultural mismatch between program leaders and content for minority populations (Magnuson & Schindler, 2016). Schools can overcome this barrier by providing digestible parent education on platforms parents already access.

The easiest way to choose the most effective method of communicating parent education to families is to survey them on preferred methods of communication. If you have a large school, it may be a good idea to disseminate information in a variety of ways such as social media posts, printed materials in folders, blog posts, videos, segments in the school newspaper, and so forth. Facebook Live can be a fun way to reach parents with casual tips that take only one to five minutes to absorb. A beloved administrator or school mental health professional could make it a regular practice to offer a parenting tip each morning or afternoon.

Research supports the value of delivering parent education online. In a meta-study of parent education programs, researchers Katherine Magnuson and Holly Schindler (2016) found that the most effective parent education programs were ones that conveyed the information in a concise and digestible manner and were delivered in an easy-to-access format like webinar, text, or e-mail. They also found that succesfull parent education programs do the following:

- Train staff to engage and work with parents

- Target specific skills or behaviors

- Focus on parenting practices clearly linked to target skills

- Give parents materials needed to implement strategies taught

- Serve other goals, such as building community and cultivating leadership

Options for Evidence-Based Parent Education Programs

To be effective, parent education programs should have a well-defined goal, properly trained staff, and be specific enough to be useful to a group of parents. The following programs have raised parent knowledge of child development, including parent responsiveness (Magnuson & Schindler, 2016):

- **Families and Schools Together (FAST)** After eight group sessions in the school building that focused on building parent-school community and parenting skills, improved parental involvement, as well as improved child social skills and behavior, were observed.

- **Parent Corps** This early childhood program focused on positive parenting skills, which were taught over thirteen group sessions. There were positive effects on parenting practices and child behavior and achievement. Pre-K and early childhood centers can apply for grants to bring this nationwide program to their schools.

- **The REDI Parenting Program** Head Start's comprehensive parenting program includes sixteen home visits, a hallmark of the most successful parenting programs. This important program helps young students transition from Head Start to Pre-K, a crucial time to intervene for parent education. When parents participated in this program, positive impacts were observed for academic performance, literacy skills, and social competence.

Five Mindful Habits to Help Parents Increase Their Family Bond

Compassionate schools can lead to more peaceful home environments that foster strong family bonds by reducing stress and increasing belonging and happiness. If parents can integrate mindfulness into their family's daily routines, over time, they will see changes that may even reduce anxiety and depression for themselves or their children.

Eventually, families could practice all five habits every day, but parents could choose one habit to start with and build on as they master each. The habits build off of each other, however families are welcome to start with the habit that most appeals to them. Schools can also follow these *Five Mindful Habits* as a structure to infuse mindful routines into the school building by modifying the suggestions for parents below.

1. **Be present**
   - Plan purposeful quality time, which may mean leaving cell phones and computers locked in a closet while doing an activity that promotes family togetherness like playing a board game or going on a hike.
   - Practice active listening, which requires everyone to make eye contact, leave judgment behind, and avoid interrupting each other during discussions, especially tense ones.

2. **Be calm**
   - Practice breathwork when a tense situation or anxiety attack creates acute stress.
   - Practice yoga and meditation daily to lower levels of stress, anxiety, and depression over time.
   - Coach your child through emotionally challenging conflicts by validating their feelings, helping them reflect on misbehaviors through perspective-taking, and brainstorming healthy solutions to conflict or processing extreme emotions.

3. **Be compassionate**
   - Model compassion as a family by doing acts of kindness for others in the family and community. During moments of disagreement, be sure to verbally model compassion for others' experiences.
   - Read books about compassion, like Carol McCloud's *Have You Filled a Bucket Today?*

4. **Be grateful**
   - Be a gratitude model for children by practicing it yourself with other family members, school staff, service providers, and anyone who helps out.
   - Start a family gratitude journal where everyone records things for which they are grateful. Younger children can draw pictures. Families can also collect mementos to turn it into a gratitude scrapbook or treasure chest.
   - Create a gratitude routine where each family member shares three things they are grateful for that day. You can do this on the car ride to school, before dinner or bed, or any time that's convenient for all members of the family to participate.

5. **Reflect**
   - Express difficult emotions through journaling, creating art, dancing, or some other way of making sense of them. This is true

for parents and children. Younger children who may not have the words to express extreme emotions can greatly benefit through art therapy.

- Find quiet moments in the day to pause, breathe, and reflect without judgment. Be grateful for the positive things and seek out a lesson in challenges without labeling them as "bad."

- Infuse the "Best/Worst Part of the Day" routine into the day, usually on the car ride home from school or around the dinner table. Everyone can share the best and worst things about their days, acknowledging that whatever made the worst list was a learning opportunity and reflecting on how to grow from the experience.

School leaders can present easy to implement routines like these to parents during an after-school workshop with parent educators—like Melanie Laguna and Dana Asby of Parent in the Moment who developed the Five Mindful Habits—or they can choose to convey these tips individually over time.

Strengths at My School

- What are the strengths of our approach to addressing mental health challenges at my school?
  _____

- How do these strengths benefit families? _____
  _____

- What else could be done? _____

Parent Teacher Associations: A Network Made to Partner With Schools

The Parent Teacher Association (PTA), with 6.5 million members in the United States, is the oldest and largest collection of unpaid child advocates in the country (White, 2020). Hearing "PTA" immediately conjures a variety of mental images, including bake sales, gift-wrapping fundraisers, angry mothers demanding extra services for their children, and more. With some relationship-building, however, PTAs can be more than just cash cows or the school board's worst enemy. Parents can assist school leaders in changing the hearts and minds of their students, teachers, and other community members as well as government officials at the local, state, and federal levels. Visioning for an ideal future for your school will be enhanced by including key members of the PTA in your core learning team (Mason, Liabenow, & Patschke, 2020).

Addressing Equity in PTAs

Not all PTAs are created equal. Some schools have large and active PTAs that raise an enormous amount of money through dues and fundraising. They use that money to purchase resources, fund field trips, and host events that schools otherwise would not be able to afford. Schools in wealthier neighborhoods are able to set higher dues, solicit donations from neighbors with disposable income, and benefit from volunteer hours of stay-at-home spouses. Parents and guardians in lower income neighborhoods may not have the funds to make donations themselves and their neighbors may be unable to purchase fundraising. Parents living in poverty are also more likely to work more than one job or work long hours. Wealthier families are also more likely to have connections to private businesses and organizations that can make large monetary donations or send volunteers to facilitate programs at schools.

This inequity in financial and social capital exacerbates the fact that certain American schools are woefully underfunded, with a widening funding gap between schools and school districts along racial lines. States see significant differences in funding, with New Jersey spending $17,379 per student while Utah only spent $6,452 per student in the 2009–2010 school year (New America, n.d.). A 2016 report found that overwhelmingly White school districts received $23 billion more than predominantly non-White school districts in state and local funding in 2016, despite serving roughly the same number of students (Meckler, 2019).

Because the majority of school funding comes from property taxes, schools or districts in the "nicer" parts of town will have more money for staffing, sports and arts programs, technology, and so forth. Parents in poorer neighborhoods may feel disenfranchised by this system, ultimately reacting combatively or apathetically, not trusting that their school community will look out for them or their child—sometimes perpetuating an attitude based on their own schooling experience.

To bring more equity to districts and schools, leaders are experimenting with fund-sharing. For example, in a diverse, urban area with working, middle, and upper-class neighborhoods, one school's PTA may be able to raise $400 for their work throughout the year, while a different school nets $1,000 of funds, goods, and services to enrich their children's education, and a third school in the same district might get over $5,000 worth of programing, donations, and other resources for the school. Some progressive districts and/or PTA organizations are building an alliance to pool all of the money collected from the schools' PTAs and redistribute it equally. If our hypothetical district implemented a fund-sharing policy, each of those schools would get $2,133. In this scenario, the wealthiest school may not be able to fund all six of the field trips they wanted to, but the poorest school is able to buy laptops and hot spots for students who do not have access to a computer or Internet service at home.

PTA vs. PTO

Some schools have a Parent Teacher Organization (PTO) instead of a Parent Teacher Association (PTA). The PTA is a longstanding national nonprofit organization that's been advocating for the rights of children in schools since 1897 (PTA, n.d.). In the 2018–2019 school year, the PTA contributed over $700,000 of funding to schools around the nation (PTA, 2019). There are local units—around 26,000 of them—at schools, councils who assists local PTAs, district units that work at the regional level, and state units.

PTOs are similar to PTAs, but they are independent from the official PTA organization and have less national structure. They are also referred to as PCCs (parent communication councils), PTGs (parent teacher groups), and HSAs (home and school associations) (Sullivan, 2019). The decision between forming a PTA and a PTO usually comes down to a school's preference between being part of a larger coalition that is fighting for the greater good versus using all of the funding raised from dues to support a local school. For schools with particularly low membership, being a part of the PTA may not be feasible. However, for schools with higher membership pools, being a local unit under the PTA umbrella can provide enormous benefits, like access to a number of grants, well-established networks between parents and state or federal officials, and conferences to gain knowledge and resources. Each school should evaluate the costs and benefits before making a decision.

Events to Increase Belonging Among School Community

- **Family Culture Fair**, where families share food, games, pictures, music, and so forth from their or their ancestors' home countries.

- **Family Reading Hour**, where families are invited to bring a blanket to spread out on the gym floor, grab some refreshments and books, and read together.

- **Family Arts Events**, where families work together to create pieces of art that can contribute to a charity art show or become masterpieces to display in their homes.

Lessons in Supporting Children and Families in Challenging Times. In 2020, educators learned a new way of communicating with and virtually supporting children and families on a day-to-day basis. The lessons we are learning simultaneously are many, but the most important is that before children need learning, they need love. In the first half of 2020, people around the globe faced mounting stress and anxiety as governments, communities, and individuals struggled to halt the spread of COVID-19. As school buildings were closed and remote classes were implemented in an effort to contain the virus, parents and children found themselves in close quarters for extended periods of time, providing the opportunity to spend more time together as a family, even as individuals practiced social distancing. Some families were better prepared to handle this challenge, and many educators and social service agencies were gravely concerned about the impact, particularly on families with greater dysfunctionality where there was a history of violence, alcohol or drug misuse, or feelings of inadequacy and despair.

In some families where the risk of infection was high or one individual appeared to have COVID-19 symptoms, children and parents lived with the ever-present reminder "not to touch." Some single parents who needed to work outside the home were faced with the burden of finding childcare for their school aged children, some parents lost jobs, and others found themselves on a daily basis venturing out into communities where they were at higher risk of being exposed to the virus. Families feared for the health and safety of loved ones and anxiety was high.

During this time, virtual communities popped up to assist one another in new ways. Churches began holding Zoom services on Sunday morning, family and friends turned frequently to the Internet as a way of connecting with the world outside their homes, and telehealth became a standard protocol for delivering mental health support services. With a virtual assist, many examples of the basic compassion, kindness, and caring went virtual, reassuring us of the basic goodness that is inherent across cultures, countries, and traditions.

Government agencies such as the CDC and SAMHSA and private organizations such as NAMI, the National Education Association, and the American Federation of Teachers developed guidelines to help individuals and families reduce stress and build their resiliency. Because these guidelines are rapidly changing, we have compiled a list of online resources that will be periodically updated on Corwin's online resource list for this book.

Parent and family needs, including needs to reduce stress and further child well-being, are shifting as our world changes and as a child grows from being a toddler to an adolescent. Many factors affect parent-child relations and communication, and educators can play a critical role in furthering positive relationships by partnering with parents and families. We can make a significant difference in reducing stress, increasing protective factors, and furthering a child's resiliency. When educators are trauma-skilled, they are also prepared to be of greater assistance to children and families during mental health crises.

Reflections on Strengthening Mental Health and Well-Being: Leverage Parent Resources to Fulfill Needs, Wants, and Dreams

A family's mental health and well-being can be furthered not only through communication and counseling but through partnering to enhance the school community. Once positive relationships have been established with families, school leaders and educators can strategize to make the most of their talents, resources, and connections.

When you bring families onto your team, you can accomplish much, supporting not only their child but others. Instead of scrambling to do the best you can with a small budget or staff, parents' involvement can turn a mediocre program or event into an impactful, memorable, and exciting one. To earn more trust and encourage greater parental involvement, build positive relationships and be intentional with how and when you ask for help.

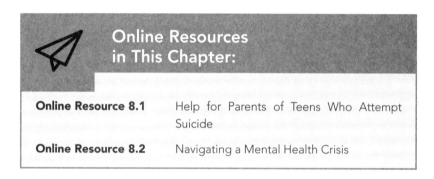

Online Resources in This Chapter:

Online Resource 8.1	Help for Parents of Teens Who Attempt Suicide
Online Resource 8.2	Navigating a Mental Health Crisis

Part 4

The Future

Reaching Our Destiny—
Overcoming Challenges
and Moving Forward

9

///

Key Principle #9

We can shape our destiny, even in the midst of strife. Mindset, self-care, thinking big, and caring are key.

Our Encounter With Destiny

The great existential and humanistic psychologist Rollo May, in the foreword to his book *Freedom and Destiny* (1999), writes, "Freedom is how we relate to our destiny, and destiny is significant only because we have freedom. In the struggle of our freedom against and with destiny, our creativity and our civilizations themselves are born" (p. xi.). The struggle "against and with destiny" is an interesting paradox—Does destiny allow for only insurmountable hardships *or* greatness? Does our destiny, the inescapable course of events, prevent or bolster our greatness? Is our lot cast at birth? Why might it be important to consider destiny right now as we envision the next steps to stem the almost universal tide of violence and trauma, to help children and schools, and, to take this from the realm of philosophy to practical, to advance specific protocol and procedures to support children and youth experiencing significant behavioral and emotional crises?

So, what are we as educators to do with our encounter with destiny? Why did we choose a career in education? Were we destined to be cogs in a wheel during a time of an increase in teenage anxiety, despair, and suicide? Do we have a role to play in shaping destiny, or is our fate sealed? In some ways, our collective sense of disenfranchisement might be compared to sleep walking or becoming a nation of automatons. How much say do we have during a time when expectations have been clearly defined with an interlocking system of matrices for standards and evaluation?

Destiny Pre-COVID-19

As the coauthors of this book met, pre-COVID-19, we discussed the destiny of school mental health systems with a strong conviction that we did not want to be responsible for simply proliferating more diagnosing and labeling. We felt schools could become submerged in the trends that are happening in education and efforts to identify and get services to the most at-risk children or that schools could step out and provide something that research shows to be more foundational: making compassion the platform undergirding services and supports. Our conviction was that we had a choice—that it was perhaps even our destiny as researchers, educators, and authors—to break out of the mold and help others to look through a new lens at options and possibilities for building resiliency and developing protective factors for all children and youth.

In the Midst

In the summer of 2020, in the midst of COVID-19, we are hopeful that our destiny will be driven by visions of a world without social distancing, pandemics, or strictly virtual learning. We are hoping that by 2021, whatever we have said about COVID-19 will be viewed more as a historical accounting rather than an ongoing day-to-day reality.

Many times in the past few months, we have paused to reflect on our world. In many ways, the world as we knew it pre-COVID-19 was "spinning out of control." We were destroying our planet with plastics killing ocean wildlife and industrial chemicals causing air and water pollution. The strife of wars that have been a reality for many were taking a toll for people in hotspots around the globe. We were complaining about long commutes in cars as we were depleting natural resources and contributing to greenhouse gases. We saw an ever-increasing cycle of violence and trauma, including school shootings, an increasing number of suicides, racially motivated police violence, and rising rates of opioid addiction. While those crises still exist, much has slowed down for many of us in the past few months as we have stayed at home with our families. Others have risked their lives to serve us and treat us in hospitals, our economy has faced its most profound crisis since the Great Depression, and many of us are facing a new and complex grief, for those who have died and what we have lost, both individually, and as a country.

Our Preparation

And yet, there are many among us who feel that our work has prepared us to meet some of these challenges. The Program for Recovery and Community Health (PRCH) at Yale University had been focused on recovery since its inception. The Center for Educational Improvement (CEI) had been meeting with key leaders for about a decade to advance compassionate leadership and our vision for compassionate schools. Even our work with the

Childhood-Trauma Learning Collaborative (C-TLC) seems to have prepared us for many aspects of the trauma, anxiety, and fear others are facing. There are many others, around the country, and the world, who have built solid foundations of work based on compassionate and courageous action, strong communities, and social action to address injustice and suffering. Was it our destiny to be prepared? To be in a place where we might have extra self-care tools to help ourselves and others through this time? To have the opportunity to learn new ways to advise others by listening closely to those we had been teaching for the past year? To be able to practice what we preached to be models for those we were mentoring?

We believe visions and destiny are intertwined and that we are not simply pulled along by invisible forces but that humans have some capacity to shift the tides in our response to those forces. The tide rolls in with mindfulness, compassion, reflection, collaboration; it makes waves with intentional and collective action. The COVID-19 pandemic is just the most recent global crisis, and one that has particularly affected the United States, but there have been, and will be, others.

Recently, Christine Mason had a fascinating discussion with Garry Turner from Bicatalyst360° and a board member of 360° Nation, in London, England, about heart centered leadership. Garry "focuses on bringing intentional, human-centered working to all walks of life." In our discussion, Garry mentioned not only his work but related efforts by HumansFirst Club a "global group of leaders, influencers and collaborators voluntarily sharing a mission to inspire positive change, fueling growth, maturity, and sustainability through stories, experiences, and open dialogue. This inspiring consortium is centered on an exceptional belief in human capacity and potential." Here is a message from their website:

> Like-hearted people gather around the world to ignite this rapidly growing global community. All of us are acutely aware of the challenges we face—with significant evidence, that the current state-of-affairs is neither desirable, nor sustainable. At HumansFirst, we believe in you—each of you—as part of this solution. HumansFirst is a place to exercise our creativity, intuition, and innovation; a place to feed our curiosity, meet and build relationships with others from around the world—who share your passion for a better future.

Christine and Garry discussed their passion for kindness, compassion, and heart centered leadership and the synchronicity of connecting at this point, each determined to advance an agenda of caring, concern, and compassion.

Our fervent wish is that by the time this book is published, that COVID-19 will be a minor postscript to a larger script that humans have crafted—a script of love, with a sensitivity toward the needs and concerns of others, and a joy that many have not only survived, but have actually learned essential lessons that will shape our destiny.

Dialogue on Destiny With Garry Turner

 As I reflect on the challenges, fear, and loss of life but also the opportunities that may emerge post COVID19, I am thinking about what we, at an individual and systemic level, should take with us, what we should let go of and the opportunities that we should seize.

Ideas to bring with us:

- We are all human beings, living a collection of single moments.
- We are all connected and interdependent as part of one singular human race.

Concepts to let go of:

- We are divided and separate from one another.
- We must operate from only our head and with logic, suppressing emotion.
- Mass inequality is simply a fact of existence.
- A financial system that serves the few and not the many is the product of the hard work of those that contribute most to society.
- An education system that prizes being right over being better produces intelligent students.
- Being busy is a badge of honor, because it means I am contributing to society.

Opportunities to seize:

- Innovative, blended approaches to education and work through remote and in-person connections make learning and professional communities more accessible.
- Education and work designed to be more heart led, whilst still acknowledging the importance of our head, leads to increased compassion and ultimately better communication and collaboration.
- Introducing a new welfare system based on unconditional basic income, where people can do the work that moves them and not just the job that pays the most, would allow our society to put our time and efforts toward what we as a whole want to see in the world rather than what those few with money and power want to see.

- Increased activism and engagement of individuals and collectives, within societal systems hold governments to account.

- We can achieve and be so much more, at home, at work and in society, when we slow down and breathe.

My overarching hope post-COVID-19 is that we balance and amplify the importance of presence, connection, and innovation, while grounding all areas of our systems in love, courage, and growth.

Source: G. Turner, personal communication, May 2020.

Time for Reflection Allows for Visioning

While the global pandemic amplified many stressors and caused a sharp increase in mental health crises, it also alleviated select stressors for some. For example, morning commutes filled with frustrating traffic jams or anxiety-inducing, packed rush-hour subway cars were replaced with an extra hour to sleep or the chance to slowly sip our morning cup of tea over the paper, luxuries many reserved for the weekend or holidays. We must acknowledge that this new luxury was not distributed equally as many essential workers had an added level of stress to their morning commute as they contemplated whether the mask and gloves they wore would protect them from the virus as they did the work so many relied on them to do to get that tea bag, water, and electricity into the homes of those given extra moments of contemplation.

For those of us blessed with small pockets of time given back to us with the cancellation of social events, sports games, and travel time, we can show our gratitude to those with less free time during this crisis by using it wisely. Many of us are experiencing extreme levels of anxiety that are exacerbated by the messages that we should be using our time productively, completing projects, cleaning our entire domicile, or learning new skills. So many are using all of our energy to merely exist in the midst of the mental unrest that comes with months of uncertainty and lack of control. *Rather than ask that people try to do more during times of crisis, we ask that people consider doing differently.*

Reflecting mindfully on how we spent our time differently when most everything had to occur over the Internet can help us understand what we missed from our old life and what we didn't. Focusing on what we like more about this new normal can help inform our vision for the future. If we felt a wave of relief to see a cheer of joy from our child when they were told the rest of the basketball season was cancelled, who was it serving? Ask yourself and your family why you were going to practice twice a week and spending half of each weekend at games and what everyone would rather spend time doing.

Our Days, Our Lives

Annie Dillard, author of *The Writing Life*, says, "How we spend our days is of course how we spend our lives. What we do with this hour and that one is what we are doing." When we look at our calendars, our to-do lists, and our goals for our lives and our families' or our classrooms, are they reflecting the values we want to instill in our students' or children's lives? If what we want to teach children most is compassion, are we participating in activities that allow us to show kindness to one another like volunteering or visiting with older relatives? If what we want to teach is community, are we modeling what it is like to think and act beyond ourselves and our own needs? If we want to teach courage, are we acting in fear, operating on a model of scarcity, and bracing for impact—or not? We have an opportunity to think more deeply about who we are in the world and how we want this world to look moving forward. Our children are watching.

Quality Time as a Tool for Purpose

Our habits define us. What we do on a regular basis becomes a deep part of our self-identity. When we learn the habits of the adults who care for us as children, we often internalize these ways of doing as natural. Although you can teach an old dog new tricks, it takes much more effort and time than instilling good habits from a young age. If we're using our daily activities as opportunities for building positive habits, we'll not only help the children we serve develop positive life skills and personality traits, we'll also reinforce these ideas for ourselves.

We challenge you to look at your calendar and see what habits you are encouraging with the way you spend your hours.

> Are the things you do with others and yourself teaching your students or family to be more grateful, kind, loving, and attentive or are they *only* teaching them to be productive, competitive, and tough?

Although none of those last three values are negative—in fact, quite the opposite—many societies around the world have come to value individuals who can do it all, better than anyone else, without shedding a tear or breaking a sweat over members of a team who work together to achieve a compassionate solution that works for all. What kind of adult are you encouraging the youth in your life to become? Is the time you spend with them *truly* quality time, instilling the values our world needs to see to become a better place?

Quality Time and Self-Care

It is rapidly becoming apparent that we are in a time of survival, a time when our lives will be enhanced as we are using our brain cells to be mindful, to avoid the virus, and to increase our sense of well-being. As we focus on doom, or become careless, our physical and mental health suffers.

To be at our optimum now requires some consideration of how to stay on top of our game, mentally and physically. Our bodies will be more disease resistant if we are doing what we can to build our own sense of vitality. Our mental health will improve as we build a sense of calmness, gratitude, and hope. Physical exercise, eating right, and mindfulness are all tools to help us live with a healthier mindset and body. Taking time for yoga, reflection, meditation, and even focusing on the good, all can not only help us relax, but help our brains be better prepared for whatever uncertainties arise.

> Our mental health will improve as we build a sense of calmness, gratitude, and hope.

School Reflections

At CEI and PRCH, we have been visioning for many of the changes that are occurring long before COVID-19 ravaged the world. We, and many of the Pre-K-12 school leaders, university educators, and expert researchers we work with, have been bringing healing practices for school mental health responses to trauma to anyone who would listen. Now, at a time when we are all understanding all too well how trauma affects our ability to be well, much less learn, we have seen an exponential rise in interest in the materials we've been producing for years. Although CEI published a blog post, from which the paragraph below is excerpted, in January of 2020, before the world truly understood how devastating this virus would be to our way of life, our vision for the future of education is even more relevant as we look toward possible futures after COVID-19.

Visioning With Intention to Change the World by Inspiring the Next Generation of Leaders

What do great schools have in common? What sets a successful school apart from a struggling one? Our decades of work in the classroom, consulting with school leaders, and looking at the research base have led us to conclude that one of the defining characteristics of an exceptional school is a sense of purpose. *Driving that sense of purpose is always a group of dedicated and tireless educators. Behind those educators is a leader who understands how to inspire their team.* To be transformational, that school leader must have a vision for their school that has been informed by the school community (Asby, 2020 January).

> *A vision is not just a picture of what could be; it is an appeal to our better selves, a call to become something more.*
>
> –Rosabeth Moss Kanter (2001)

Rainbow Community School Vision for Online Learning

 One of the board members at the Center for Educational Improvement, Renee Owen, is also the executive director of the Rainbow Community School in Asheville, NC.

At Rainbow, when we were moving quickly into remote learning, we recognized that it was easy to focus on the logistics of remote learning. After all, everyone had a steep learning curve, and we had to learn quickly how to run the technology, and so forth. We were in an environment of fear, including fear around what online learning would look like.

Fortunately, we also recognized that we needed to step back for one moment to clarify how we would uphold our school's mission during remote learning. Thanks to our Dynamic Governance system of decision making, we engaged in a circle consent decision-making process to consider a vision statement of goals for online learning.

Below is what we developed and what the faculty circle approved. As soon as the vision was understood and shared by all, I could feel the tension in the room ease. Our vision for online learning gave teachers a groundedness in what was most important. The vision affirmed that connection, meaning, a love of learning, and well-being were our core values (just like when we are teaching in person). Although converting to remote learning wasn't easy, taking the time to create a shared vision took away a lot of the fear because there were fewer unknowns (because we all knew what we were aiming for). This inspired us and freed up emotional space for creativity. The online work our teachers have been doing is incredibly creative. Families have been immensely grateful for how well our remote learning program has helped the whole family.

Rainbow Community School Vision for Online Learning

Our vision to achieve our mission as we move to remote learning:

- To nurture authentic connections to the Rainbow community and our individual classrooms, despite physical isolation

- To continue to inspire a love of learning

- To encourage students and families in creating a daily and weekly rhythm that
  - highlights learning opportunities.
  - includes meaning and purpose.
  - fosters holistic well-being.

Thinking Big and Thinking Small: Setting the Stage for Success

Change happens when someone sees an opportunity for improvement and convinces other people that the hard work necessary to make things better will be worth the effort. In a school building, this person is often the principal; however, any educator—a school psychologist, a nurse, a classroom teacher, a paraprofessional—can take on the role of change agent. The first step on the journey to transformation is identifying what needs to be different. Often, those in charge can see clearly where improvements could made, but when the lens of a leader doesn't include the perspective of the entire group, the vision will be incomplete. Nel Noddings (2015), an educational philosopher and professor emerita at Stanford University, suggests that the future will see a shift away from quantifiable measures of performance. Instead, Noddings suggests that the new vision of schools will encompass all aspects of students' lives: intellectual, physical, moral, spiritual, social, vocational, aesthetic, and civic.

When visioning for success, leaders must think broadly of the big picture without forgetting about all the little details.

Sharing the Burden of the Weight of the World

The process of transforming your school into a compassionate community where everyone in the building is thriving, growing, and making a difference in their neighborhood and beyond can easily become overwhelming, if you're the only one steering the effort.

Luckily, every school has the most important resources needed for radical change: people who care. Many young people around the world are already demanding change. Swedish climate activist Greta Thunberg won't let us forget that the way we are treating our Earth will lead to disaster. Pakistani education activist Malala Yousafzai won't rest until the whole world agrees that girls deserve an education. Water conservation activist Autumn Peltier won't stand silent as oil companies pollute water supplies across the United States. These teenagers demand we take action now, because each of them has a unique vision built on lived experience.

When we embark on a visioning journey, we're not just raising test scores and lowering suspension rates; we're transforming the lives of children, adults, and entire communities. We're drawing out leaders who have been waiting in the shadows. We're giving young people, middle-aged

(Continued)

(Continued)

folks, and those in their golden years the opportunity to make their mark on the world and make it a better place in the process. In her book *Becoming* (2018), Michelle Obama repeated something she often heard her husband say to inspire people on the South Side of Chicago when he was a community organizer, "Do we settle for the world as it is, or do we work for the world as it should be?" (p. 118).

Reflections on Strengthening Mental Health and Well-Being

School leaders wishing to move their schools from stagnant to thriving *must* bring in voices to represent as many community stakeholders as possible, and students and families are essential voices in that process. The sooner in the process those voices are heard, the more inclusive of everyone's needs the vision will be. This will also make it much easier to recruit a group of peers committed to bringing the ideas you formed together into fruition. In addition, everyone involved is given an opportunity to exercise their leadership skills. When a heart centered leader models compassionate leadership, they give their colleagues a safe space to take risks and be creative as they cultivate their own leadership skills.

We are interconnected. Even as we socially distance, we are acutely aware of countries "opening back up," of the death rates in Italy and risks in Sweden. We are tuned into science and economics hour to hour as we hear from governors, researchers, and public health officials. We are seeing the greatness of lightning-quick transformations from auto to face shield and incubator production. Even as inequities are called out right now, others are calling for justice, reduction in disparities, and more kindness and compassion.

With a focus on trauma right now, we invite you to focus as well on healing: healing rifts, healing wounds, healing children, healing families, and healing yourself. As you do this, think not of shiny packages, checklists, regulations, and old habits. Think beyond small, to large.

Destiny? An unusual, not oft used, word. We challenge you to think of our children, to uplift teachers and schools, and consider individual well-being for all as foundational. Dream large, hope eternally, and do your part, in whatever way you can, to help us heal, thrive, and move forward into a realm of greater kindness, greater caring, and greater humanity. Now is the time to be great—not in a big, audacious, boastful way, but in the small, humble way of doing what's right. Doing what's right, one mindful step, one mindful breath, at a time. This is what is required for a brighter destiny and brighter future, for all.

References

Abbott, B. (2019, October 17). Youth suicide rate increased 56% in decade, CDC says. *The Wall Street Journal*. https://www.wsj.com/articles/youth-suicide -rate-rises-56-in-decade-cdc-says-11571284861

Abel, M., & Sewell, J. (1999). Stress and burnout in rural and urban secondary school teachers. *Journal of Educational Research, 92*, 287–293. https://doi .org/10.1080/00220679909597608

Abrams, A., Goyal, M., & Badolato, G. (2019). Racial disparities in pediatric mental health-related emergency department visits: A five-year multi-institutional study. *Pediatrics 144*(2). DOI: https://doi.org/10.1542/peds.144.2_MeetingAbstract.414

Access Pittsfield. (2020). Positive health and wellness: Episode 7. http://www .pittsfieldtv.net/CablecastPublicSite/search?channel=1&query=rivers%20 murphy

Achenbach, T. M., & Rescorla, L. A. (2001). *Manual for the ASEBA school-age forms and profiles*. University of Vermont, Research Center for Children, Youth, & Families

Adair, B. (2019). *The emotionally connected classroom: Wellness and the learning experience*. Corwin.

Adams, D., Shahrun, S., & Zainol, A. (2018). Transactional and transformational leadership: complementary or opposites? *Mastering Theories of Educational Leadership and Management*, 107–114.

Adams, J. M. (2013, June 21). *New push for mental health training for teachers and principals*. EdSource. https://edsource.org/2013/task-force -recommends-including-mental-health-training-in-teacher-credential/33503

Addis, S. (2020). *Trauma-skilled literacy: What's the connection?* EdWeb. https://home.edweb.net/webinar/differentiate20200123/

Adelman, H. S., & Taylor, L. (2010). *Mental health in schools: Engaging learners, preventing problems, and improving schools*. Corwin.

Adoption and Foster Care Analysis and Reporting System (AFCARS). (2019). *The AFCARS Report*, FY2018 data. U.S. Department of Health and Human Services, Administration for Children and Families, Administration on Children, Youth and Families, Children's Bureau.

Aguilar, E. (2018). *Onward: Cultivating emotional resilience in educators*. Wiley.

Alegria, M., Vallas, M., & Pumariega, A. J. (2010). Racial and ethnic disparities in pediatric mental health. *Child and Adolescent Psychiatric Clinics of North America*, *19*(4), 759–774. https://doi.org/10.1016/j.chc.2010.07.001

Al-Kenai, A., & Graham, J. R. (2016). Help-seeking: Traditional and modern ways of knowing, and insights for mental health practice. In M. M. Amer & G. H. Awad (Eds.), *Handbook of Arab American Psychology* (pp. 263–274). Routledge/Taylor & Francis Group.

Allegretto, S., & Mishel, L. (2018, September 5). *The teacher pay penalty has hit a new high*. Economic Policy Institute. https://www.epi.org/publication/teacher-pay-gap-2018/

Al-Mateen, C. S., & Rogers, K. M. (2018). Suicide among African-American and other African-origin youth. In *Suicide Among Diverse Youth*. Springer International Publishing AG.

Amador, A. (2019, November). *Comprehensive behavioral health model in the Boston Public Schools*. [PowerPoint slides; see related information at https://cbhmboston.com/.]

Amador, A. (2020). *Schools should be more proactive and preventive in helping students with behavioral issues. Committee for Children*. https://www.cfchildren.org/about-us/what-is-sel/andria-amador/

Amato, N. (2015, March 26). A lack of resources for many classrooms. *The New York Times*. https://www.nytimes.com/roomfordebate/2015/03/26/is-improving-schools-all-about-money/a-lack-of-resources-for-many-classrooms

American Academy of Child and Adolescent Psychiatry (AACAP). (n.d.). *What is child and adolescent psychiatry?* https://www.aacap.org/AACAP/Medical_Students_and_Residents/Medical_Students/What_is_Child_and_Adolescent_Psychiatry.aspx

American Academy of Child and Adolescent Psychiatry. (2017, July). *Talking to kids about mental illnesses*. https://www.aacap.org/AACAP/Families_and_Youth/Facts_for_Families/FFF-Guide/Talking-To-Kids-About-Mental-Illnesses-084.aspx

American Academy of Sleep Medicine. (2016, June 13). *Video game playing negatively influences adequate sleep and bedtimes: Over 67 percent of gamers reported missed sleep due to playing*. ScienceDaily. http://www.sciencedaily.com/releases/2016/06/160613144656.htm

American Federation of Teachers (AFT). (2017). *2017 educator quality of life survey*. https://www.aft.org/sites/default/files/2017_eqwl_survey_web.pdf

American Psychiatric Association. (2013). *Diagnostic and statistical manual of mental disorders (DSM-5®)*. American Psychiatric Pub.

American Psychiatric Association (APA). (2020). *Mental health 2020: A presidential initiative for mental health.* https://www.psychiatry.org/File%20 Library/Psychiatrists/Advocacy/Federal/Mental-Health-2020-A-Presidential -Initiative-for-Mental-Health.pdf

American Psychological Association (APA). (2011, January). *Stressed in America.* https://www.apa.org/monitor/2011/01/stressed-america

American Psychological Association (APA). (2018). *The road to resilience.* https://www.apa.org/topics/resilience

American School Counselor Association's (ASCA). (2015). The school counselor and student mental health.

Anderson, M., & Cardoza, K. (2016, August 31). *Mental health in schools: A hidden crisis affecting millions of students.* NPREd. https://www.npr.org/ sections/ed/2016/08/31/464727159/mental-health-in-schools-a-hidden-crisis -affecting-millions-of-students

Ansley, B. M., Meyers, J., McPhee, K., & Varjas, K. (2018, March 2). *The hidden threat of teacher stress.* The Conversation. http://theconversation.com/the -hidden-threat-of-teacher-stress-92676

Arenas, F. J. (2019). *A casebook of transformational and transactional leadership.* Routledge.

Arthur-Mensah, N., & Zimmerman, J. (2017). Changing through turbulent times– why adaptive leadership matters. *The Journal of Student Leadership, 1*(2), 1–13.

Asarnow, J. R., Babeva, K., & Horstmann, E. (2017). The emergency department: Challenges and opportunities for suicide prevention. *Child and Adolescent Psychiatric Clinics, 26*(4), 771–783.

Asby, D. (2019, October 15a). *School mental health screening part I: The benefits and cautions of universal mental health screening.* http://www .edimprovement.org/2019/10/part-i-the-benefits-and-cautions-of-universal -mental-health-screening/

Asby, D. (2019, October 15b). *School mental health screening part II: Trauma-informed recommendations.* Center for Educational Improvement. http://www .edimprovement.org/2019/10/part-ii-school-mental-health-screening-trauma -informed-recommendations/

Asby, D. (2019, November 11). *Featured fellow: Addressing trauma with Joan Cavallo, St. Albans City school principal.* Center for Educational Improvement.

http://www.edimprovement.org/2019/11/featured-fellow-addressing-trauma-with-joan-cavallo-st-albans-city-school-principal/

Asby, D. (2020, January 14). *Visioning with intention to change the world by inspiring the next generation of leaders*. Center for Educational Improvement. http://www.edimprovement.org/2020/01/visioning-with-intention-to-change-the-world-by-inspiring-the-next-generation-of-leaders/

Asby, D. (2020, April 3). *Part II: Five mindful habits for families and schools to increase happiness and connection – compassion, gratitude, and reflection.* Center for Educational Improvement. http://www.edimprovement.org/2020/04/__trashed/

Asby, D. (2020, April 4). *Featured fellow: Andrea Elliot – bringing compassion to New Hampshire high schoolers*. Center for Educational Improvement. http://www.edimprovement.org/2020/04/featured-fellow-andrea-elliot-bringing-compassion-to-new-hampshire-high-schoolers/

Asby, D., & Mason, D. (2020). *Heart centered learning focus groups*. New England Mental Health Technology Transfer Center.

Asby, D., & Rueda, D. (2018). S-CCATE: *A more effective classroom climate measurement tool*. Center for Educational Improvement. http://www.edimprovement.org/2018/12/s-ccate-measurement-tool/

Ashe, A. (2001). *Arthur Ashe quotes*. BrainyQuote. https://www.brainyquote.com/quotes/arthur_ashe_371527

Augustine, C. H., Engberg, J., Grimm, G. E., Lee, E., Wang, E. L., Christianson, K., & Joseph, A. A. (2018). *Can restorative practices improve school climate and curb suspensions? An evaluation of the impact of restorative practices in a mid-sized urban school district*. Santa Monica, CA: RAND Corporation. https://www.rand.org/pubs/research_reports/RR2840.html

Averill, O. H., Rinaldi, C., & Collaborative, U. S. E. L. (2011). Multi-tier system of supports (MTSS). *District Administration, 48*(8), 91-95. https://www.researchgate.net/profile/Claudia_Rinaldi/publication/257943832_Research_Brief_Multitier_System_of_Supports_MTSS_Urban_Special_Education_Leadership_Collaborative_From_RTI_and_PBIS_to_MTSS/links/00b7d52669fbe69ded000000.pdf

Baker, C. N., Brown, S. M., Wilcox, P. D., Overstreet, S., & Arora, P. (2016). Development and psychometric evaluation of the attitudes related to trauma-informed care (ARTIC) scale. *School Mental Health, 8*(1), 61-76. doi.org/10.1007/s12310-015-9161-0

Bakosh, L. S., Snow, R. M., Tobias, J. M., Houlihan, J. L., & Barbosa-Leiker, C. (2016). Maximizing mindful learning: Mindful awareness intervention improves elementary school students' quarterly grades. *Mindfulness, 7*(1), 59–67.

Barnard-Brak, L., & Shiu, W. (2010). Classroom Community Scale in the blended learning environment: A psychometric review. *International Journal on E-learning*, *9*(3), 303–311.

Baškarada, S., Watson, J., & Cromarty, J. (2017). Balancing transactional and transformational leadership. *International Journal of Organizational Analysis*, *25*(3), 506–515.

Bass, B.M. (2008). *The Bass handbook of leadership, theory, research, and managerial applications*. Free Press.

Bassuk, E. L., DeCandia, C. J., Beach, C. A., & Berman, F. (2014). *America's youngest outcasts: A report card on child homelessness*. American Institutes for Research.

BBC News. (2017, May 31). *"One in two" young online gamers bullied, report finds*. https://www.bbc.com/news/technology-40092541

Bear, G. G., Gaskins, C., Blank, J., & Chen, F. F. (2011). Delaware School Climate Survey—Student: Its factor structure, concurrent validity, and reliability. *Journal of School Psychology*, *49*(2), 157–174.

Beck, J.S., Beck, A.T., Jolly, J.B., & Steer, R.A. (2005). *Beck Youth Inventories second edition for children and adolescents manual*. PsychCorp.

Bell, L., & Bolam, R. (2010). Teacher professionalism and continuing professional development: Contested concepts and their implications for school leaders. In T. Bush, L. Bell, & D. Middlewood (Eds.), *The principles of educational leadership and management* (2nd edition), pp. 89–111. SAGE.

Berkowitz, R., Moore, H., Astor, R. A., & Benbenishty, R. (2017). A research synthesis of the associations between socioeconomic background, inequality, school climate, and academic achievement. *Review of Educational Research*, *87*(2), 425-469. doi:10.3102/0034654316669821

Bernstein, J. Y., & Watson, M. W. (1997). Children who are targets of bullying. *Journal of Interpersonal Violence, 12*(4), 483–498. doi: 10.1177/088626097012004001

Bimpong, M. (2017, April 30). Untreated mental illnesses: The causes and effects. *Princeton Public Health Review*. https://pphr.princeton.edu/2017/04/30/untreated-mental-illnesses-the-causes-and-effects/

Black, M. C., Basile, K. C., Breiding, M. J., Smith, S. G., Walters, M. L., Merrick, M. T., Chen, J., & Stevens, M. R. (2011). *The national intimate partner and sexual violence survey: 2010 summary report*. National Center for Injury Prevention and Control, Centers for Disease Control and Prevention.

Boston Children's Hospital Neighbor Program (BCHNP). (2017). *Break free from depression*. http://www.childrenshospital.org/Centers-and-Services/Programs/

A-_-E/boston-childrens-hospital-neighborhood-partnerships-program/break-free-from-depression-program

Bowen, E. A., & Murshid, N. S. (2016). Trauma-informed social policy: A conceptual framework for policy analysis and advocacy. *American Journal of Public Health, 106*(2), 223–229.

Boys Town. (n.d.). *History.* https://www.boystown.org/about/our-history/Pages/default.aspx

Brach, T. (2020, January 1). *RAIN: A practice of radical compassion.* https://www.tarabrach.com/rain-practice-radical-compassion/

Bradley, S., & Levin, K. (n.d.) *Understanding and addressing principal turnover.* National Association of Secondary School Principals and Learning Policy Associates.

Bradshaw, C. P., Debnam, K. J., Lindstrom Johnson, S., Pas, E. T., Hershfeldt, P., Alexander, A., Barrett, S., & Leaf, P. J. (2014). Maryland's evolving system of social, emotional, and behavioral interventions in public schools: The Maryland Safe and Supportive Schools Project. *Adolescent Psychiatry, 4*(3), 194–206.

Bradshaw, C. P., Waasdorp, T. E., Debnam, K. J., & Johnson, S. L. (2014). Measuring school climate in high schools: A focus on safety, engagement, and the environment. *Journal of School Health, 84*(9), 593–604.

Braun, G., Kumm, S., Brown, C., Walte, S., Hughes, M. T., & Maggin, D. M. (2018). Living in Tier 2: educators' perceptions of MTSS in urban schools. *International Journal of Inclusive Education,* 1–15.

Breslau, N., Koenen, K. C., Luo, Z., Agnew-Blais, J., Swanson, S., Houts, R. M., . . . & Moffitt, T. E. (2014). *Childhood maltreatment, juvenile disorders and adult post-traumatic stress disorder: a prospective investigation. Psychological medicine,* 44(9), 1937–1945. doi: 10.1017/S0033291713002651

Breslau, N., Peterson, E. L., Poisson, L. M., Schultz, L. R., & Lucia, V. C. (2004). Estimating post-traumatic stress disorder in the community: Lifetime perspective and the impact of typical traumatic events. *Psychological Medicine, 34*(5), 889–898.

Bridge J. A., Horowitz L. M., Fontanella C. A., Sheftall, A. H., Greenhouse, J., Kelleher, K. J., & Campo, J. V. (2018). Age-related racial disparity in suicide rates among US youths from 2001 through 2015. *JAMA Pediatrics, 172*(7):697–699. doi:10.1001/jamapediatrics.2018.0399

Brigham Young University. (2009, January 25). *Video games linked to poor relationships with friends, family.* ScienceDaily. http://www.sciencedaily.com/releases/2009/01/090123075000.htm

Brixval, C. S., Rayce, S. L., Rasmussen, M., Holstein, B. E., & Due, P. (2012). Overweight, body image and bullying—an epidemiological study of 11 to 15-years olds. *The European Journal of Public Health, 22*(1), 126-130.

Brody, G. H., Dorsey, S., Forehand, R., & Armistead, L. (2002). Unique and protective contributions of parenting and classroom processes to the adjustment of African American children living in single-parent families. *Child Development, 73*(1), 274–286. doi:10.1111/1467-8624.00405

Brofenbrenner, U. (1977). Toward an experimental ecology of human development. *American Psychologist, 32*(7), 513-31.

Brookline Center for Community Mental Health. (2018). *BRYT notes: Changing school culture to support mental health.* https://www.brooklinecenter.org/wp-content/uploads/2018/09/BRYTNotesReport_FromTheBrooklineCenter.pdf. Retrieved September 10, 2019.

Brookline Center for Community Mental Health (2019). *How BRYT works.* https://www.brooklinecenter.org/services/school-based-support/bryt-program/how-bridge-programs-work/ Retrieved September 10, 2019.

Brookline Center for Community Mental Health. (2020). *Welcome to BRYT: Bridge for resilient youth in transition.* https://www.brooklinecenter.org/services/school-based-support/bryt-program/

Brown, B. (2010, June). *The power of vulnerability.* TEDx. https://www.ted.com/talks/brene_brown_the_power_of_vulnerability?language=en

Brown, D. W., Anda, R. F., Tiemeier, H., Felitti, V. J., Edwards, V. J., Croft, J. B., & Giles, W. H. (2009). Adverse childhood experiences and the risk of premature mortality. *American Journal of Preventive Medicine, 37*(5), 389–396. doi:10.1016/j.amepre.2009.06.021

Brown, V., & Olson, K. (2014). *The mindful school leader: Practices to transform your leadership and school.* Corwin.

Bruhn, A. L., Woods-Groves, S., & Huddle, S. (2014). A preliminary investigation of emotional and behavioral screening practices in K–12 schools. *Education and Treatment of Children, 37*(4), 611–634.

Bryant, P., Butcher, J., & O'Connor, J. (2016). Improving school leadership: The connection of transformation leadership and psychological well-being of the followers. *School Leadership Review, 11*(2), 46–58.

Bunting, M. (2016). *The mindful leader: 7 practices for transforming your leadership, your organisation and your life.* Wiley.

Burch, K. (2018, January 25). *Principals: We need to talk about student mental health.* We Are Teachers. https://www.weareteachers.com/school-mental-health/

Burns, J.M. (1978). *Leadership.* Harper and Row.

Camera, L. (2019, April 29). Teacher salaries fell 4.5% over the last decade. *US News.* https://www.usnews.com/news/education-news/articles/2019-04-29/teacher-salaries-fell-45-over-the-last-decade

Canfield, J., & Hansen, M. V. (2012). *Chicken soup for the teenage soul: The real deal challenges: Stories about disses, losses, messes, stresses & more*. Simon and Schuster.

Castro, R.M. (2018, April 12). *Teachers can help reduce mental health problems in children, study finds*. MedicalXpress. https://medicalxpress.com/news/2018 -04-teachers-mental-health-problems-children.html

Centers for Disease Control and Prevention (CDC). (n.d). *Children's mental disorders*. https://www.cdc.gov/childrensmentalhealth/symptoms.html

Centers for Disease Control and Prevention (CDC). (2018, June 7). *Suicide rising across the US*. https://www.cdc.gov/vitalsigns/suicide/index.html

Centers for Disease Control and Prevention (CDC). (2020, March 23). *Coronavirus disease 2019 (COVID-19): Manage anxiety and stress*. https://www.cdc.gov/ coronavirus/2019-ncov/prepare/managing-stress-anxiety.html

Centers for Disease Control and Prevention (CDC). (2020a). *Stress and coping*. https://www.cdc.gov/coronavirus/2019-ncov/daily-life-coping/managing-stress -anxiety.html

Centers for Disease Control and Prevention (CDC). (2020b). *Symptoms and test-ing*. https://www.cdc.gov/coronavirus/2019-ncov/symptoms-testing/index.html

Center for Educational Improvement (2020, April). *Focus group on Heart Centered Learning*. Unpublished report.

Center for Mindfulness Studies. (2015). *Ending mental health stigma through mindfulness*. https://www.mindfulnessstudies.com/ending-mental-health -stigma-through-mindfulness/

Center on Positive Behavioral Intervention and Supports. (n.d). *What is PBIS?* https://www.pbis.org/

Chatterjee, R. (2019, November 5). *CDC: Childhood trauma is a public health issue and we can do more to prevent it*. NPR. https://www.npr.org/sections/ health-shots/2019/11/05/776550377/cdc-childhood-trauma-is-a-public-health -issue-and-we-can-do-more-prevent-it

Child Trends. (2019). *Key facts about foster care*. https://www.childtrends.org/ indicators/foster-care

Collaborative for Social and Emotional Learning (CASEL). (n.d.). *SEL and assessment*. https://casel.org/sel-assessment/

Collaborative for Social and Emotional Learning (CASEL). (2020). *What is social and emotional learning?* https://schoolguide.casel.org/what-is-sel/what-is-sel/

Committee on the Assessment of Ongoing Effects in the Treatment of Posttraumatic Stress Disorder; Institute of Medicine. (2012). *Treatment for posttraumatic stress disorder in military and veteran populations: Initial assessment*. National Academies Press.

Cooper, J. L., Masi, R., Dababnah, S., Aratani, Y., & Knitzer, J. (2007). *Strengthening policies to support children, youth, and families who experience trauma.* National Center for Children in Poverty. https://www.theannainstitute. org/SAMHSA%20Manual.pdf

Corbit, K. (2005). Inadequate and inappropriate mental health treatment and minority overrepresentation in the juvenile justice system. *Hastings Race & Poverty Law Journal, 3*(1), 75–94.

Courageous Conversation. (n.d.). *Courageous conversations about race.* https://courageousconversation.com/about/

Cuijpers, P., Weitz, E., Karyotaki, E., Garber, J., & Andersson, G. (2015). The effects of psychological treatment of maternal depression on children and parental functioning: A meta-analysis. *European Child & Adolescent Psychiatry, 24*(2), 237–245.

Crosby, S. D. (2016). Trauma-informed approaches to juvenile justice: A critical race perspective. *Juvenile and Family Court Journal, 67*(1), 5–18.

Daryanani, I., Hamilton, J. L., Abramson, L. Y., & Alloy, L. B. (2016). Single mother parenting and adolescent psychopathology. *Journal of Abnormal Child Psychology, 44*(7), 1411–1423.

Davidson, L. (2003). *Living outside mental illness: Qualitative studies of recovery in schizophrenia.* New York University Press.

Davidson, L., Tondora, J., Lawless, M. S., O'Connell, M. J., & Rowe, M. (2009). *A practical guide to recovery-oriented practice: Tools for transforming mental health care.* Oxford University Press.

Davidson, R. J., Kabat-Zinn, J., Schumacher, J., Rosenkranz, M., Muller, D., Santorelli, S. F., Urbanowski, F., Harrington, A., Bonus, K., & Sheridan, J. F. (2003). Alterations in brain and immune function produced by mindfulness meditation. *Psychosomatic Medicine, 65*(4), 564–570.

Dela Cruz, K. (2019, May 29). *LGBTQ youth mental health: A perpetual issue hidden in the shadows.* http://www.edimprovement.org/2019/05/lgbtq-youth -mental-health-a-perpetual-issue-hidden-in-the-shadows/

DePaoli, J. L., Atwell, M. N., & Bridgeland, J. (2017). *Ready to Lead: A national principal survey on how social and emotional learning can prepare children and transform schools.* Retrieved from https://files.eric.ed.gov/ fulltext/ED579088.pdf

Diehl, A. (2019, September 5). *The after-school restraint collapse: Helping your child overcome their emotional buildup from school.* Rice Psychology Group. https://ricepsychology.com/behavior/the-after-school-restraint-collapse-helping-your-child-overcome-their-emotional-buildup-from-school/

Dillard, A. (1989). Landmark essays on writing process. In A. Dillard, *The writing life* (pp. 212–220). Harper & Row.

Dillard, C. (2017). *Multi-tiered system of supports (MTSS) and implementation science.* California State University.

Doheny, K. (2020, May 6). *Gay blood donors: Eager to help, but face barriers.* https://www.webmd.com/lung/news/20200506/gay-blood-donors-eager-to-help-but-face-barriers

Donohoo, J. (2017). *Collective efficacy: How educator beliefs impact student learning.* Corwin.

DoSomething.org. (n.d.). *11 facts about cyberbullying.* https://www.dosomething.org/us/facts/11-facts-about-cyber-bullying

Dougherty, C. (2020, May 1). 31% can't pay the rent: "It's only going to get worse". *The New York Times.* https://www.nytimes.com/2020/04/08/business/economy/coronavirus-rent.html

Dreher, A. (2018, May 9). *How the wage gap affects single moms.* Jackson Free Press. https://www.jacksonfreepress.com/news/2018/may/09/how-wage-gap-affects-single-moms/

Dunin, D. (2019, September 14). *Understanding self-harm in students (Part I and II).* Center for Educational Improvement. http://www.edimprovement.org/2019/09/understanding-self-harm-in-students-part-1/

Durlak, J.A., & Mahoney, J.L. (2019, April 28). The practical benefits of an SEL program. CASEL.

Durlak, J. A., Weissberg, R. P., Dymnicki, A. B., Taylor, R. D., & Schellinger, K. B. (2011). The impact of enhancing students' social and emotional learning: A meta-analysis of school-based universal interventions. *Child Development, 82*(1), 405–432.

Eagle, J. W., Dowd-Eagle, S. E., Snyder, A., & Holtzman, E. G. (2015). Implementing a multi-tiered system of support (MTSS): Collaboration between school psychologists and administrators to promote systems-level change. *Journal of Educational and Psychological Consultation, 25*(2–3), 160–177.

Education Advisory Board (EAB). (2019). *Breaking bad behavior: The rise of classroom disruptions in early grades and how districts are responding.* http://pages.eab.com/rs/732-GKV-655/images/BreakingBadBehaviorStudy.pdf

Edwards, D., Evans, N., Gillen, E., Longo, M., Pryjmachuk, S., Trainor, G., & Hannigan, B. (2015). What do we know about the risks for young people moving into, through and out of inpatient mental health care? Findings from an evidence synthesis. *Child and Adolescent Psychiatry and Mental Health, 9*(1), 55.

Eilers, E. (2018). *How trauma-informed schools help every student succeed.* Crisis Prevention Institute. https://www.crisisprevention.com/Blog/Trauma-Informed-Schools

Elmore, R. F. (2004). *School reform from the inside out: Policy, practice, and performance*. Harvard Education Press.

Emerson, R. W. (2020). *Quotable quote*. GoodReads. https://www.goodreads .com/quotes/49592-the-secret-of-education-lies-in-respecting-the-pupil-it

Ercan, R., & Yaman, T. (2015). Human rights attitude scale: A validity and reliability study. *Journal of Education and Training Studies, 3*(6), 220–231.

Erikson, E. (2020). *Quotable quote*. GoodReads. https://www.goodreads.com/ quotes/209039-children-love-and-want-to-be-loved-and-they-very

Esfahani Smith, E. (2020, April 26). *The 4 pillars of meaning that will help us emerge from the pandemic better than before*. https://mariashriver.com/the -4-pillars-of-meaning-that-will-help-us-emerge-from-the-pandemic-better -than-before/

Espelage, D. L., Merrin, G. J., & Hatchel, T. (2018). Peer victimization and dating violence among LGBTQ youth: The impact of school violence and crime on mental health outcomes. *Youth Violence and Juvenile Justice, 16*(2), 156–173.

Evans, K.R., & Lester, J.N. (2013). Restorative justice in education: What we know so far. *Middle School Journal, 44*(5), 57-63. https://doi.org/10.1080/00 940771.2013.1146187

Evenson, L. (1997, February 2). Sunday interview - Seymour Papert. *SFGate*. https://www.sfgate.com/news/article/SUNDAY-INTERVIEW-Seymour -Papert-Computers-In-2856685.php

Every Town for Gun Safety. (n.d.). *Who we are*. https://everytown.org/who-we-are/

Fagan, C. (2019, December 4). *The impact of mass school shootings on the mental health of survivors: What parents need to know*. Psycom. https://www .psycom.net/mental-health-wellbeing/school-shooting-survivor-mental-health/

Fantuzzo, J., Sutton-Smith, B., Atkins, M., Meyers, R., Stevenson, H., Coolahan, K., Weiss, A., & Manz, P. (1996). Community-based resilient peer treatment of withdrawn maltreated preschool children. *Journal of Consulting and Clinical Psychology, 64*(6), 1377.

Faraz, N. A., Yanxia, C., Ahmed, F., Estifo, Z. G., & Raza, A. (2018). The influence of transactional leadership on innovative work behavior—a mediation model. *European Journal of Business and Social Sciences, 7*(01), 51–62.

Farrise, K. (2019, November 11). *National school mental health curriculum launched to help school districts support student mental health*. Center for Educational Improvement. http://www.edimprovement.org/2019/11/national -school-mental-health-curriculum-launched-to-help-school-districts-support -student-mental-health/

Feather, A. (2019, September 2). *State of mind: Teacher stress levels on the rise.* WWMT. https://wwmt.com/news/i-team/state-of-mind-teacher-stress-levels-on-the-rise

Felitti, V. J. (2019). Health appraisal and the Adverse Childhood Experiences study: National implications for health care, cost, and utilization. *The Permanente Journal, 23,* 18-026. doi:10.7812/TPP/18-026

Felitti, V. J., Anda, R. F., Nordenberg, D., Williamson, D. F., Spitz, A. M., Edwards, V., Koss, M. P., & Marks, J. S. (1998). Relationship of childhood abuse and household dysfunction to many of the leading causes of death in adults: The Adverse Childhood Experiences (ACE) Study. *American Journal of Preventive Medicine, 56*(6), 774–786.

Fernando, R. (2013). *Measuring the efficacy and sustainability of a mindfulness-based in-class intervention.* https://www.mindfulschools.org/wp-content/uploads/2019/10/Mindful-Schools-Study-Highlights.pdf

Feuer, V., Rocker, J., Saggu, B. M., Andrus, J. M., & Wormley, M. (2018). Best practices in managing child and adolescent behavioral health emergencies [digest]. *Pediatric Emergency Medicine Practice, 15*(1), 1–28.

Flemming, M., & Aronson, L. (2016). *The relationship between non-suicidal self-injury and child maltreatment.* Information Brief Series, Cornell Research Program on Self Injury and Recovery. Cornell University.

Flook, L., Goldberg, S. B., Pinger, L., Bonus, K., & Davidson, R. J. (2013). Mindfulness for teachers: A pilot study to assess effects on stress, burnout, and teaching efficacy. *Mind, Brain, and Education, 7*(3), 182–195. https://doi.org/10.1111/mbe.12026

Flook, L., Smalley, S. L., Kitil, M. J., Galla, B. M., Kaiser-Greenland, S., Locke, J., Ishijima, E., & Kasari, C. (2010). Effects of mindful awareness practices on executive functions in elementary school children. *Journal of Applied School Psychology, 26*(1), 70–95.

Foley, W. (2019, November 14). *Creating peace, healing trauma. Center for Educational Improvement.* http://www.edimprovement.org/2019/11/14/

Ford, M. (2015, June 8). America's largest mental hospital is a jail. *The Atlantic.* https://www.theatlantic.com/politics/archive/2015/06/americas-largest-mental-hospital-is-a-jail/395012/

Ford, J. D., & Courtois, C. A. (Eds.). (2013). *Treating complex traumatic stress disorders in children and adolescents: Scientific foundations and therapeutic models.* Guilford Press.

Fox, H. L. (2016). Reality and resiliency: The educational needs and strengths of former foster youth. *Office of Community College Research and Leadership, 2*(2).

Fox, M. (2018, November 2). *More kids are showing up in ERs with mental health crises*. NBC News. https://www.nbcnews.com/health/health-news/more -kids-are-showing-ers-mental-health-crises-n930506

Fox 12 Staff. (2019). *Ore. high schoolers push for bill allowing students to call in sick for mental health*. Fox 12 Oregon. https://www.kptv.com/news/ore-high-schoolers-push-for-bill-allowing-students-to-call/article_af8c435c-655b-11e9-8aa8-2bfe3679bc4c.html

Frame, S. (2020, March 17). *Washington woman, 106, who lived through 1918 Spanish flu shares coronavirus advice*. K5 News. https://www.king5.com/ article/news/local/106-year-old-washington-resident-lived-through-the-spanish -flu-of-1918/281-819e6bfb-c209-4bbd-9a52-529a2746c8c8

Franco, C., Mañas, I., Cangas, A. J., & Gallego, J. (2010, September). The applications of mindfulness with students of secondary school: Results on the academic performance, self-concept and anxiety. In *World Summit on Knowledge Society* (pp. 83-97). Springer International Publishing AG.

Frank, J. L., Bose, B., & Schrobenhauser-Clonan, A. (2014). Effectiveness of a school-based yoga program on adolescent mental health, stress coping strategies, and attitudes toward violence: Findings from a high-risk sample. *Journal of Applied School Psychology, 30*(1), 29–49.

Frank, J. L., Kohler, K., Peal, A., & Bose, B. (2016, October). Effectiveness of a school-based yoga program on adolescent mental health and school performance: Findings from a randomized controlled trial. *Mindfulness*, 1–10. doi: 10.1007/s12671-016-0628-3

Franzen, M., Keller, F., Brown, R. C., & Plener, P. L. (2019). Emergency presentations to child and adolescent psychiatry: Nonsuicidal self-injury and suicidality. *Frontiers in Psychiatry, 10*(979).

Fristad, M. A., Gavazzi, S. M., & Soldano, K. W. (1998). Multi-family psychoeducation groups for childhood mood disorders: A program description and preliminary efficacy data. *Contemporary Family Therapy, 20*(3), 385–402.

Fristad, M. A., Goldberg-Arnold, J. S., & Gavazzi, S. M. (2003). Multi-family psychoeducation groups in the treatment of children with mood disorders. *Journal of Marital and Family Therapy, 29*(4), 491–504.

Fryers, T., & Brugha, T. (2013). Childhood determinants of adult psychiatric disorder. *Clinical Practice and Epidemiology in Mental Health, 9*, Article 1–50. https://doi.org/10.2174/1745017901309010001

Fuller, D. A., Lamb, H. R., Biasotti, M., & Snook, J. (2015, December). Overlooked in the undercounted: The role of mental illness in fatal law enforcement encounters. *Office of Research and Public Affairs*. https://www.treatment

advocacycenter.org/storage/documents/overlooked-in-the-undercounted
.pdf

Gagnon, D. J., & Mattingly, M.J. (2016). *Most U.S. school districts have low access to school counselors: Poor, diverse, and city school districts exhibit particularly high student-to-counselor ratios.* University of New Hampshire, Carsey School of Public Policy. https://scholars.unh.edu/cgi/viewcontent.cgi?article=1285&context=carsey

Gallego, J., Aguilar-Parra, J. M., Cangas, A. J., Langer, Á. I., & Mañas, I. (2014). Effect of a mindfulness program on stress, anxiety and depression in university students. *The Spanish Journal of Psychology, 17*(109), 1–6. doi:10.1017/sjp.2014.102

Gilbert, P. (Ed.). (2005). *Compassion: Conceptualisations, research and use in psychotherapy.* Routledge.

Gillis. M. E. (2019, September 21). *Cyberbullying on rise in US: 12-year-old was "all-American little girl" before suicide.* Fox News. https://www.foxnews.com/health/cyberbullying-all-american-little-girl-suicide

Gleeson, J. P., Hsieh, C. M., & Cryer-Coupet, Q. (2016). Social support, family competence, and informal kinship caregiver parenting stress: The mediating and moderating effects of family resources. *Children and Youth Services Review, 67,* 32–42.

Gluck, S. (2019, June 21). *Self injury, self harm statistics and facts.* HealthyPlace. https://www.healthyplace.com/abuse/self-injury/self-injury-self-harm-statistics-and-facts

Goldston, D. B., Molock, S. D., Whitbeck, L. B., Murakami, J. L., Zayas, L. H., & Hall, G. C. N. (2008). Cultural considerations in adolescent suicide prevention and psychosocial treatment. *American Psychologist, 63*(1), 14.

Goleman, D., & Boyatzis, R. (2008). Social intelligence and the biology of leadership. *Harvard Business Review, 86*(9), 74–81.

Goleman, D., Boyatzis, R. E., & McKee, A. (2002). *The new leaders: Transforming the art of leadership into the science of results.* Little Brown.

Goleman, D., Boyatzis, R. E., & McKee, A. (2013). Primal leadership: Unleashing the power of emotional intelligence. Harvard Business Press.

Goleman, D., & Senge, P. (2014). *The triple focus: A new approach to education.* More Than Sound.

Government of Ireland: Department of Education and Skills. (2019, October). *Wellbeing policy statement and framework for practice.* https://www.education.ie/en/Schools-Colleges/Information/wellbeingineducation/

Grant, A. (2014, March 17). *Why girls get called bossy, and how to avoid it.* https://www.psychologytoday.com/intl/blog/give-and-take/201403/why-girls-get-called-bossy-and-how-avoid-it

Grant, S., Hamilton, L. S., Wrabel, S. L., Gomez, C. J., Whitaker, A., Leschitz, J. T., & Harris, M. G. (2017). *Social and emotional learning interventions under the Every Student Succeeds Act: Evidence review. Research report.* (RR-2133-WF). Santa Monica, CA: https://eric.ed.gov/?id=ED581645

Green, H. (2017, September 26). *Help for parents of teens who attempt suicide.* How to Adult. https://howtoadult.com/parents-teens-attempt-suicide-6826.html

Greenberg, M. (2018, September 29). How PTSD and trauma affect your brain functioning. *Psychology Today.* https://www.psychologytoday.com/us/blog/the-mindful-self-express/201809/how-ptsd-and-trauma-affect-your-brain-functioning

Gregory, A., & Clawson, K. (2016). The potential of restorative approaches to discipline for narrowing racial and gender disparities. In R.J. Skiba, K. Mediratta, & M.K. Rausch (Eds.), *Inequality in school discipline: Research and practice to reduce disparities* (pp. 153–170). Palgrave MacMillan.

Gregory, A., & Evans, K.R. (2020). *The starts and stumbles of restorative justice in education: Where do we go from here?* National Education Policy Center. http://nepc.colorado.edu/publication/restorative-justice

Guan, K., Fox, K. R., & Prinstein, M. J. (2012). Nonsuicidal self-injury as a time-invariant predictor of adolescent suicide ideation and attempts in a diverse community sample. *Journal of Consulting and Clinical Psychology, 80*(5), 842–849.

Guo, P., Choe, J., & Higgins-D'Alessandro, A. (2011). *Report of construct validity and internal consistency findings for the comprehensive school climate inventory.* Fordham University. https://safesupportivelearning.ed.gov/survey/comprehensive-school-climate-inventory

Haas, A. P., Eliason, M., Mays, V. M., Mathy, R. M., Cochran, S. D., D'Augelli, A. R., Silverman, M. M., Fisher P. W., Hughes, T., Rosario, M., Russell, S. T., Malley, E., Reed, J., Litts, D. A., Haller, E., Sell, R. L., Remafedi, G., Bradford, J., Beautrais, A. L., . . . Clayton, P. J. (2011). Suicide and suicide risk in lesbian, gay, bisexual, and transgender populations: review and recommendations. *Journal of Homosexuality, 58*(1), 10–51. http://doi.org/10.1080/00918369.2011.534038

Hair, N. L., Hansen, J. L., Wolfe, B. L., & Pollack S. D. (2015). Association of child poverty, brain development, and academic achievement. *JAMA Pediatrics, 169*(9), 822–829. doi:10.1001/jamapediatrics.2015.1475

Hallinger, P. (2003). Leading educational change: Reflections on the practice of instructional and transformational leadership. *Cambridge Journal of Education, 33*(3), 329–352.

Hameed, S., Sadiq, A., & Din, A. U. (2018). The increased vulnerability of refugee population to mental health disorders. *Kansas Journal of Medicine, 11*(1), 1–12.

Hammond, Z. (2014). *Culturally responsive teaching and the brain: Promoting authentic engagement and rigor among culturally and linguistically diverse students.* Corwin.

Handle With Care. (n.d.). *Overview.* https://handlewithcare.com/

Hanson, R., (2013). *Hardwiring happiness: The new brain science of contentment, calm, and confidence.* Harmony.

Hanson, R., & Hanson, F. (2020). *Resilient: How to grow an unshakable core of calm, strength, and happiness.* Harmony.

Hanson, T., & Voight, A. (2014). The appropriateness of a California student and staff survey for measuring middle school climate. *National Center for Education Evaluation (NCES).* http://files.eric.ed.gov/fulltext/ED546900.pdf

Hartas, D. (2019). Assessing the foundational studies on adverse childhood experiences. *Social Policy and Society, 18*(3), 435–443. doi:10.1017/S1474746419000034

Harvard Center on the Developing Child. (2017). *Three principles to improve outcomes for children and families.* https://developingchild.harvard.edu/resources/three-early-childhood-development-principles-improve-child-family-outcomes/#responsive-relationships

Hashim, A., Strunk, K., & Dhaliwal, T. (2018). Justice for all? Suspension bans and restorative justice programs in the Los Angeles Unified School District. *Peabody Journal of Education, 93*(2), 174–89. https://doi.org/10.1080/0161956X.2018.1435040

Hawkley, L. C., & Capitanio, J. P. (2015). Perceived social isolation, evolutionary fitness and health outcomes: A lifespan approach. *Philosophical Transactions of the Royal Society B: Biological Sciences, 370*(1669), doi/10.1098/rstb.2014.0114.

Hebert, L., Peterson, K., & Dunsmore, K. (2019). *A leader's guide to trauma-sensitive schools and whole-child literacy.* NORC University of Chicago Leadership Organization Capacity Initiative. https://partnership4resilience.org/wp-content/uploads/2019/05/Publisher_SEL-White-Paper_v2.pdf

HealthEngine. (2010, April 9). Balancing working and parenting. https://healthengine.com.au/info/balancing-working-and-parenting

Health Resources and Services Administration. (n.d.). The "loneliness epidemic." https://www.hrsa.gov/enews/past-issues/2019/january-17/loneliness-epidemic

Hill, R.A. (2020). Wraparound: A key component of school-wide culture competence to support academics and socio-emotional well-being. Peabody *Journal of Education. 95*(1): 66–72.

Hillier, A., & Torg, E. (2019). Parent participation in a support group for families with transgender and gender-nonconforming children: "Being in the company of others who do not question the reality of our experience." *Transgender Health*, *4*(1), 168–175.

Hollar, M. (2001). The impact of racism on the delivery of healthcare and mental health services. *Psychological Quarterly*, *72*(4), 337

Holm-Hadulla, R. M., & Koutsoukou-Argyraki, A. (2015). Mental health of students in a globalized world: Prevalence of complaints and disorders, methods and effectivity of counseling, structure of mental health services for students. *Mental Health & Prevention*, *3*(1–2), 1-4. http://dx.doi.org/10.1016/j.mhp.2015.04.003

Horowitz, J. L., & Garber, J. (2006). The prevention of depressive symptoms in children and adolescents: A meta-analytic review. *Journal of Consulting and Clinical Psychology, 74*(3), 401.

HumansFirst.club. (2018). Opening hearts and multiplying impact. https://humansfirst.club/

Individuals with Disabilities Education Act (IDEA). Section 1401(3). https://sites.ed.gov/idea/statute-chapter-33/subchapter-i/1401/3

Individuals with Disabilities Education Act. (2004). https://sites.ed.gov/idea/

Jackson, Y. (2015). *The pedagogy of confidence: Inspiring high intellectual performance in urban schools*. Teachers College Press.

Jain, S., Bassey, H., Brown, M.A., & Karla, P. (2014). *Restorative justice in Oakland schools. Implementation and impact: An effective strategy to reduce racially disproportionate discipline, suspensions, and improve academic outcomes*. Data in Action. https://www.ousd.org/cms/lib/CA01001176/Centricity/Domain/134/OUSD-RJ%20Report%20revised%20Final.pdf

Jennings, P. A., Frank, J. L., Snowberg, K. E., Coccia, M. A., & Greenberg, M. T. (2013). Improving classroom learning environments by cultivating awareness and resilience in education (CARE): Results of a randomized controlled trial. *School Psychology Quarterly*, *28*(4), 374.

Jeong, S. (2011). *Long-term effects of restorative justice conferencing on future criminality: The Indianapolis experiment*. Michigan State University.

Johnson, B., & Stevens, J. J. (2006). Student achievement and elementary teachers' perceptions of school climate. *Learning Environments Research*, *9*(2), 111–122.

Johnson, S. R. (2016, December 31). Demand for mental health services soars amid provider shortage. https://www.modernhealthcare.com/article/20161231/TRANSFORMATION03/161229942/demand-for-mental-health-services-soars-amid-provider-shortage

Kabat-Zinn, J. (2012). *Mindfulness for beginners:* Explore the infinite potential that lies within this very moment. Sounds True. https://www.soundstrue.com/products/mindfulness-for-beginners

Kalb, L. G., Stapp, E. K., Ballard, E. D., Holingue, C., Keefer, A., & Riley, A. (2019). Trends in psychiatric emergency department visits among youth and young adults in the US. *Pediatrics*, *143*(4).

Kanter, R. M. (2001). Rosabeth Moss Kanter quotes. *BrainyQuote*. https://www.brainyquote.com/quotes/rosabeth_moss_kanter_390507

Kark, R., Van Dijk, D., & Vashdi, D. R. (2018). Motivated or demotivated to be creative: The role of self-regulatory focus in transformational and transactional leadership processes. *Applied Psychology*, *67*(1), 186–224.

Karr-Morse, R., Felitti, V., & Wiley, M. S. (2013). *Ghosts from the nursery: Tracing the roots of violence* (Revised and updated. ed.). The Atlantic Monthly Press. https://groveatlantic.com/book/ghosts-from-the-nursery/

Keating, D. P. (2017, August 15). Dealing with stress at school in an age of anxiety. *Psychology Today.* https://www.psychologytoday.com/us/blog/stressful-lives/201708/dealing-stress-school-in-age-anxiety

Kennedy, C. M. (2018). *Principal leadership of Tier 3 school-wide positive behavior interventions and supports.* (Dissertation). University of New England. https://dune.une.edu/cgi/viewcontent.cgi?referer=https://scholar.google.com/&httpsredir=1&article=1152&context=theses

Kessler, R. C., & Bromet, E. J. (2013). *The epidemiology of depression across cultures. Annual Review of Public Health*, 34, 119-138.

Kim-Cohen, J., Caspi, A., Moffitt, T. E., Harrington, H., Milne, B. J., & Poulton, R. (2003). Prior juvenile diagnoses in adults with mental disorder: Developmental follow-back of a prospective-longitudinal cohort. *Archives of General Psychiatry*, *60*(7), 709–717.

King, C. A., Arango, A., & Foster, C. E. (2018). Emerging trends in adolescent suicide prevention research. *Current Opinion in Psychology*, *22*, 89–94.

Kinsella, S. (2014). *Finding Audrey*. Delacorte Press.

Knight, D., & Wadhwa, A. (2014). Expanding opportunity through critical restorative justice: Portraits of resilience at the individual and school level. *Schools*, *11*(1), 11–33.

Kohl, D., Recchia, S., & Steffgen, G. (2013). Measuring school climate: An overview of measurement scales. *Educational Research*, *55*(4), 411–426.

Kokkinos, C.M. (2007). Job stressors, personality and burnout in primary school teachers. *British Journal of Educational Psychology*, *77*, 229–243. https://doi.org/10.1348/000709905X90344

Kotter, J. P. (1996). *Leading change*. Harvard Business School Press.

Lai, A. (2011). Transformational-transactional leadership theory. 2011 AHS Capstone Projects. Paper 17. https://www.academia.edu/11691701/ Transformational_Transactional_Leadership_Theory

Lander, J. (2018, September 26). *Helping teachers manage the weight of trauma.* Harvard Graduate School of Education. https://www.gse.harvard.edu/ news/uk/18/09/helping-teachers-manage-weight-trauma

Lantieri, L., Nambiar, M., Harnett, S., Kyse, E.N. (2016) Cultivating inner resil- ience in educators and atudents: The Inner Resilience Program. In K. Schonert- Reichl, R. Roeser (eds.) *Handbook of mindfulness in education.* Springer International Publishing AG.

Laye-Gindhu, A., & Schonert-Reichl, K. A. (2005). Nonsuicidal self-harm among community adolescents: Understanding the "whats" and "whys" of self-harm. *Journal of Youth and Adolescence, 34*(5), 447–457.

Leavey, J. E. (2015). *Living recovery: Youth speak out on "owning" mental illness.* Wilfrid Laurier University Press.

Ledbetter, J. (2018, April 8). *Restorative justice: Preschool style.* Stories from school. http://www.storiesfromschoolaz.org/restorative-justice-preschool-style/

Lee, J. (2020). Mental health effects of school closures during COVID-19. *Child & Adolescent Health.* https://doi.org/10.1016/S2352-4642(20)30109-7

Lerner, D., Adler, D. A., Rogers, W. H., Lapitsky, L., McLaughlin, T., & Reed, J. (2010). Work performance of employees with depression: The impact of work stressors. *American Journal of Health Promotion, 24*(3), 205–213. https://dx .doi.org/10.4278%2Fajhp.090313-QUAN-103

Lima, N. N. R., Do Nascimento, V. B., De Carvalho, S. M. F., De Abreu, L. C., Neto, M. L. R., Brasil, A. Q., ... & Reis, A. O. A. (2013). Childhood depression: A systematic review. *Neuropsychiatric Disease and Treatment, 9,* 1417.

Liu, Y., Carney, J. V., Kim, H., Hazler, R. J., & Guo, X. (2020). Victimization and students' psychological well-being: The mediating roles of hope and school connectedness. *Children and Youth Services Review, 108.* doi:10.1016/ j.childyouth.2019.104674

Longhi, D., Brown, M., Barila, T., Reed, S. F., & Porter, L. (2019). How to increase community-wide resilience and decrease inequalities due to adverse childhood expe- riences (ACEs): Strategies from Walla Walla, Washington. *Journal of Prevention and Intervention in the Community.* doi:10.1080/10852352.2019.1633071

Lorenzo, A., & Poulisse, A. (2020, February 21). School shooting drills, lockdowns affect students' mental health, Osceola County school board member says. *WFTV.* https://www.wftv.com/news/local/osceola-county/school-shooting-drills -lockdowns-affect-students-mental-health-osceola-county-school-board -member-says/CXCAQNHXIZFOBM74AG7BH4XMMU/

Macklem, G. L. (2014). *Preventive mental health at school, evidence-based services for students*. Springer International Publishing AG.

MacNeil, A. J., Prater, D. L., & Busch, S. (2008). The effects of school culture and climate on student achievement. *International Journal of Leadership in Education*, *12*(1), 73–84.

MacNeill, N., Silcox, S., & Boyd, R. (2018). Transformational and transactional leadership: A false dichotomy of leadership in schools. *Education Today*, 10–12.

Madjar, N., Shabat, S. B., Elia, R., Fellner, N., Rehavi, M., Rubin, S. E., Segal, N., & Shoval, G. (2017). Non-suicidal self-injury within the school context: Multilevel analysis of teachers' support and peer climate. *European Psychiatry*, *41*, 95-101.

Magnuson, K., & Schindler, H.S. (2016). Parent programs in pre-k through third grade. *Future of Children*, *26* (2), 209–221.

Mahfouz, J. (2018a). Mindfulness training for school administrators: Effects on well-being and leadership. *Journal of Educational Administration*, *56*(6), 602–619. https://doi.org/10.1108/JEA-12-2017-0171

Mahfouz, J. (2018b). Principals and stress: Few coping strategies for abundant stressors. *Educational Management Administration & Leadership*, *48*(3), 440–458. https://doi.org/10.1177/1741143218817562

Mahon, M. A., Mee, L., Brett, D., & Dowling, M. (2017). Nurses' perceived stress and compassion following a mindfulness meditation and self compassion training. *Journal of Research in Nursing*, *22*(8), 572–583.

Martins, C. & Gaffan, E. A. (2000). Effects of early maternal depression on patterns of infant-mother attachment: A meta-analytic investigation. *Journal of Child Psychology and Psychiatry, 41*(6), 737–746.

Maslow, A. (1968). Some educational implications of the humanistic psychologies. *Harvard Educational Review, 38*(4), 685–696.

Mason, C. (2020, January 14). *Destiny, education, and next steps to address mental health challenges*. Center for Educational Improvement. http://www.edimprovement.org/ 2020/01/destiny-education-and-next-steps-to-address-mental-health-challenges/

Mason, C., Asby, D., Dunin, D., & Staeheli, M. (2020, May). Stress, school, and self-care: COVID-19 highlights inequities, mental health challenges, systemic needs, and possible solutions. *A Childhood Trauma Collaborative Issue Brief*. https://mhttcnetwork.org/centers/new-england-mhttc/product/c-tlc-stress-school-and-self-care-covid-19-highlights-inequities

Mason, C., Liabenow, P., & Patschke, M. (2020). *Visioning onward: A guide for ALL schools*. Corwin.

Mason, C., Rivers Murphy, M., Bergey, M., Sawilowsky, S., Mullane, S., & Asby, D. (2018). *School compassionate culture analytic tool for educators (S-CCATE) and*

S-CCATE supplement user manual, instrument development, psychometrics.
https://www.s-ccate.org/static/media/manual.782a06fb.pdf

Mason, C., Rivers Murphy, M., & Jackson, Y. (2019). *Mindfulness practices: Cultivating heart centered communities where students thrive and flourish.* Solution Tree. https://www.solutiontree.com/mindfulness-practices.html

Mason, C., Rivers Murphy, M. M., & Jackson, Y. (2020). *Mindful school communities: The five Cs of nurturing heart centered learning.* Solution Tree Press.

Massachusetts Department of Elementary and Secondary Education. (2016). *Educator effectiveness guidebook for inclusive practice.* Retrieved April 30, 2019.

Massachusetts Department of Elementary and Secondary Education (2018). *Multi-tiered system of support: Blueprint for MA.* Retrieved April 30, 2019.

May, R. (1999). *Freedom and destiny.* W.W. Norton & Company.

Mazza, J. J., Dexter-Mazza, E. T., Miller, A. L., Rathus, J. H., & Murphy, H. E. (2016). *DBT? Skills in schools: Skills training for emotional problem solving for adolescents (DBT Steps-A).* Guilford Press.

McBride, R. S. (2020). A literature review of the secondary school experiences of trans youth. *Journal of LGBT Youth*, 1–32.

McClelland, M. M., Acock, A. C., & Morrison, F. J. (2006). The impact of kindergarten learning-related skills on academic trajectories at the end of elementary school. *Early Childhood Research Quarterly, 21*(4), 471–490. doi:10.1016/j.ecresq.2006.09.003

McCloud, C. (2016). *Have you filled a bucket today.* Bucket Fillosophy. www.bucketfillers101.com

McDougal, J., Bardos, A., & Meier, S. (2011). *Behavioral intervention monitoring and assessment system (BIMAS).* Multi-Health Systems.

McGah, J., & Saavedra, E. (2015, December). *Homelessness and education cross-system collaboration: Applied research summary and tools.* National Center for Homeless Education. https://nche.ed.gov/wp-content/uploads/2018/11/res-summ-cross-system.pdf

McGoey, K.E., Rispoli, K.M., Venesky, L.G., Schaffner, K.F., McGuirk, L., & Marshall, S. (2014). A preliminary investigation into teacher perceptions of the barriers to behavior intervention implementation. *Journal of Applied School Psychology, 30* (4), 375–390. https://doi.org/10.1080/15377903.2014.950441

McGuire, T. G., & Miranda, J. (2008). New evidence regarding racial and ethnic disparities in mental health: Policy implications. *Health Affairs, 27*(2), 393–403. https://doi.org/10.1377/hlthaff.27.2.39

McInerney, M., & McKlindon, A. (2014, December). *Unlocking the door to learning: Trauma-informed classrooms and transformational schools.* Education

Law Center. https://www.elc-pa.org/wp-content/uploads/2015/06/Trauma-Informed-in-Schools-Classrooms-FINAL-December2014-2.pdf

McKinney-Vento Homeless Assistance Act. (Reauthorized 2015, December). https://uscode.house.gov/view.xhtml?path=/prelim@title42/chapter119/subchapter6/partB&edition=prelim

Meador, D. (2019, January 29). *How principals can provide teacher support.* *ThoughtCo.* https://www.thoughtco.com/suggestions-for-principals-to-provide-teacher-support-3194528

Meadows, K. (2016, December 9). *From one parent to another: How to help your child.* National Alliance on Mental Illness. https://www.nami.org/Blogs/NAMI-Blog/December-2016/From-One-Parent-to-Another-How-to-Help-Your-Child

Mechammil, M., Boghosian, S., & Cruz, R. A. (2019). Mental health attitudes among Middle Eastern/North African individuals in the United States. *Mental Health, Religion & Culture, 22*(7), 724–737. https://doi.org/10.1080/13674676.2019.1644302

Meckler, L. (2019, February 25). Report finds $23 billion racial funding gap for schools. *The Washington Post.* https://www.washingtonpost.com/local/education/report-finds-23-billion-racial-funding-gap-for-schools/2019/02/25/d562b704-3915-11e9-a06c-3ec8ed509d15_story.html

Menas, A. (2018, May 2). The widening mental health treatment gap in schools. *NEA News.* https://www.nea.org/advocating-for-change/new-from-nea/widening-mental-health-treatment-gap-schools

Mental Health Technology Transfer Center (MHTTC). (2019, April 2). *After a school tragedy . . . readiness, response, recovery, and resources.* https://mhttcnetwork.org/centers/mhttc-network-coordinating-office/product/after-school-tragedyreadiness-response-recovery

Mental Health Technology Transfer Center (MHTTC). (2020). *School mental health initiative: Childhood-Trauma Learning Collaborative.* https://mhttcnetwork.org/centers/new-england-mhttc/school-mental-health-initiative-childhood-trauma-learning-collaborative

Mental Health Technology Transfer Center (MHTTC). (2020, January 14). *Supporting student mental health: Resources to prepare educators.* https://mhttcnetwork.org/centers/mhttc-network-coordinating-office/supporting-student-mental-health

Meredith, J., & Anderson, L. (2015). *Analysis of the impacts of city year's whole school whole child model on partner schools' performance.* Policy Study Associates. https://www.cityyear.org/wp-content/uploads/2019/10/PSAstudy2015.pdf

Metzl, J. M., & Roberts, D. E. (2014). Structural competency meets structural racism: Race, politics, and the structure of medical knowledge. *The Virtual Mentor, 16*(9), 674–690. doi:10.1001/virtualmentor.2014.16.09.spec1-1409

Milaniak, I., & Widom, C. S. (2015). Does child abuse and neglect increase risk for perpetration of violence inside and outside the home? *Psychology of Violence, 5*(3), 246–255. doi:10.1037/a0037956

Miller, D. N. (2018). Suicidal behavior in children: Issues and implications for elementary schools. *Contemporary School Psychology*, 1-10.

MindWise. (2020). *Suicide prevention programs overview*. https://www.mind wise.org/what-we-offer/suicide-prevention-programs/

Minero, E. (2017, October 4). When students are traumatized, teachers are too. *Edutopia*. https://www.edutopia.org/article/when-students-are-traumatized -teachers-are-too

Mohatt, D. (2018, May). Mental health and rural America: Challenges and opportunities. National Institute of Mental Health Office for Research on Disparities and Global Mental Health 2018 webinar series. https://www.nimh.nih .gov/news/media/2018/mental-health-and-rural-america-challenges-and-opportunities.shtml

Montoya, S. (2018, October 1). *New data reveal that poor youth are among the most vulnerable to bullying*. Global Partnership for Education. https://www .globalpartnership.org/blog/new-data-reveal-poor-youth-are-among-most -vulnerable-bullying

Moon, J., Williford, A., & Mendenhall, A. (2017). Educators' perceptions of youth mental health: Implications for training and the promotion of mental health services in schools. *Children and Youth Services Review, 73*, 384–391.

Morgan, P. L., Staff, J., Hillemeier, M. M., Farkas, G., & Maczuga, S. (2013). Racial and ethnic disparities in ADHD diagnosis from kindergarten to eighth grade. *Pediatrics, 132*(1), 85–93. doi:https://doi.org/10.1542/peds.2012-2390

Morrison, N. (2019, June 27). Number of teachers quitting the classroom after just one year hits all-time high. *Forbes*. https://www.forbes.com/sites/ nickmorrison/2019/06/27/number-of-teachers-quitting-the-classroom-after -just-one-year-hits-all-time-high/#496eb11f60e5

Murphy, D., Bandy, T., Schimtz, H., & Moore, K. A. (2013, December). Caring adults: Important for positive child well-being. *ChildTrends*.

National Alliance on Mental Illness (NAMI). (n.d.). *Mental health facts: Children and teens*. https://www.nami.org/nami/media/nami-media/infographics/ children-mh-facts-nami.pdf

National Alliance on Mental Illness (NAMI). (2018). *Navigating a mental health crisis.* https://www.nami.org/About-NAMI/Publications-Reports/Guides/Navigating-a-Mental-Health-Crisis/Navigating-A-Mental-Health-Crisis.pdf?utm_source=website&utm_medium=cta&utm_campaign=crisisguide

National Alliance on Mental Illness (NAMI). (2020a). *Getting treatment during a crisis.* https://www.nami.org/Learn-More/Treatment/Getting-Treatment-During-a-Crisis

National Alliance on Mental Illness (NAMI). (2020b). Say it out loud. https://www.nami.org/Extranet/Education,-Training-and-Outreach-Programs/Outreach-and-Advocacy/Say-It-Out-Loud

National Association of Elementary School Principals (NAESP). (2018). *The pre-k-8 school leader in 2018: A 10-year study.* https://www.naesp.org/sites/default/files/NAESP%2010-YEAR%20REPORT_2018.pdf

National Association of School Psychologists (NASP). (2010). *Model for comprehensive and integrated school psychological services.* https://www.nasponline.org/Documents/Standards%20and%20Certification/Standards/2_PracticeModel.pdf

National Association of School Psychologists (NASP). (2013). *A framework for successful schools.* https://www.nasponline.org/Documents/Research%20and%20Policy/Advocacy%20Resources/Framework_for_Safe_and_Successful_School_Environments.pdf

National Association of School Psychologists (2016). *School-based mental health services: Improving student-learning and well-being.* https://www.nasponline.org/resources-and-publications/resources-and-podcasts/mental-health/school-psychology-and-mental-health/school-based-mental-health-services. Retrieved April 28, 2020.

National Association of School Psychologists (NASP). (2019). *Mitigating psychological effects of lockdowns.* https://www.nasponline.org/resources-and-publications/resources-and-podcasts/school-climate-safety-and-crisis/systems-level-prevention/mitigating-psychological-effects-of-lockdowns

National Center for Child Poverty (NCCP). (2019). *Child poverty.* https://www.nccp.org/

National Center for Mental Health in Schools. (2016). *Improving ESSA planning for student and learning supports.* UCLA. http://smhp.psych.ucla.edu/pdfdocs/improveessa.pdf

National Center of Safe Supportive Learning Environments. (2020). *Trauma sensitive schools training package.* https://safesupportivelearning.ed.gov/trauma-sensitive-schools-training-package

National Center for School Mental Health. (2020). *The SHAPE system.* University of Maryland School of Medicine. http://www.theshapesystem.com

National Center for School Mental Health and MHTTC Network Coordinating Office. (2019). *Trainer manual, National School Mental Health Curriculum.* MHTTC Network Coordinating Office.

National Center for School Mental Health and MHTTC Network Coordinating Office. (2019, July 8). *MHTTC National School Mental Health Curriculum.* https://mhttcnetwork.org/now-available-school-mental-health-curriculum

National Child Traumatic Stress Network. (2013). *Child welfare trauma training toolkit.* https://www.nctsn.org/resources/child-welfare-trauma-training-toolkit

National Domestic Violence Hotline. (n.d.). *"Why don't they just leave?"* https://www.thehotline.org/is-this-abuse/why-do-people-stay-in-abusive -relationships/

National Educational Psychological Service. (2015). *Guidelines for mental health promotion: Well-being in primary schools.* Department of Education and Skills of the Irish Government. https://www.education.ie/en/Publications/ Education-Reports/Well-Being-in-Primary-Schools-Guidelines-for-Mental -Health-Promotion.pdf

National Institutes of Health (NIH). (2002, September 9). *Stress system malfunction could lead to serious, life threatening disease.* https://www.nichd .nih.gov/newsroom/releases/stress

National Institutes of Health. (2020). *Bipolar disorder.* https://ghr.nlm.nih.gov/ condition/bipolar-disorder#inheritance

National Institute of Mental Health (NIMH). (2018, May 30). *Mental health and rural America: Challenges and opportunities.* https://www.nimh.nih .gov/news/media/2018/mental-health-and-rural-america-challenges-and -opportunities.shtml

National Research Council and Institute of Medicine Committee on Depression. (2009). *Parenting practices, and the healthy development of children.* National Academies Press.

Neff, K., & Germer, C. (2018). *The mindful self-compassion workbook: A proven way to accept yourself, build inner strength, and thrive.* Guilford Press.

New America. (n.d.). *Funding disparities.* New America. https://www.newamerica .org/education-policy/topics/school-funding-and-resources/school-funding/ funding-disparities/

New England Mental Health Technology Transfer Center (2019). *Guiding principles: Resiliency and recovery.* https://mhttcnetwork.org/centers/new -england-mhttc/product/guiding-principles-resiliency-and-recovery

New England Mental Health Technology Transfer Center. (2020, April). *Bringing compassionate practices to New England schools through the Childhood - Trauma Learning Collaborative: 2019-2020 survey of C-TLC fellows.* https://

mhttcnetwork.org/centers/new-england-mhttc/product/c-tlc-2019-2020-survey-childhood-trauma-learning-collaborative-c

Noble, R., Sornberger, M., Toste, J., Heath, N., & McLouth, R. (2011). Safety first: The role of trust and school safety in non-suicidal self-injury. *McGill Journal of Education*, *46*(3), 423–441.

Noddings, N. (2015). Back to the whole. In M. Scherer (Ed.), *Keeping the whole child healthy and safe*. ASCD.

Obama, M. (2018). *Becoming*. Penguin Random House, LLC.

Office of the Assistant Secretary for Planning and Evaluation (ASPE). (2020). *Poverty guidelines*. https://aspe.hhs.gov/poverty-guidelines

Office of the Surgeon General. (2001, August). *Mental health: Culture, race, and ethnicity*. National Institute of Mental Health. https://www.ncbi.nlm.nih.gov/books/NBK44249/

Offner, D. (2018, May 14). *Ensuring your child is supported at school*. https://nami.org/Blogs/NAMI-Blog/May-2018/Ensuring-Your-Child-is-Supported-at-School

Olcoń, K., Kim, Y., & Gulbas, L. E. (2017). Sense of belonging and youth suicidal behaviors: What do communities and schools have to do with it? *Social Work in Public Health*, *32*(7), 432–442.

Olivet, J., Dones, M., & Richard, M. (2019). The intersection of homelessness, racism, and mental illness. In *Racism and psychiatry* (pp. 55–69). Springer International Publishing AG.

O'Mara, C. (2018, May 29). Kids do not spend nearly enough time outside. Here's how (and why) to change that. *The Washington Post*. https://www.washingtonpost.com/news/parenting/wp/2018/05/30/kids-dont-spend-nearly-enough-time-outside-heres-how-and-why-to-change-that/

Ortega, L., Lyubansky, M., Nettles, S., & Espelage, D. L. (2016). Outcomes of a restorative circles program in a high school setting. *Psychology of Violence*, *6*(3), 459.

Osher, D., Cantor, P., & Caverly, S. (2019). The relational, ecological, and phenomenological foundations of school safety, mental health, wellness, and learning. *Keeping Students Safe and Helping Them Thrive: A Collaborative Handbook on School Safety, Mental Health, and Wellness* (2 volumes), 29.

Osofsky, J. D., & McAlister Groves, B (2018). *Violence and trauma in the lives of children* (2 volumes). Praeger Publishers.

Ozer, E. J., & Weinstein, R. S. (2004). Urban adolescents' exposure to community violence: The role of support, school safety, and social constraints in a school-based sample of boys and girls. *Journal of Clinical Child and Adolescent Psychology*, *33*(3), 463–476. doi:10.1207/s15374424jccp3303_4

Parent Teacher Association (PTA). (n.d.). *History.* https://www.pta.org/ home/About-National-Parent-Teacher-Association/Mission-Values/National -PTA-History

Parent Teacher Association (PTA). (2019). *Impact: 2018-2019* annual report. http://online.fliphtml5.com/dtoi/qjpy/#p=1

Parlakian, R. (2018, July 18). *What you need to know: Early intervention. Parenting Resource.* Zero to Three. https://www.zerotothree.org/resources/ 2335-what-you-need-to-know-early-intervention

PCTV. (2020). Episode 7: Living with heart. *Positive Health & Wellness Series.*

Pearrow, M.M., Amador, A., & Dennery, S. (2016, November). Boston's comprehensive behavioral health model. *Communique, 45*(3).

Pearrow, M.M., Amador, A., Dennery, S., Zortman Cohen, M., Snyder, J., & Shachmut, L. (2016, December). Boston's comprehensive behavioral health model: Organizational structures. *Communique, 45*(4).

Pepper, K. (2010). Effective principals skillfully balance leadership styles to facilitate student success: A focus for the reauthorization of ESEA. *Planning and Changing, 41,* 42–56.

Perfect, M. M., Turley, M. R., Carlson, J. S., Yohanna, J., & Saint Gilles, M. P. (2016). School-related outcomes of traumatic event exposure and traumatic stress symptoms in students: A systematic review of research from 1990 to 2015. *School Mental Health, 8*(1), 7–43. https://doi.org/10.1007/s12310 -016-9175-

Perry, B. D. (2001). The neurodevelopmental impact of violence in childhood. In *Textbook of Child and Adolescent Forensic Psychiatry* (221–238). American Psychiatric Press.

Perry, B. D. (2009). Examining child maltreatment through a neurodevelop-mental lens: Clinical applications of the neurosequential model of therapeutics. *Journal of Loss and Trauma, 14*(4), 240–255. DOI: 10.1080/15325020903004350

Plumb, J. L., Bush, K. A., & Kersevich, S. E. (2016). *Trauma-sensitive schools: An evidence-based approach. 40, 2,* 37–60. http://www.communityschools.org/ assets/1/AssetManager/TSS.pdf

Polack, E. (2018, May 1). *New Cigna study reveals loneliness at epidemic levels in America.* Cigna. https://www.cigna.com/newsroom/news-releases/ 2018/new-cigna-study-reveals-loneliness-at-epidemic-levels-in-america

Poliner, R., & Benson, J. (2017). *Teaching the whole teen: Everyday practices that promote success and resilience in school and life.* Corwin.

Profe, W., & Wild, L. G. (2017). Mother, father, and grandparent involvement: Associations with adolescent mental health and substance use. *Journal of Family Issues, 38*(6), 776–797.

Rainbow Community Schools. (2020). *Vision for online learning*. http://rainbow communityschool.org/rainbow-community-school-vision-for-online-learning/

Rao, U., & Chen, L. A. (2009). Characteristics, correlates, and outcomes of childhood and adolescent depressive disorders. *Dialogues in Clinical Neuroscience, 11*(1), 45–62.

Ravitch, D. (2016). *The death and life of the great American school system: How testing and choice are undermining education*. Basic Books. https://www .basicbooks.com/titles/dianc-ravitch/the-death-and-life-of-the-great-american -school-system/9780465097999/

Read, J., Fosse, R., Moskowitz, A., & Perry, B. (2014). The traumagenic neurodevelopmental model of psychosis revisited. *Neuropsychiatry, 4*(1), 65–79. doi:10.2217/npy.13.89

Read, J., Perry, B. D., Moskowitz, A., & Connolly, J. (2001). The contribution of early traumatic events to schizophrenia in some patients: A traumagenic neurodevelopmental model. *Psychiatry, 64*(4), 319–345. doi:10.1521/psyc.64.4.319.18602

Remeis, K. (2020, January 14). *Featured fellow: Jaime Ela, a Maine principal implementing trauma-informed learning in the classroom*. Center for Educational Improvement. http://www.edimprovement.org/2020/01/featured -fellow-jaime-ela-a-maine-principal-implementing-trauma-informed-learning -in-the-classroom/

Remick, K., Gausche-Hill, M., Joseph, M. M., Brown, K., Snow, S. K., Wright, J. L., American Academy of Pediatrics Committee on Pediatric Emergency Medicine and Section on Surgery, American College of Emergency Physicians Pediatric Emergency Medicine Committee, and Emergency Nurses Association Pediatric Committee. (2018). Pediatric readiness in the emergency department. *Pediatrics, 142*(5). https://doi.org/10.1542/peds.2018-2459

Reynolds, C.R., & Kamphaus, R.W. (2015). *Behavior assessment system for children* (3rd ed.) *[Assessment instrument]*. Pearson.

Richardson, H. (2014). Poor parent-child bonding "hampers learning." BBC News. Retrieved from https://www.bbc.com/news/education-26667036

Rihmer, Z. (2001). Can better recognition and treatment of depression reduce suicide rates? A brief review. *European Psychiatry, 16*(7), 406–409. doi: 10.1016/ s0924-9338(01)00598-3

Rogers, J., Franke, M. Yun, J.E., Ishimoto, M., Diera, C., Geller, R., Berryman, A., Brenes, T. (2017). *Teaching and learning in the age of Trump: Increasing stress and hostility in America's high schools*. UCLA's Institute for Democracy, Education, and Access.

Rones, M., & Hoagwood, K. (2000). School-based mental health services: A research review. *Clinical Child and Family Psychology Review, 3*(4), 223–241.

Rosen, C., Jones, N., Longden, E., Chase, K. A., Shattell, M., Melbourne, J. K., Keedy, S. K., & Sharma, R. P. (2017). Exploring the intersections of trauma, structural adversity, and psychosis among a primarily African-American sample: A mixed-methods analysis. *Frontiers in Psychiatry, 8*(57). https://doi .org/10.3389/fpsyt.2017.00057

Rosenbach, W. E. (2018). *Contemporary issues in leadership.* Routledge.

Rousseau, D. (2018). *Manifestation of childhood trauma.* http://sites.bu.edu/ daniellerousseau/2018/08/13/the-manifestation-of-childhood-trauma/

Rueda, D. (2019, March 18). *Cyberbullying in the information age.* Center for Educational Improvement. http://www.edimprovement.org/2019/03/cyber bullying-in-the-information-age/

Ryan, C., Huebner, D., Diaz, R. M., & Sanchez, J. (2009). Family rejection as a predictor of negative health outcomes in white and Latino lesbian, gay, and bisexual young adults. *Pediatrics, 123*(1), 346–352.

Schatell, E. (2017, July 10). *Challenging multicultural disparities in mental health.* National Alliance on Mental Illness. https://www.nami.org/blogs/nami -blog/july-2017/challenging-multicultural-disparities-in-mental-he

Schonert-Reichl, K. A., & Lawlor, M. S. (2010). The effects of a mindfulness-based education program on pre-and early adolescents' well-being and social and emotional competence. *Mindfulness, 1*(3), 137–151.

Second Step. (2020). *Social-emotional learning program.* https://www.second step.org/second-step-social-emotional-learning

Seltzer, L.F. (2015, July 8). Trauma and the freeze response: Good, bad, or both? *Psychology Today.* https://www.psychologytoday.com/us/blog/evolution -the-self/201507/trauma-and-the-freeze-response-good-bad-or-both

Senge, P. (2006). T*he fifth discipline: The art and practice of the learning organization.* Doubleday.

Senge, P. M., Cambron-McCabe, N., Lucas, T., Smith, B., & Dutton, J. (2012). *Schools that learn (updated and revised): A fifth discipline fieldbook for educators, parents, and everyone who cares about education.* Crown Business.

Seppala, E. (2009). *Loving-kindness meditation: A tool for increasing social connectedness.* Stanford University.

Sergiovanni, T. (2007). *Rethinking leadership: A collection of articles.* (2nd ed.). Corwin.

Seto, C. (2019, September 4). After-school restraint collapse is a real thing—here's how to deal with it. *Today's Parent.* https://www.todaysparent.com/kids/school -age/after-school-restraint-collapse-is-a-real-thing-heres-how-to- deal-with-it/

Shannahan, R., & Fields, S. (2016). *Services in support of community living for youth with serious behavioral health challenges: Mobile crisis response and stabilization services.* Substance Abuse and Mental Health Services Administration. https://wraparoundohio.org/wp-content/uploads/2018/01/MobileCrisisResponseStabilizationServicesMay2016.pdf

Sheidow, A. J., Henry, D. B., Tolan, P. H., & Strachan, M. K. (2014). The role of stress exposure and family functioning in internalizing outcomes of urban families. *Journal of Child and Family Studies, 23*(8), 1351–1365. https://doi.org/10.1007/s10826-013-9793-3

Sheridan, D. C., Spiro, D. M., Fu, R., Johnson, K. P., Sheridan, J. S., Oue, A. A., Wang, W., Van Nes, R., & Hansen, M. L. (2015). Mental health utilization in a pediatric emergency department. *Pediatric Emergency Care, 31*(8), 555.

Shirley, D. (2009). *The fourth way: The inspiring future of educational change.* Corwin.

Shonkoff, J. P., Garner, A. S., Siegel, B. S., Dobbins, M. I., Earls, M. F., Garner, A. S., McGuinn, L., Pascoe, J., & Wood, D. L. (2011). The lifelong effects of early childhood adversity and toxic stress. *Pediatrics, 129*(1). doi: 10.1542/peds.2011-2663

Short, A. T. O., & Nemeroff, C. B. (2014). *Suicide: Phenomenology and neurobiology.* Springer International Publishing AG

Siegel, D. (2010). *Mindsight: The new science of personal transformation.* Bantam Books.

Silver, D., & Stafford, D. (2017). *Teaching kids to thrive: Essential skills for success.* Corwin.

Singh, N. N., Lancioni, G. E., Winton, A. S., Karazsia, B. T., & Singh, J. (2013). Mindfulness training for teachers changes the behavior of their preschool students. *Research in Human Development, 10*(3), 211–233.

Singleton, G., & Linton, C. (2006). *A field guide for achieving equity in schools: Courageous conversations about race.* Corwin.

Skaar, N. R., Freedman, S., Carlon, A., & Watson, E. (2016). Integrating models of collaborative consultation and systems change to implement forgiveness-focused bullying interventions. *Journal of Educational and Psychological Consultation, 26*(1), 63–86.

Smith, M., & Davey, M. (2019, October 31). Chicago teachers' strike, longest in decades, ends. *The New York Times.* https://www.nytimes.com/2019/10/31/us/chicago-cps-teachers-strike.html?login=smartlock&auth=login-smartlock

Smylie, M., Murphy, J., & Seashore Louis, K. (2020). *Caring school leadership.* Corwin.

Spitzer, D. L. (2005). Engendering health disparities. *Canadian Journal of Public Health, 96*(SUPPL. 2). http://www.scopus.com/scopus/inward/record.url?eid=2-s2.0-21644434947&partnerID=40

Stamm, B. H. (2010). *The concise ProQOL manual.* https://programs.caringsafely .org/wp-content/uploads/2018/01/ProQOL_Concise_2ndEd_12-2010.pdf

Steinberg, A. M., Brymer, M. J., Decker, K. B., & Pynoos, R. S. (2004). The University of California at Los Angeles post-traumatic stress disorder reaction index. *Current Psychiatry Reports, 6*(2), 96–100.

Substance Abuse and Mental Health Services Administration (SAMHSA). (n.d.) *About us.* https://www.samhsa.gov/about-us

Substance Abuse and Mental Health Services Administration (SAMHSA). (2010) *What a difference a friend makes.* http://www.mhaac.org/uploads/documents/ What%20A%20Difference-ENG.pdf

Substance Abuse and Mental Health Services Administration (SAMHSA). (2014). *A treatment improvement protocol. Trauma-Informed care in behavioral health services.* U.S. Department of Health and Human Services. https://www .ncbi.nlm.nih.gov/books/NBK207201/pdf/Bookshelf_NBK207201.pdf

Substance Abuse and Mental Health Services Administration (SAMHSA). (2016, June). *DSM-5 changes: Implications for child serious emotional disturbances.* CBHSQ Methodology Report. Center for Behavioral Health Statistics and Quality, Substance Abuse and Mental Health Services Administration, Rockville, MD https://www.ncbi.nlm.nih.gov/books/NBK519708/

Substance Abuse and Mental Health Services Administration (SAMHSA). (2017). *Suicide clusters within American Indian and Alaska Native communities: A review of the literature and recommendations.* https://store.samhsa.gov/sites/ default/files/d7/priv/sma17-5050.pdf

Substance Abuse and Mental Health Services Administration (SAMHSA). (2017, November). *Measuring progress towards becoming a trauma-informed school.* https://www.nhstudentwellness.org/uploads/5/3/9/0/53900547/measuring_ trauma_informed_schools_11.10.17.pdf

Substance Abuse and Mental Health Services Administration (SAMHSA). (2018a). *Behavioral health conditions in children and youth exposed to natural disasters.* https://www.samhsa.gov/sites/default/files/srb-childrenyouth-8-22-18.pdf

Substance Abuse and Mental Health Services Administration (SAMHSA). (2018b). *Evidence-based practices resource center.* https://www.samhsa.gov/ ebp-resource-center

Substance Abuse and Mental Health Services Administration (SAMHSA). (2018c). *Key substance use and mental health indicators in the United States: Results from the 2017 National Survey on Drug Use and Health.* https://www .samhsa.gov/data/report/2017-nsduh-annual-national-report

Suicide Prevention Resource Center (SPRC). (2011, March). *Suicide and bullying issue brief.* http://www.sprc.org/sites/default/files/migrate/library/Suicide_ Bullying_Issue_Brief.pdf

Suicide Prevention Resource Center (SPRC). (2018). *Racial and ethnic dispari-ties.* https://www.sprc.org/racial-ethnic-disparities

Suicide Prevention Resource Center (SPRC). (2019). *Preventing suicide: The role of high school teachers.* https://www.sprc.org/resources-programs/role-high-school-teachers-preventing-suicide-sprc-customized-information-page

Sullivan, T. (2019, December 31). What's the difference between PTA and PTO? *PTO Today.* https://www.ptotoday.com/pto-today-articles/article/292-pto-vs-pta-whats-the-difference

Takeuchi, D. T., Williams, D. R., & Adair, R. K. (1991). Economic stress in the family and children's emotional and behavioral problems. *Journal of Marriage and the Family, 53*(4), 1031–1041. https://doi.org/10.2307/353006

Taliaferro, L. A., McMorris, B. J., Rider, G. N., & Eisenberg, M. E. (2019). Risk and protective factors for self-harm in a population-based sample of transgender youth. *Archives of Suicide Research, 23*(2), 203–221.

Tanap, R. (2019, July 25). *Why Asian-Americans and Pacific Islanders don't go to therapy.* National Alliance on Mental Illness. https://www.nami.org/Blogs/NAMI-Blog/July-2019/Why-Asian-Americans-and-Pacific-Islanders-Don-t-go-to-Therapy

Tate, E. (2019, May 7). *Why social-emotional learning is suddenly in the spotlight.* EdSurge. https://www.edsurge.com/news/2019-05-07-why-social-emotional-learning-is-suddenly-in-the-spotlight

Taylor, R. D., Oberle, E., Durlak, J. A., & Weissberg, R. P. (2017). Promoting positive youth development through school-based social and emotional learning interventions: A meta-analysis of follow-up effects. *Child Development, 88*(4), 1156–1171.

Taylor, Z. E., & Conger, R. D. (2017). Promoting strengths and resilience in single-mother families. *Child Development, 88*(2), 350–358.

Thomason, M. E., Marusak, H. A., Tocco, M. A., Vila, A. M., McGarragle, O., & Rosenberg, D. R. (2015). Altered amygdala connectivity in urban youth exposed to trauma. *Social Cognitive and Affective Neuroscience, 10*(11), 1460–1468. doi:10.1093/scan/nsv030

THRIVE. (2010). *Guide to trauma-informed organizational development.* https://www.maine.gov/dhhs/ocfs/cbhs/webinars/documents/THRIVE-Guide-to-Trauma-Informed-Organizational-Development.pdf

Time to Change. (2017, August 18). *Being judged for my mental illness was so damaging.* https://www.time-to-change.org.uk/blog/being-judged-my-mental-illness-was-so-damaging

Toom, A. (2018). School culture, leadership and relationships matter. *Teachers and Teaching, 24*(7): 745–748. https://doi.org/10.1080/13540602.2018.1503855

Tschannen-Moran M., & Hoy, A. (2001). Teacher efficacy: Capturing an elusive construct. *Teaching and Teacher Education, 17*, 783–805. https://doi.org/10.1016/S0742-051X(01)00036-1

Twenge, J. (2019, March 20). *Teens have less face time with their friends – and are lonelier than ever*. The Conversation. https://theconversation.com/teens-have-less-face-time-with-their-friends-and-are-lonelier-than-ever-113240

Ullman, P. (2018). *Eight steps to an authentic life: Ancient wisdom for modern times*. Archway Publishing.

UNESCO. (2020). Education response. https://en.unesco.org/covid19/educationresponse

Unite for Sight (2016). *Module 6: Barriers to mental health care*. Global Health University. https://www.uniteforsight.org/mental-health/module6

University of Missouri-Columbia. (2020, January 27). Nearly all middle school teachers are highly stressed: Education experts suggest findings indicate a need to reduce burden of teaching. *ScienceDaily*. http://www.sciencedaily.com/releases/2020/01/200127134722.htm

U.S. Department of Education Office for Civil Rights. (n.d.). *Civil rights data collection* (CRDC). https://www2.ed.gov/about/offices/list/ocr/data.html

U.S. Department of Health and Human Services (HHS). (2018). Adolescent Health. https://www.hhs.gov/ash/oah/facts-and-stats/national-and-state-data-sheets/adolescent-mental-health-fact-sheets/united-states/index.html

U.S. Department of Health and Human Services (HHS). (2019, March 25). *Communicating*. https://www.hhs.gov/ash/oah/adolescent-development/healthy-relationships/parents-child/communicating/index.html

U.S. Department of Health and Human Services, Administration for Children and Families, Administration on Children, Youth and Families, Children's Bureau. (2018). *Child maltreatment 2016*. https://www.acf.hhs.gov/cb/research-data-technology/statistics-research/child-maltreatment

van der Kolk, B. A. (2007). *The Developmental Impact of Childhood Trauma*. Cambridge University Press.

Varathan, P. (2018, June 1). The US is having a hard time keeping teachers in their jobs. *Quartz*. https://qz.com/1284903/american-teachers-leave-their-jobs-at-higher-rates-than-other-countries-with-top-ranked-school-systems/

Vitoroulis, I., & Georgiades, K. (2017). Bullying among immigrant and non-immigrant early adolescents: School- and student-level effects. *Journal of Adolescence, 61*, 141–151. doi: 10.1016/j.adolescence.2017.10.008

Walker, T. (2014, November 2). NEA survey: Nearly half of teachers consider leaving profession due to standardized testing. *NEAToday.* https://www.nea.org/advocating-for-change/new-from-nea/survey-70-percent-educators-say-state-assessments-not

Walker, T. (2018, September 13). Are schools ready to tackle the mental health crisis? *NEAToday.* http://neatoday.org/2018/09/13/mental-health-in-schools/

Wang, M. T., & Degol, J. L. (2016). School climate: A review of the construct, measurement, and impact on student outcomes. *Educational Psychology Review, 28*(2), 315–352.

Waters, S. F., West, T. V., & Mendes, W. B. (2014). Stress contagion. *Psychological Science, 25*(4), 934–942. doi: 10.1177/0956797613518352

WeAreTeachers Staff. (2019, January 15). *What teachers need to know about restorative justice.* https://www.weareteachers.com/restorative-justice/

Weist, M., Rubin, M., Moore, E., Adelsheim, S., & Wrobel, G. (2007). Mental health screening in schools. *Journal of School Health, 77*(2), 53–58.

Weisz, J. R., Sandler, I. N., Durlak, J. A., & Anton, B. S. (2005). Promoting and protecting youth mental health through evidence-based prevention and treatment. *American psychologist, 60*(6), 628.

Wells, C. M. (2015). Conceptualizing Mindful Leadership in Schools: How the Practice of Mindfulness Informs the Practice of Leading. Education Leadership Review of Doctoral Research, 2(1), 1-23. https://files.eric.ed.gov/fulltext/EJ1105711.pdf

Welsh, J. W., Rappaport, N., & Tretyak, V. (2018). The opioid epidemic: 7 things educators need to know. *Educational Leadership, 75*(4), 18–22.

Wexler, R. (2017, September 20). *Abuse in foster care: Research vs. the child welfare system's alternative facts.* YouthToday. https://youthtoday.org/2017/09/abuse-in-foster-care-research-vs-the-child-welfare-systems-alternative-facts/

Whalen, J. (2018, May 15). Youth suicidal behavior is on the rise, especially among girls. *The Wall Street Journal.* https://www.wsj.com/articles/youth-suicidal-behavior-is-on-the-rise-especially-among-girls-1526443782

White, Jenna. (2020). Parent power: Partnering to create trauma-informed schools [PowerPoint slides]. Creating Trauma-Sensitive Schools Conference.

Whitmore, L. M., & Smith, T. C. (2018). Isolating the association of sleep, depressive state, and other independent indicators for suicide ideation in United States teenagers. *Archives of Suicide Research, 23*(3), 471–490.

Williams, D. R. (2012). Miles to go before we sleep: Racial inequities in health. *Journal of Health and Social Behavior, 53*(3), 279–295. doi:10.1177/0022146512455804

Williams, D. R., Priest, N., & Anderson, N. B. (2016). Understanding associations among race, socioeconomic status, and health: Patterns and prospects. *Health Psychology, 35*(4), 407–411. doi:10.1037/hea0000242

Williams, M.T. (2011, November 2). Why African Americans avoid psychotherapy. *Psychology Today*. https://www.psychologytoday.com/us/blog/culturally-speaking/201111/why-african-americans-avoid-psychotherapy

Willis, S., Clarke, S., & O'Connor, E. (2017). Contextualizing leadership: Transformational leadership and Management-By-Exception-Active in safety-critical contexts. *Journal of Occupational and Organizational Psychology, 90*(3), 281–305.

Wilson, C. J., & Deane, F. P. (2001). Adolescent opinions about reducing help-seeking barriers and increasing appropriate help engagement. *Journal of Educational & Psychological Consultation, 12*(4), 345–364.

Wilson, J. (2019, January 28). *Screen time before bed puts children at risk of anxiety, obesity, and poor sleep.* Imperial College London. https://www.imperial.ac.uk/news/190011/screen-time-before-puts-children-risk/

Wolf-Prusan, L., O'Malley, M., & Hurley, N. (2015). Restorative practices: Approaches at the intersection of school discipline and school mental health. Now Is The Time Technical Assistance Center. http://files.ctctcdn.com/bde05f96001/ec0c1e04-3a0c-49b2-8561-2713c08b511c.pdf

Worsley, D., Barrios, E., Shuter, M., Pettit, A. R., & Doupnik, S. K. (2019). Adolescents' experiences during "boarding" hospitalization while awaiting inpatient psychiatric treatment following suicidal ideation or suicide attempt. *Hospital Pediatrics, 9*(11), 827–833.

Yang, M. (2019, July 1). Balancing expectations with mental health. *National Alliance on Mental Illness*. https://www.nami.org/Blogs/NAMI-Blog/July-2019/Balancing-Expectations-with-Mental-Health

Yeager, D. S., & Dweck, C. S. (2012). Mindsets that promote resilience: When students believe that personal characteristics can be developed. *Educational Psychologist, 47*(4), 302–314.

Youth Restoration Project. (2016). *The benefits of restorative practices.* https://yrpofri.org/benefits-of-restorative-practices/

Yu, E., & Cantor, P. (2014). Turnaround for children, poverty, stress, and schools: Implications for research, practice, and assessment. Retrieved from http://www .turnaroundusa.org/wp-content/uploads/2016/05/Turnaround-for-Children -Poverty-Stress-Schools.pdf

Zayas, L. H., & Heffron, L. C. (2016, November). Disrupting young lives: How detention and deportation affect US-born children of immigrants. *American Psychological Association.* https://www.apa.org/pi/families/resources/news letter/2016/11/detention-deportation

Zelazo, P.D., & Cunningham, W.A. (2007). Executive function: Mechanisms underlying emotion regulation. In J. J. Gross (Ed.), *Handbook of Emotion Regulation* (135–158). Guilford Press.

Zelazo, P. D., & Lyons, K. E. (2011). Mindfulness training in childhood. *Human Development, 54*(2), 61–65.

Zelazo, P. D., & Lyons, K. E. (2012). The potential benefits of mindfulness training in early childhood: A developmental social cognitive neuroscience perspective. *Child Development Perspectives, 6*(2), 154–160.

Zepeda, M., Varela, F., & Morales, A. (2004). Promoting positive parenting practices through parenting education. *UCLA Center for Healthier Children, Families and Communities.*

Zero to Three. (2020). *How to communicate with parents.* https://www .zerotothree.org/resources/92-how-to-communicate-with-parents

Zolkoski, S. M., & Bullock, L. M. (2012). Resilience in children and youth: A review. *Children and Youth Services Review, 34*(12), 2295–2303.

Zolli, A. (2012). Learning to bounce back. *The New York Times.* http://www.uvm .edu/~epscor/pdfFiles/2013_workshop/Forget_Sustainability.pdf

Index

A SAGE Publishing Company

Helping educators make the greatest impact

CORWIN HAS ONE MISSION: to enhance education through intentional professional learning.

We build long-term relationships with our authors, educators, clients, and associations who partner with us to develop and continuously improve the best evidence-based practices that establish and support lifelong learning.